THE
BASIC/NOT BORING
MIDDLE GRADES
MATH
BOOK

Grades 6–8⁺

Inventive Exercises to Sharpen
Skills and Raise Achievement

Series Concept & Development
by Imogene Forte & Marjorie Frank

Incentive Publications, Inc.
Nashville, Tennessee

Acknowledgment:
Many thanks to Terri Breeden and Andrea Sukow,
whose adapted exercises are included in this book.

Illustrated by Kathleen Bullock
Cover art by Mary Patricia Deprez, dba Tye Dye Mary®
Cover design by Marta Drayton and Joe Shibley
Edited by Angela Reiner

ISBN 0-86530-459-9

2   3   4   5   6   7   8   9   10   07   06   05

PRINTED IN THE UNITED STATES OF AMERICA
www.incentivepublications.com

TABLE OF CONTENTS

INTRODUCTION

Do basic skills have to be boring? Absolutely not! Mastery of basic skills provides the foundation for exciting learning opportunities for students. Content relevant to their everyday life is fascinating stuff! Kids love learning about topics such as sporting and Olympic events, midnight snacks and temperature, famous athletes and mountain climbing, football and fishing, games and golf and more. It is on acquired knowledge bases that they develop basic skills which enable them to ponder, process, grow, and achieve school success.

Acquiring, polishing, and using basic skills and content is a cause for celebration—not an exercise in drudgery. *The BASIC/Not Boring Middle Grades Math Book* invites you to celebrate with students as you help them sharpen their abilities in the essentials of math.

As you examine *The BASIC/Not Boring Middle Grades Math Book*, you will see that it is filled with attractive age-appropriate student exercises. These pages are no ordinary worksheets! *The BASIC/Not Boring Middle Grades Math Book* contains hundreds of inventive and inviting ready-to-use lessons based on a captivating theme that invites the student to join an adventure, solve a puzzle, practice a sport, or tackle a problem. Additionally, each fittingly illustrated exercise provides diverse tools for reinforcement and extension of basic and higher-order thinking skills.

The BASIC/Not Boring Middle Grades Math Book contains the following components:

- **A clear, sequential list of skills for 6 different content areas**
  Checklists of skills begin each content section. These lists correlate with the exercises, identifying page numbers where specific skills can be practiced. Students can chart their progress by checking off each skill as it is mastered.

- **Nearly 250 pages of student exercises**
  Each exercise page:
      . . . addresses a specific basic skill or content area.
      . . . presents tasks that grab the attention and curiosity of students.
      . . . contains clear directions to the student.
      . . . asks students to use, remember, and practice a basic skill.
      . . . challenges students to think creatively and analytically.
      . . . requires students to apply the skill to real situations or content.
      . . . takes students on learning adventures in a variety of exciting sporting adventures!

- **A ready-to-use assessment tool**
  Six skills tests, one for each content area, follow each series of exercises. The tests are presented in parts corresponding to the skills lists. Designed to be used as pre- or post-tests, individual parts of these tests can be given to students at separate times, if needed.

- **Complete answer keys**
  Easy-to-find-and-use answer keys for all exercises and skills tests follow each section.

HOW TO USE THIS BOOK:

The exercises contained in *The BASIC/Not Boring Middle Grades Math Book* are to be used with adult assistance. The adult may serve as a guide to ensure the student understands the directions and questions.

The BASIC/Not Boring Middle Grades Math Book is designed to be used in many diverse ways. Its use will vary according to the needs of the students, the form of instruction, and the structure of the learning environment.

The skills checklists may be used as:
>. . . record-keeping tools to track individual skills mastery.
>. . . planning guides for the teacher's instruction.
>. . . progress reports to share with parents.
>. . . a place for students to proudly check off accomplishments.

Each exercise page may be used as:
>. . . a pre-test or check to see how well a student has mastered a skill.
>. . . a tool around which the teacher may build a mini-skills based lesson.
>. . . one of many resources or exercises for teaching a lesson or unit.
>. . . a way to practice or polish a skill that has been taught.
>. . . a review of a skill taught earlier.
>. . . reinforcement of a single basic skill, skills cluster, or content base.
>. . . a preview to help the teacher identify instructional needs.
>. . . an assessment for a skill that a student has practiced.

The exercises are flexibly designed for presentation in many formats and settings. They are useful for individual instruction or independent work. They can also be used under the direction of the teacher with small groups or an entire class. Groups of exercises on related skills may make up the practice materials for a series of lessons or may be used as a unit enhancement.

The skills tests may be used as:
>. . . pre-tests to gauge instructional or placement needs.
>. . . information sources to help teachers adjust instruction.
>. . . post-tests to review student mastery of skills and content areas.

The BASIC/Not Boring Middle Grades Math Book is not intended to be a complete curriculum guide or textbook. It is a collection of inventive exercises to sharpen skills and provide students and teachers with tools for reinforcing concepts and skills, and for identifying areas that need additional attention. This book offers a delightful assortment of tasks that give students just the practice they need—and to get that practice in a manner that will definitely be remembered as non-boring.

As your students take on the challenges of the enticing adventures in this book, they will increase their comfort level with the use of fundamental geometry, algebra, and general math skills and concepts. Watching your students check off the skills they have sharpened will be cause for celebration!

WHOLE NUMBERS & INTEGERS

Skills Exercises

1,000,000

X = -10 ÷

-3 X -5 = 15

SKILLS CHECKLIST FOR WHOLE NUMBERS & INTEGERS

✔	SKILL	PAGE(S)
	Read and write whole numbers	18
	Identify place value of whole numbers	19
	Write whole numbers in expanded form	20
	Compare and order whole numbers	21
	Round whole numbers	22
	Add and subtract whole numbers	23–25
	Identify and use properties of operations	26
	Identify and use properties of numbers	27
	Identify and understand multiples of numbers	28, 29
	Find common multiples and least common multiples	29
	Multiply whole numbers	30–32
	Divide whole numbers	33, 34
	Understand divisibility and identify factors	35
	Identify prime and composite factors	36
	Read and write numbers with exponents	37
	Read, write, and use numbers which are powers of ten	38–40
	Multiply by powers of ten	39
	Divide by powers of ten	40
	Solve word problems with whole numbers	41–43
	Estimate answers to whole number operations	44, 45
	Solve equations with whole numbers	46, 47
	Select the proper operation for a given computation	48
	Read, write, compare, and order integers	49–51
	Place integers on a number line	50, 51
	Add and subtract integers	52
	Multiply integers	53
	Divide integers	54
	Solve equations with integers	55

YOU NEED A BIG CITY

Professional baseball is a big-city game. Only a large metropolitan area can provide enough money and fans to support a team. Complete the following exercises that describe some major league cities.

I. Write in words the population of these National League Baseball locales.

Team Name	Population	
1. Chicago Cubs	2,783,726	_____
2. New York Mets	7,322,564	_____
3. Philadelphia Phillies	1,585,587	_____

II. Write the population of these National League Baseball locales in standard form.

Team Name	Population	
4. Atlanta Braves	Two million, eight hundred thirty-three thousand, five hundred eleven	_____
5. Cincinnati Reds	One million, seven hundred forty-four thousand, one hundred twenty-four	_____
6. Houston Astros	Three million, seven hundred eleven thousand, forty-three	_____
7. Los Angeles Dodgers	Eight million, eight hundred sixty-three thousand, one hundred sixty-four	_____

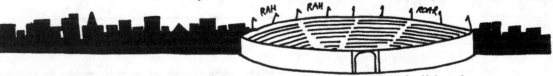

III. Write in words the population of these American League Baseball locales.

Team Name	Population	
8. Baltimore Orioles	2,382,172	_____
9. Cleveland Indians	1,831,122	_____
10. Detroit Tigers	4,382,297	_____
11. Milwaukee Brewers	1,607,183	_____

IV. Write the population of these American League Baseball locales in standard form.

Team Name	Population	
12. Kansas City Royals	One million, five hundred sixty-six thousand, two hundred eighty	_____
13. Oakland Athletics	Three hundred seventy-two thousand, two hundred forty-two	_____
14. Seattle Mariners	One million, nine hundred seventy-two thousand, nine hundred sixty-one	_____

Name _____

BIG MONEY FOR BIG ATHLETES

You've heard about multimillion dollar contracts for athletes, haven't you? Read about these big salaries in professional sports while you practice your knowledge of place value.

1. In 1995, Chris Miller of the St. Louis Rams was forced to give up the game and his nine million dollars in salary. He had suffered his sixth concussion in fourteen months. Write his salary in standard form.

   _____

2. The professional basketball player Juwan Howard was pursued by several teams. The Bullets were able to get him to join their team with a $105,000,000 offer. What is the value of the 5 in his salary?

   _____

3. Tiger Woods is the man to watch in professional golf. In one year he received $60,000,000 in sports endorsement contracts. What place value position does the 6 hold in this large number?

   _____

4. Alex Rodriguez, an American League MVP, negotiated a new contract with the Seattle Mariners. He signed a three-year extension for $10,250,000. What place value position does the 5 hold?

   _____

5. Mark Brooks, a professional golfer, made $1,430,000 in one year. What is the value of the 4 in his earnings?

   _____

6. Mike Tyson, heavyweight boxer, beat Bruce Sheldon in a 109-second fight. Mike Tyson earned $137,615 per second. What is the value of the 6 in his earnings?

   _____

7. The Lakers' contract with Shaquille O'Neal is worth $120 million. What is the value of the 1 in O'Neal's contract?

   _____

8. Michael Jordan received the richest one-year contract in the history of sports. He was paid $25,000,000 for a one-year deal. What digit is in the ten millions place in this figure?

   _____

9. In a very unfriendly game between the Oilers and the Steelers, the teams' fines totaled $145,000. What is the place value of the 1 in this large number?

   _____

10. Jarome Iginla, a professional hockey player, signed a three-year contract worth $850,000. What is the value of the 8 in this number?

   _____

Name _____

FANS LOVE STATS

Sports are filled with interesting statistics (they're called stats). Read the stats below and then write the given number in expanded form.

1. Dave "Tiger" Williams piled up 3,966 penalty minutes in hockey. Write 3,966 in expanded form.

   _____

2. In 1945 the penalty for punching an umpire was lifetime banishment from baseball. Write 1945 in expanded from.

   _____

3. When Team USA defeated Canada in the hockey World Cup only 767,200 U.S. households watched the game. Write 767,200 in expanded form.

   _____

4. Did you know that there are 162 games in a full season of baseball? Write 162 in expanded form.

   _____

5. In 1996 there were 4,962 home runs hit. Write 4,962 in expanded form.

   _____

6. When Kirby Puckett announced his retirement from baseball, he stood before 51,011 fans. Write 51,011 in expanded form.

   _____

7. Ohio State University has a great football team. In only six games into the 1996 season their total offensive output was 2,962 yards. Write 2,962 in expanded form.

   _____

8. Frank Eliscu was the sculptor of the Heisman Trophy. He died in 1996 at the age of 83. Determine the year of his birth, and write it in expanded form.

   _____

9. When the famous racehorse, Cigar, won the Arlington Race, over $200,000,000 worth of tickets went uncashed. The memento of the ticket was worth more than the payoff. Write 200,000,000 in expanded form.

   _____

10. In 1996, the Celtics basketball team took 6,942 shots. Write 6,942 in expanded form.

    _____

11. Courtside seats at the Los Angeles Lakers game cost $600 each. This price includes a program and waiter service. Determine how much it would cost to attend six games. Write this answer in expanded form.

    _____

12. Jason Kidd became the sixth player in NBA history to register 783 assists and 553 rebounds. Total these two numbers and write your answer in expanded form.

    _____

Name _____

20

BIG BUCKS FOR GOOD SEATS

If you've never tried to buy tickets to an NBA (National Basketball Association) game, you may be shocked at these ticket prices. But this is the kind of money you'll need to have, if you want to get up close to the action and sit at courtside!

COURTSIDE SEAT PRICES:

CHARLOTTE HORNETS $180. 100276534

CHICAGO BULLS $400. ZN103

COURTSIDE $375.00 HOUSTON ROCKETS

LOS ANGELES CLIPPERS $275.00

MINNESOTA TIMBERWOLVES COURTSIDE 174.

COURTSIDE TICKET L.A. LAKERS $600.

N.Y. KNICKS $1000.00

1. List the team and the ticket prices from most expensive to least expensive.

Team	Ticket Price
_____	_____
_____	_____
_____	_____
_____	_____
_____	_____
_____	_____
_____	_____

2. Which would cost more, three tickets to a Chicago Bulls game or five tickets to a Charlotte Hornets game? How much more? _____

3. Which would cost more, two tickets to see the Los Angeles Lakers or five tickets to a Chicago Bulls game? How much more? _____

4. Which would cost more, three tickets to a Los Angeles Clippers game or four tickets to a Charlotte Hornets game? How much more? _____

5. Which would cost more, five tickets to a Houston Rockets game or two tickets to a Los Angeles Lakers game? _____

6. Mrs. Martinez's class of 25 students wants to go to see a professional team play. If they raise $10,000 for tickets, which teams could they see for one game? _____
_____

7. William won $5,000 in a radio sports contest. The money had to be spent on tickets. He has four good friends that he wants to take to the game with him. On the back of this page, write a possible budget to spend his winnings. (Don't forget to include William's tickets.)

Name _____

BALLPARK FIGURES

The expression "ballpark figure" means an estimate or a round number. For instance, you might ask your mom to give you a ballpark figure for how much time you have to work on your homework before dinner. Follow the directions to get a ballpark figure for each number below.

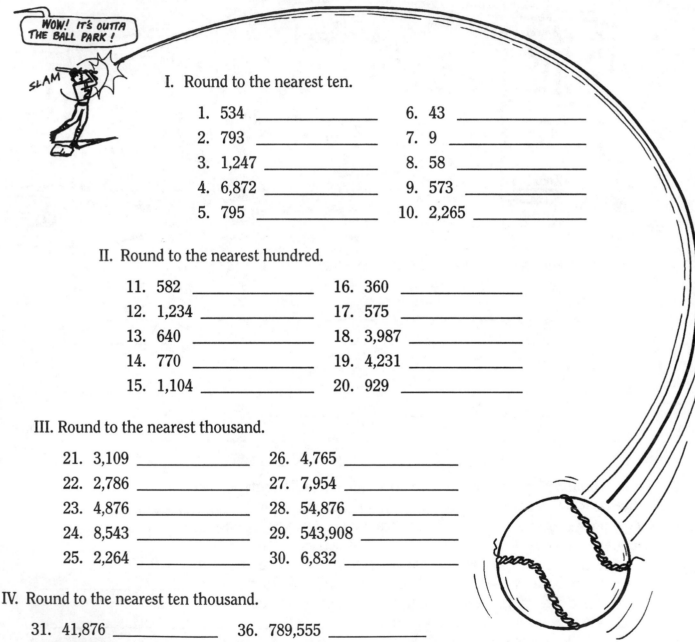

I. Round to the nearest ten.

1. 534 _____   6. 43 _____
2. 793 _____   7. 9 _____
3. 1,247 _____   8. 58 _____
4. 6,872 _____   9. 573 _____
5. 795 _____   10. 2,265 _____

II. Round to the nearest hundred.

11. 582 _____   16. 360 _____
12. 1,234 _____   17. 575 _____
13. 640 _____   18. 3,987 _____
14. 770 _____   19. 4,231 _____
15. 1,104 _____   20. 929 _____

III. Round to the nearest thousand.

21. 3,109 _____   26. 4,765 _____
22. 2,786 _____   27. 7,954 _____
23. 4,876 _____   28. 54,876 _____
24. 8,543 _____   29. 543,908 _____
25. 2,264 _____   30. 6,832 _____

IV. Round to the nearest ten thousand.

31. 41,876 _____   36. 789,555 _____
32. 260,098 _____   37. 86,452 _____
33. 91,975 _____   38. 755,555 _____
34. 207,865 _____   39. 7,643 _____
35. 462,876 _____   40. 54,321 _____

Name _____

FEARSOME FELINES

Not all cats are the kind you want to curl up with by the fire. Many cats are college and professional sports teams fighting out competitive battles on the fields or courts. Solve the problems to get a number code for each letter below. Then use the codes to find the "cat" names of the teams described below.

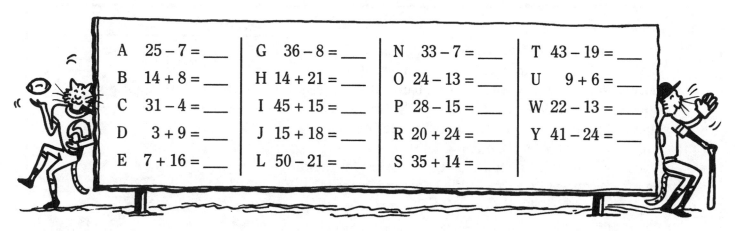

A   25 − 7 = ___   G   36 − 8 = ___   N   33 − 7 = ___   T   43 − 19 = ___

B   14 + 8 = ___   H   14 + 21 = ___   O   24 − 13 = ___   U   9 + 6 = ___

C   31 − 4 = ___   I   45 + 15 = ___   P   28 − 15 = ___   W   22 − 13 = ___

D   3 + 9 = ___   J   15 + 18 = ___   R   20 + 24 = ___   Y   41 − 24 = ___

E   7 + 16 = ___   L   50 − 21 = ___   S   35 + 14 = ___

___ ___ ___ ___ ___ ___ ___ ___
9 60 29 12 27 18 24 49

1. Mascot name shared by Villanova, University of Arizona, Kansas State, and Northwestern University

___ ___ ___ ___ ___ ___ ___
22 23 26 28 18 29 49

2. Cincinnati's pro football team

___ ___ ___ ___ ___
29 60 11 26 49

3. Penn State's famed Nittany _____ ; Detroit's pro football team

___ ___ ___ ___ ___ ___ ___ ___
13 18 26 24 35 23 44 49

4. Carolina's pro football team and University of Pittsburgh's mascot

___ ___ ___ ___ ___ ___
24 60 28 23 44 49

5. Detroit's pro baseball team; mascot of Tennessee State, Princeton, and Louisiana State (although these are "fighting")

___ ___ ___ ___ ___ ___ ___
22 11 22 27 18 24 49

6. University of Ohio and Southwest Texas State mascot

___ ___ ___ ___ ___ ___ ___
27 11 15 28 18 44 49

7. Washington State and University of Houston mascot

___ ___ ___ ___ ___ ___ ___
33 18 28 15 18 44 49

8. Southern Baton-Rouge University mascot

Name _____

STRIKES, SPARES, & SCORES

Sylvia, Mark, Jana, and Jay have decided to spend the afternoon bowling. While some lanes have computers that keep score for the bowlers, the four friends have chosen to go to the lanes where the competitors get to keep their own score. Each bowler's turn involves trying to knock down all ten pins with at most two balls. Each player's turn is scored in one frame.

EXAMPLE:

On her first turn, Jana knocked down all ten pins with one ball. That's a STRIKE (scored with an X). On her next turn she knocked down five pins with the first ball and three pins with the second. To calculate her score for the first frame she gets to add the ten points from her strike to the total pins for her next two balls (10 + 5 + 3 = 18).

So her score after frame one is 18. To get her score for frame two she adds her previous score to the total pins knocked down by her next two balls (18 + 5 + 3 = 26), so her score after two frames is 26.

FRAME 1   FRAME 2

18   X   5 3
           26

 **1.** In the first frame Sylvia knocked down eight pins with her first ball and one pin with her second ball. In the second frame she knocked down three pins with the first ball and four pins with the second ball. Calculate her score in each of the first two frames.

FRAME 1   FRAME 2

8 1   3 4

 **2.** Mark rolled a gutter ball on his first throw and knocked down all ten pins with his second ball—that's a SPARE (scored with a /). In the second frame, he knocked down six and two with his two rolls.

  a. To score the first frame, add ten pins from his spare to his first ball (six pins) from the second frame.

  b. To score the second frame, add his score from the first frame (part a) to the pins from his two rolls in the second frame.

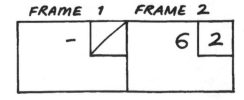

FRAME 1   FRAME 2

- /   6 2

Use with page 25.

Name _____

STRIKES, SPARES, & SCORES, CONTINUED

Use with page 24.

3. Jay knocked down two pins on his first roll and knocked down the other eight with his second ball (that's a _____). In the second frame, he knocked down nine pins with his first ball and zero with his second. Calculate his score for these two frames.

FRAME 1	FRAME 2
2 ◿	9 –

4. After the first game the players decide to compare scores.

Player's names	After 5 frames	Final scores
Sylvia	59	118
Mark	84	135
Jana	72	124
Jay	68	136

a. What was the difference in Sylvia and Jana's score after five frames? _____

b. By how many pins did Mark's final score exceed Sylvia's? _____

c. If Sylvia and Mark were partners, how much did the sum of their scores lead Jana and Jay's after five frames? _____

d. By the end of the first game Jana and Jay were the winners. By how many pins did they win? _____

5. Below are the first five frames for the second game played by the four friends. Total up their scores for each of the frames.

1. | 4 | 2 | – | 9 | ⊠ | 6 ◿ | 8 | 1 | **Sylvia:** _____

2. | 3 | 5 | 7 ◿ | 7 | – | 5 ◿ | 6 | 2 | **Mark:** _____

3. | – | 8 | 4 ◿ | ⊠ | 1 | 7 | 3 | 5 | **Jana:** _____

4. | ⊠ | 9 | – | 2 ◿ | 8 | 1 | 6 | 3 | **Jay:** _____

Name _____

KNOWING THE GAME PLAN

In football, the coach can call many different plays. Each player needs to know what the plays are, or all the plans and rules won't do much good. Each play requires each player to know how, when, and where to perform his assigned tasks. In math, the properties of operations are kind of like football plays. They tell each player (number) what tasks they can do. You'll need to use three properties of operations: **commutative, associative,** and **distributive,** to solve these problems.

1. Mark thinks of the commutative property as the order of his daily travels from home to school and then from school to home. Fill in the missing numbers to complete the following examples of the commutative property.

   (a) $7 + 3 = \_\_\_ + 7$

   (b) $5 \times \_\_\_ = 8 \times 5$

2. Tonya considers the grouping of the associative property to be like driving to pick up her two best friends. Sometimes she picks up Jessica first and then Mary, and other times she picks up Mary first and then Jessica. Either way, all three friends get to their activities. Complete the following equations using the associative property.

   (a) $(2 \times 5) \times 7 = 2 \times (5 \times \_\_\_)$

   (b) $(3 + \_\_\_) + 8 = 3 + (7 + 8)$

3. If the order of the numbers is what changes, think *commutative*. If the grouping of the numbers changes, think *associative*. Identify the following as commutative (**C**) or associative (**A**) property examples.

   (a) $2 + (4 + 9) = 2 + (9 + 4)$ _____

   (b) $(3 \times 5) \times 10 = 3 \times (5 \times 10)$ _____

   (c) $(1 + 6) + 8 = 8 + (1 + 6)$ _____

   (d) $(7 + 4) + 3 = 7 + (4 + 3)$ _____

   (e) $2 \times (8 \times 9) = (8 \times 9) \times 2$ _____

   (f) $(8 \times 6) \times 5 = 8 \times (6 \times 5)$ _____

4. Complete the following examples using the distributive property.

   (a) $7(3+1) = \_\_\_ \times 3 + \_\_\_ \times 1$

   (b) $5 \times 8 + 5 \times 2 = \_\_\_ (8+2)$

5. Rearrange the following equations using the given property.

   a) associative $12 + (7 + 3) = $ _____

   b) associative $6 \times (8 \times 2) = $ _____

   c) commutative $(5 + 11) + 9 = $ _____

   d) distributive $10 (4 + 3) = $ _____

   e) distributive $6 \times 5 + 6 \times 2 = $ _____

   f) associative $1 + (9 + 5) = $ _____

   g) commutative $12 \times (4 \times 7) = $ _____

   h) commutative $(2 \times 7) \times 11 = $ _____

   i) associative $(8 \times 10) \times 2 = $ _____

   j) commutative $(3 + 8) + 14 = $ _____

Name _____

THE RULES OF THE GAME

All sports have rules. Whether it's an individual sport such as golf, tennis, or speed skating, or a team sport such as baseball or volleyball, participants get into trouble if they don't know and follow the rules of the game. In math, the properties of numbers are a lot like game rules. Properties tell you what numbers can and cannot do as a part of the game plan. Here are some of the properties that you need to know well in order to correctly solve math equations.

Identity Property	**Property of Zero**	**Inverse Property of One**
$5 + 0 = 5$	$6 \times 0 = 0$	$2 \times (\frac{1}{2}) = 1$
$7 \times 1 = 7$		

1. Complete the following equations using identity, inverse, and zero properties.

   (a) ___ $+ 3 = 3$ (c) ___ $\times 8 = 0$ (e) $(\frac{1}{4}) \times$ ___ $= 1$

   (b) $0 +$ ___ $= 2$ (d) $5 \times$ ___ $= 1$ (f) $1 \times$ ___ $= 9$

2. Identify whether the following are examples of the identity, inverse, or zero properties.

   (a) $(\frac{2}{3}) \times (\frac{3}{2}) = 1$ (d) $0 + 4 = 4$ (g) $0 = 6 \times 0$

   _____   _____   _____

   (b) $12 \times 0 = 0$ (e) $2 = 2 \times 1$ (h) $1 = 7 \times 1$

   _____   _____   _____

   (c) $11 \times 1 = 11$ (f) $1 = (\frac{1}{5}) \times 5$ (i) $2 = 0 + 2$

   _____   _____   _____

3. Select the letter below that correctly identifies what property the equations illustrate.

   A. Identity   C. Zero Property   E. Commutative
   B. Inverse   D. Distributive   F. Associative

   _____ 1. $5 + 1 = 1 + 5$ _____ 5. $(3 + 9) + 10 = 3 + (9 + 10)$

   _____ 2. $0 = 0 \times 7$ _____ 6. $(2 \times 5) \times 8 = 8 \times (2 \times 5)$

   _____ 3. $2 \times 3 + 2 \times 7 = 2 (3+7)$ _____ 7. $(4 + 9) = (4 + 9) + 0$

   _____ 4. $6 \times (\frac{1}{6}) = 1$ _____ 8. $1 \times (11 \times 6) = (11 \times 6)$

Name _____

SPORTING MULTIPLES

Athletes love multiples—as long as you're talking about multiple scores or points, and not injuries! Use your knowledge of multiples to solve these problems.

1. Too Tall Tom is great at three-pointers in basketball. Write the first ten multiples of 3.

   _____

2. The Big Bruisers are great at touchdowns. Write the first ten multiples of 6.

   _____

3. The Much-Muscle Football Team always makes the extra point each time they score a touchdown. Write the first ten multiples of 7.

   _____

4. Each time Sugar Foot Steve shoots the basketball from the left side of the court, he scores 2 points. Write the first ten multiples of 2.

   _____

5. Fill in the scoreboards for these games.

a. Cougars: 4 touchdowns (6 pts each); 3 extra points
               (1 pt each); 3 field goals (3 pts each)
   Panthers: 5 touchdowns (6 pts each); 1 extra point
               (1 pt each); 1 field goal (3 pts each)

SCORE	
COUGARS	
PANTHERS	

b. Bobcats: 29 goals (2 pts each); 6 three-point goals
               (3 pts each); 18 free throws (1 pt each)
   Wildcats: 35 goals (2 pts each); 5 three-point goals
               (3 pts each); 5 free throws (1 pt each)

SCORE	
BOBCATS	
WILDCATS	

c. Lions: 9 innings; 4 runs in each inning
   Tigers: 9 innings; 3 runs in each of four innings;
            5 runs in each of the other innings

SCORE	
LIONS	
TIGERS	

d. Cougars: 44 goals (2 pts each); 22 free throws (1 pt each)
   Jaguars: 39 goals (2 pts each); 19 free throws (1 pt each)

SCORE	
COUGARS	
JAGUARS	

Name _____

CMs & LCMs

How are you with your CMs and your LCMs? Do you remember what these are?

A **common multiple** is a multiple that 2 or more numbers have in common.
  Ex: 12 is a **common multiple** for 2, 3, 4, and 6.

A **least common multiple** is the smallest number that is a common multiple for 2 or more numbers.
  Ex: 4, 8, 12, and 16 are **common multiples** for 2 and 4, but 4 is the **least common multiple**.

1. The Wildcats Football Team made the extra point after every touchdown for 7 points each time they scored. The Cougars made only the touchdown each time they scored, for 6 points each time.
   What is the lowest score at which the game would be tied? _____

2. The Hit-A-Homer Baseball Company ships their baseballs in cases of 6. The Super Slugger Baseball Company ships their baseballs in cases of 8. What is the fewest baseballs you would have to order to get the same number of balls from each company in full cases? _____

3. Molly Muscle is putting weights on her machine. Each of her weights are 5 pounds. Pump-It-Up Polly wants to have the same amount of weight on her machine as Molly, but her weights are 12 pounds each. What is the least amount of weight that could be placed on both machines so that the women are lifting the same amount? _____

4. The Burros have scored only 2-pointers in the basketball game and the Tornadoes have scored only 3-pointers in the game. Is it possible for the score to be tied at 18 to 18? _____

Write 5 common multiples for each of these sets of numbers:

5. 4, 5 _____ _____ _____   6. 2, 5, 6 _____ _____ _____   7. 3, 7 _____ _____ _____

8. 6, 4 _____ _____ _____   9. 3, 15 _____ _____ _____   10. 2, 16 _____ _____ _____

Find the least common multiples for the following numbers:

11. 14, 22 _____   12. 12, 20 _____

13. 9, 15 _____   14. 12, 25 _____

15. 10, 15 _____   16. 4, 7, 9 _____

17. 3, 5, 12 _____   18. 6, 16, 26 _____

19. 150, 375 _____

Name _____

CYCLE THE DISTANCE

Tom, Jane, and Jonathan ride their bicycles on the paths around town, each riding several miles a day. Below is a map of the points around town. Also listed are the distances between points on the map. Draw lines between points that are connected, and write in the distance in miles between the points on the map. Help our cyclists to compute the distances and times for their bike rides to answer the questions on the next page (page 31).

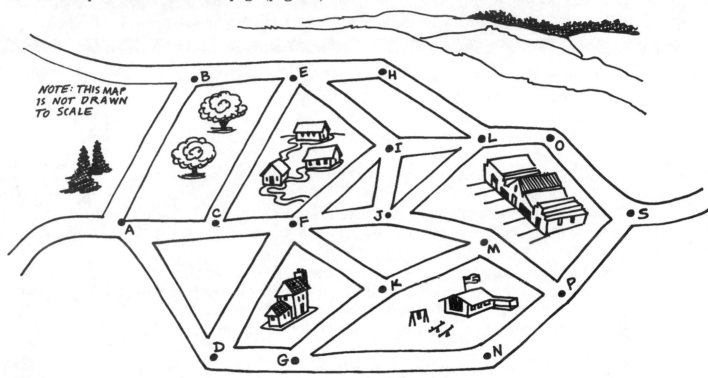

NOTE: THIS MAP IS NOT DRAWN TO SCALE

From	To	Distance	From	To	Distance	From	To	Distance
A	B	3 miles	E	I	4 miles	J	L	4 miles
A	C	1 mile	F	I	6 miles	J	M	4 miles
A	D	2 miles	F	J	5 miles	K	M	3 miles
B	E	2 miles	F	K	4 miles	L	O	6 miles
C	E	4 miles	G	K	6 miles	M	P	5 miles
C	F	5 miles	G	N	10 miles	N	P	4 miles
D	F	3 miles	H	L	2 miles	O	S	3 miles
D	G	3 miles	I	J	2 miles	P	S	4 miles
E	H	5 miles	I	L	3 miles			

Use with page 31.

Name

CYCLE THE DISTANCE, CONTINUED

Use with page 30.

1. Tom is considering three different paths to bike from point A to point L. Find the distance in miles for each path.

   I.   A – D – F – J – L = 2 + 3 + 5 + 4 = _____ miles

   II. A – C – F – I – L = _____ miles

   III. A – B – E – H – L = _____ miles

2. If Tom bikes at a rate of 7 minutes per mile, calculate how long it will take him to cycle each of the three routes above.

   I.   14 miles x 7 minutes per mile = 98 minutes

   II. _____ miles x 7 minutes per mile = _____ minutes

   III. _____ miles x 7 minutes per mile = _____ minutes

3. Jane is considering three different routes from point A to point P. Calculate the miles for each route.

   I.   A – B – E – I – J – M – P = _____ miles

   II. A – C – F – K – M – P = _____ miles

   III. A – D – G – N – P = _____ miles

4. Jane is able to ride at a speed of 1 mile every 6 minutes. Calculate her time for each of the 3 paths in question 3.

   I.   _____ miles x 6 minutes per mile = _____ minutes

   II. _____ miles x 6 minutes per mile = _____ minutes

   III. _____ miles x 6 minutes per mile = _____ minutes

5. Find the shortest path in miles from point A to point S.

   I. Give the path in letters: A _____ S

   II. What is the length of the path in miles? _____ miles

6. If Jonathan rides at a speed of 1 mile every 5 minutes, how long will it take him to ride from point A to point S using the shortest route that you found in question five?

   _____

7. Every morning Jonathan regularly rides this route: D-F-I-E-C-A-D. How far does he ride each time?

   _____

Name _____

MOUNTAINS OF MEMORABILIA

Sarah, Jake, and Mark are great sports fans. They love to watch their favorite athletes and teams on TV or at live sporting events. But they also enjoy collecting memorabilia that was used by famous sports personalities or collectibles that commemorate their famous accomplishments.

1. Sarah has an interest in the Triple Crown of Racing: the Kentucky Derby, the Preakness Stakes, and the Belmont Stakes. She collects the official race day glasses from the three races and she also collects figurines of the horses that have won the races. Sarah has decided to total the value of the multiples in her collection.

Number in Collection	Description of the item	Value of one item	Total Value
5	1995 Kentucky Derby glass	$2	_____
3	1994 Triple Crown glasses (set)	$9	_____
7	1989 Belmont Stakes cups	$4	_____
4	Triple Crown horses (set)	$23	_____
8	Secretariat figurines	$6	_____
Total value			_____

2. Jake is a baseball fan, and his blood runs "Cincinnati Red." He collects rookie cards, signed baseballs, programs, and felt pennants.

Number in Collection	Description of the item	Value of one item	Total Value
9	Baseballs signed by Opening Day starters	$12	_____
6	Complete Rookie Card Sets (1995)	$29	_____
7	1994 World Series Programs	$5	_____
27	Felt Pennants 1993 (assorted teams)	$4	_____
3	Baseballs signed by Hal Morris	$7	_____
Total value	_____		

3. Mark is a golfing fan. Since he hails from Georgia, his favorite tournament is the Masters at Augusta. His current favorite golfer is Tiger Woods.

Number in Collection	Description of the item	Value of one item	Total Value
5	Programs from the 1995 Masters	$3	_____
3	1996 Masters passes signed by Greg Norman	$14	_____
7	Golf balls used by Lee Trevino	$6	_____
2	Golf hats worn by Tiger Woods	$58	_____
9	Golf tees used by Tiger Woods	$2	_____
Total value	_____		

Name _____

HOW MUCH IS ONE PLAYER WORTH?

Professional sports is a big money item. Star players or franchise players command multimillion dollar salaries that are paid out over several years. Below are some of the salaries negotiated and signed in 1996. Answer these questions about money earned by athletes.

_____ 1. Before being dethroned as the heavyweight boxing champion in a stunning upset by Evander Holyfield, Mike Tyson earned $75 million for three fights. On average, what did Mike earn per fight?

_____ 2. Alan Houston, who was coached by his father when he played basketball at the University of Tennessee, became a talented shooting guard in the NBA. The New York Knicks convinced him to sign a seven-year deal that was worth $56 million. On average, how much would Alan be earning per year?

_____ 3. Alonzo Mourning, nicknamed Zo by the media and his teammates, played his college hoops for John Thompson at Georgetown University. Under his new contract with the Miami Heat of the NBA he would be paid $112 million over the next seven years. How much would Zo be making on average each year?

_____ 4. Kenny Anderson signed a basketball contract with the Portland Trailblazers that would pay him $50 million over the next seven years. To the nearest dollar, how much would Kenny be paid on average for each of the next seven years?

_____ 5. The Seattle Mariners have one of the premier shortstops in major league baseball in Alex Rodriguez. Under a recent contract he would be paid $105 million over the next three years. On average, how much would Alex's yearly salary be?

_____ 6. The high scorer among the Washington Bullets for the 1995–1996 season was Juwan Howard with 1789 points. His contract stipulated that he would be paid $105 million over the next seven years. How much is Juwan's average annual salary?

_____ 7. The Atlanta Hawks of the NBA have been pleased with the play of Dikembe Mutumbo. He signed a five-year contract with them that would pay him a total of $50 million. Compute his average yearly salary in millions of dollars.

_____ 8. The Los Angeles Lakers convinced Shaquille O'Neal to leave the Orlando Magic by paying him over $120 million dollars. Since the Shaq weighed in at 300 pounds, how much did Los Angeles pay per pound for this marquee player?

9. Michael Jordan, who many consider the greatest basketball player ever, signed a one-year contract with the Chicago Bulls for $25 million.

_____ a. Although the regular season is 82 games long, the Bulls would almost certainly be in the playoffs again. Assuming that they could play as many as 100 games in all, calculate what the Bulls would be paying Michael for each game.

_____ b. In the 1995–1996 basketball season, Michael scored 2491 points. If he scored 2500 points in the next season, how much would he be earning per point?

Name _____

QUOTE ME!

One of the greatest slogans of sports is:

" *What matters is not the size of the dog in the fight, but the size of the fight in the dog!* "

To discover who made this statement, work each exercise below. Each time the answer appears, write the matching letter below it.

7⟌630	8⟌5600	24⟌72	53⟌424	12⟌48	91⟌819	44⟌264
C	T	O	N	A	Y	H

12⟌7584	41⟌31,734	31⟌899	65⟌780	24⟌744	41⟌902
R	P	U	L	B	E

	90	3	4	90	6		774	4	29	12	
___	___	___	___	___	___		___	___	___	___	
"	31	22	4	632	"		31	632	9	4	8	700
___	___	___	___	___			___	___	___	___	___	___

Name

DIVIDE THE SAVINGS

Here's a quick review of some divisibility rules. You'll need them to solve the problems below.

If a number is divisible by:

. . . 2, then the ones digit is even

. . . 3, then the sum of the digits is divisible by 3

. . . 4, then the number formed by the last two digits is divisible by 4

. . . 5, then the ones digit is 0 or 5

. . . 6, then the number is divisible by 2 and 3

. . . 10, then the ones digit is 0

The Goal Post Sports Store is having a Midnight Madness Sale. Read the ad and answer the questions that follow.

MIDNIGHT MADNESS SALE

MEN'S SUPER TENNIS SHOES $15.00

FOOTBALL T-SHIRTS ONLY $12.00

TIGER GOLF CLUBS $150.00

PRO TEAM CAPS $4.45 !!

aqua shoes $17.00

Soccer Shoes $25.00

We pay all sales tax during this sale!

____ 1. Could you pay for the Men's New Super Tennis Shoes with all five-dollar bills and receive no change back?

____ 2. If you wanted the football T-Shirt and the Aqua Shoes, could you pay with all ten-dollar bills and receive no change back?

____ 3. If you had only nickels, could you pay for the Pro Team Cap and receive no change back?

____ 4. If six friends wanted to buy a set of Tiger Golf Clubs together, could they split the bill evenly with no one having to pay extra?

____ 5. If four sisters wanted to buy their father a pair of Aqua Shoes, a pair of Men's New Super Tennis Shoes, and a football T-Shirt, could they split the bill evenly with no one having to pay extra?

Using the divisibility rules above, determine whether each number is divisible by 2, 3, 4, 5, 6, or 10. If it is divisible by a number, place an X in the appropriate row.

	58	153	228	523	80	104	180	89	532	90
2										
3										
4										
5										
6										
10										

Name

PRIME-TIME SCOREBOARD

This scoreboard changes images during intermissions and other breaks. When it's not showing the score, it's showing a message to the crowd. Shade in all the prime numbers with a red marker and shade all composite numbers with a blue marker to read the message it's flashing today.

Name

FOOTBALL MATCHUPS

Athletes are often given nicknames. Here are some nicknames of some famous football players. To match the nicknames with the athletes, find the letter (A-J) that matches the exponential number (1–10).

____ 1. 5^4 Deion Sanders

____ 2. 4^3 Jeff Hostetler

____ 3. 1^{40} Willie Anderson

____ 4. 2^5 REGGIE WHITE

____ 5. 13^2 DESMOND HOWARD

____ 6. 8^3 Red Grange

____ 7. 9^4 John Riggins

____ 8. 6^1 Andy Nelson

____ 9. 7^2 Fred Evans

____ 10. 6^4 BART BUETOW

A. 64   Hoss

B. 32   The Minister Of Defense

C. 6561   The Diesel

D. 625   Prime Time

E. 6   Bones

F. 49   Dippy

G. 1   Flipper

H. 169   Magic

I. 1296   The Mad Scientist

J. 512   The Galloping Ghost

SUPER STAR PROBLEMS

Find the value of each expression.

11. $2^3 \cdot 7^2$ _____

12. $5^2 \cdot 8^2 \cdot 3^3$ _____

13. 100^3 _____

14. $5 \cdot 6^3 \cdot 10^3$ _____

15. $3^2 \cdot 4^3$ _____

16. $5^3 \cdot 100^2$ _____

17. $2^2 \cdot 7^2$ _____

18. $5^0 \cdot 5^2$ _____

19. $9^2 \cdot 2^2 \cdot 3^2$ _____

20. $10 \cdot 4 \cdot 6^2$ _____

21. $25^2 \cdot 2^3$ _____

22. $4^2 \cdot 10^2$ _____

Name _____

THREE KEYS TO SPORTS SUCCESS

Nick knows that great ability at running, jumping, and throwing are the keys to success in many sports. As a trivia fan, he likes to keep up with the running, jumping, and throwing records set by both man and beast. The following facts are some that Nick finds most interesting. See how many you know.

_____ 1. Michael Johnson won gold medals in the men's 200 m and 400 m sprints at the 1996 Olympic Games held in Atlanta. Write 200 m and 400 m as powers of ten.

2. In a tournament situation, one of the best Frisbee™ throwers in the world tossed the Frisbee™ 500 feet or 6000 inches. Write these two distances as powers of ten.

3. One of the fastest land animals is the cheetah, which has been clocked at speeds of 100,000 mm per hour. Write this rate as a power of ten.

4. The men's water-ski jumping record is over 6×10^1 m or 6×10^4 mm. Write these two distances without using powers of ten.

5. The men's Olympic high jump record was set by American Charles Austin at the Atlanta games with a mark of 2.39×10^3 mm. The long jump record is still held by American Bob Beamon with a jump of 8.9×10^2 cm which he set at the Mexico Olympics. Write these two distances without using powers of ten.

6. The Olympic record in the marathon is held by Carlos Lopes of Portugal and was set at the Los Angeles Olympics with a time of 7761 seconds. Round these seconds to the nearest thousand and write them as a power of ten.

7. A marathon race is 26 miles and 385 yards long. It commemorates a Greek messenger's run from the city of Marathon to Athens to proclaim a great victory over the Persians. This distance in yards is 46,145. Round this number to the nearest ten thousand and write it as a power of ten.

8. Secretariat was one of the greatest horses ever to win the triple crown. His record winning time for the Kentucky Derby was 119.4 seconds (set in 1973). The distance for the Derby race is 2310 yards.

   a. Round the time to the nearest ten and write it as a power of ten.

   b. Round the distance to the nearest hundred and write as a power of ten.

9. The highest jump by any animal is an estimated thirty-foot leap by a Mako shark. This height in millimeters would be about 9414. Round this number to the nearest thousand and write it as a power of ten.

10. The Olympic record in the javelin was set in 1976 by Miklos Nemeth of Hungary with a throw of 9.458×10^4 mm. Round this distance to the nearest thousand and write it without using a power of ten.

Name _____

ERRANDS ON SKIS

Anne has been snowed in at the cabin for several days. She wants to plan a trip so that when she is able to get out she can run all of her errands and get back to the cabin using the shortest route. She has a diagram of the area (not drawn to scale).

Below are the distances measured from a map. These distances need to be converted to yards. The scale of the map is 1 mm = 100 yards and 1 cm = 1000 yards.

C = cabin
D = drugstore
G = grocery
R = restaurant
S = ski lodge
V = video store

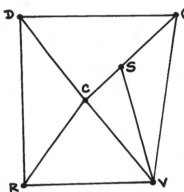

CR = 9.2 mm
VG = 1.4 cm
CD = 6.8 mm
VR = 2.7 cm
CS = 8.9 mm
VS = 3.1 cm
CV = 7.3 mm
SG = 8.7 cm
DR = 9.5 cm
GD = 10.6 cm

Convert the above measurements to yards.

1. Cabin to restaurant _____

2. Cabin to drugstore _____

3. Cabin to ski lodge _____

4. Cabin to video store _____

5. Drugstore to restaurant _____

6. Video store to grocery _____

7. Video store to restaurant _____

8. Video store to ski lodge _____

9. Ski lodge to grocery _____

10. Grocery to drugstore _____

Find the shortest route in yards that begins at the cabin, visits each site once, and returns to the cabin. Describe the shortest route and give its distance in yards.

11. Route _____

_____

_____

_____

_____

_____

12. Length of route in yards _____

Name _____

RACING RATES

Nakia has the need for speed. She loves things that are fast. Her fascination has led her to read everything she can find about speeds achieved in air, on water, and on land. Here are some facts that she has found. Convert each to kilometers per hour.

_____ 1. Parachutists can reach speeds of 298,000 meters per hour in a skydiving free fall. Divide this number by 1000 to find out the parachutist's speed in kph.

_____ 2. Racing pigeons flying in windless conditions have achieved speeds of 9.7×10^6 centimeters per hour. Divide this speed by 100,000 to find the pigeon's speed in kph.

_____ 3. In 1976 an official world air speed record was set by a jet plane traveling 3,529,560 meters per hour. Divide the jet's speed by 10^3 to find the rate in kph.

_____ 4. An unofficial world record was set in water skiing in 1979 when a speed of 2.06×10^8 millimeters per hour was measured. Divide this rate by one million to find its rate in kph.

_____ 5. In 1977 an unlimited hydroplane set an unofficial world water speed record by traveling at a speed of 55,600 dekameters. Dividing by a hundred will give the speed in kph.

_____ 6. A board sailing world mark was set in 1980 when a speed of 4.5 million centimeters per hour was recorded. To find the rate in kph divide by 100,000.

_____ 7. The world speed record for ice yachting was set in 1938 when a speed of 2.3×10^6 decimeters per hour was reached. The rate in kph can be found by dividing by 10,000.

_____ 8. Craig Breedlove hopes to bring the world land speed record for jet-powered vehicles back to the United States. He is developing a new vehicle called the Spirit of America that he hopes will break the sound barrier by traveling at a rate of 1.224 million meters per hour. By dividing this number by 10^3 the rate in kph can be found.

_____ 9. The top speeds achieved by skateboarders in a standing position are so fast that they would outpace both speed skaters and racehorses. A world speed record set in 1978 clocked the rate of a standing skateboarder to be 8.6 million centimeters per hour. Divide this speed by 100,000 to find the answer in kph.

10. If the previous 9 speedsters were to be ranked by their speeds in kph, put a rank beside them where 1 would be the fastest and 9 would be the slowest.

☐ Parachutist	☐ Water skier	☐ Ice yacht
☐ Racing pigeon	☐ Hydroplane	☐ Jet vehicle
☐ Jet plane	☐ Board sailer	☐ Skate boarder

Name _____

PROBLEMS WITH WHEELS

Biking is one of the fastest growing and most popular sports around the country for competition and for recreation. Solve these problems about folks on wheels.

_____ 1. Almost 100,000 bike riders are members of the League of American Cyclists. If the club magazine is bundled in packages of 10, how many bundles will there be to mail?

_____ 2. The bicycle was introduced to the United States in 1866. How many years ago did this happen?

_____ 3. In 1983, Laurent Fignon won the Tour de France in a little more than 105 hours. If the race was 2,315 miles long, what was his average speed per hour?

A bicycle store is having a sale. Using the sales flyer at right, solve the following problems.

_____ 4. Mark wants a new 10-speed bike, a deluxe helmet, and a water bottle. What is his total bill?

_____ 5. Evan is trying to watch his budget. He decides to buy a rebuilt 3-speed bike, a basic helmet, handle grips, and a water bottle. What is his total bill?

_____ 6. Abby wants a new 3-speed bike and a deluxe helmet. The bike store owner will take her old bike as a trade-in. How much will she owe the bike store if the owner gives her $50 for her old bike?

Cycle City
Spring Sale
NEW 10-SPEED BIKES: $350.00
NEW 3-SPEED BIKES: $200.00

REBUILT BIKES
10-SPEED $175.00
3-SPEED $100.00

DELUXE HELMETS: $75.00
BASIC HELMETS: $25.00
HANDLE GRIPS: $15.00
WATER BOTTLES: only....$5.00

_____ 7. Ramon wants to buy a new 10-speed bike, a basic helmet, and a water bottle. He doesn't have enough money now, but the owner says he will put these items on layaway for him. To place these items on layaway it will cost an additional $10. What is his total bill? He wants to pay in 3 installments for the items. How much will he have to pay each time?

_____ 8. Hilary works at the bike store and receives $25 off on any item she buys over $50. If she wants to buy a new 3-speed bike and a basic helmet, how much is her total bill?

Name _____

RIVER TRIP

Sam's dad has offered to take him on a trip to a river lodge. Sam is allowed to bring David and Mike with him if the three friends will split their expenses. Solve the problems on this page and the next (page 43) about their trip.

1. On the way to the river Sam's dad fills the car with gas and the bill comes to $22. If he contributes $7, how much will each of the three boys need to pay for gas?

2. At dinner, each of the boys orders separately. Sam's hamburger platter and milkshake comes to $6. David's chicken sandwich, onion rings, and drink cost $7. Mike's spaghetti, milk, and pie total $8. If Sam's dad gathers the money and pays the total bill with $30, then how much did his dinner cost?

3. At the lodge, the three boys share a room. The charge for Thursday night's stay will be $75, but the room rate for Friday and Saturday is $93 a night. What is the total room charge for their three-night stay, and what is each boy's share of the bill?

4. On Friday morning Sam's dad treats the boys to a pancake breakfast and asks what their plans are for the day. David outlines the boys' plans below.

TIME:	ACTIVITY:	CHARGES:	COST:
9:00 – 11:00	Mountain biking	$4. per bike	
11:00 – 12:00	Swimming	no charge	
12:00 – 1:00	Picnic with Ice cream	$14. total	
1:00 – 2:00	Water sliding	$6. each	
2:00 – 3:00	Jet Skiing	$100. total	
3:00 – 4:00	Basketball	no charge	
4:00 – 5:00	Video games	$3. each	
5:00 – 6:00	Buffet dinner	$25. total	
6:00 – 7:30	Bowling	$9. each	
7:30 – 9:30	Watching movies	$5. total	

a. Give the total amount that the three boys will owe for the day if they participate in all of these activities.

b. Give the share for each boy.

Use with page 43.

Name

RIVER TRIP, CONTINUED

Use with page 42.

5. On Saturday, Sam's dad offers to treat the boys to a float trip on the river.
If innertube rental with life jacket and insurance is $14 per person, round-trip transportation is $5 per person, and the picnic at the waterfall is $7 per person, what will the trip for four cost? If Sam's dad pays with two fifties and a twenty, how much change should he receive?

6. After dinner, the three friends decide to take a river cruise featuring fire-works and a beach bonfire hosted by the lodge's entertainment staff. If the cost is $14 per person, how much will David and Mike have to pay if they decide to pay Sam's way?

7. At breakfast on Sunday, the three friends decide to treat Sam's dad to the lodge's special brunch buffet. If the cost is $12 per person, how much will each boy have to pay to settle the bill for four if a $6 tip is added?

8. After the Sunday brunch, the three friends pool their remaining cash. It totals $31. Kayak rental with helmet, paddle, and life vest is $13 per person for a half day. How much will they need to borrow from Sam's dad to be able to kayak?

9. On the way home, Sam's dad reminds the boys that they have not saved any money to pay for gas and dinner on the way home. By the time they get home from the river, the boys are in debt to dad for $36. If he offers to pay each boy $2 an hour for yard work, how many hours will each of the three friends need to work for Sam's dad to pay off their river trip?

10. When the boys go to develop their pictures, they find that they have each taken 6 rolls of 36 pictures each.

   a. How many pictures will they have to have developed?

   b. If each boy spends $48, how much will each picture cost to develop?

Name _____

GEARING UP

While surfing the Internet, Will found a store that sold authentic team wear. He printed the price list. Study the prices and then estimate the cost of the items that he may purchase. Solve all problems on this page and the next page (page 45).

1. When Will found this site he told his mom about it. She suggested that he determine approximately how much it would cost to buy his family hooded sweatshirts. His family included the following members:

Family Member	Adult Size	Favorite Team
Dad	XXL	Titans
Mom	L	Titans
Claire (sister)	S	Giants
Eric (brother)	M	Steelers
Will	M	Vikings

About how much would it cost to buy one sweatshirt for each person and pay for the shipping?

_____

Use with page 45.

Name

GEARING UP, CONTINUED

Use with page 44.

2. It's hard to buy presents for Grandpa. He is an XXL and enjoys the 49ers. Mom told Will that he could order Grandpa's Christmas presents if he did not spend more than $120. Write two estimated orders for Grandpa and don't forget to include the shipping charges.

3. Will loves authentic team wear. He was wondering how much it would cost to buy one of every item for himself. About how much would it cost for Will to order everything that the sport store has in Viking sportswear ?

4. Will has drawn his cousin's name in the family gift exchange. The price limit for the gift is around $25. What could Will buy for his cousin with this budget?

5. Uncle Mark is a former linebacker for the Chicago Bears. He is 6'4" tall and weighs 350 pounds. He is a size 52 or 3XL. Mom told Will to order Uncle Mark one of whatever the store has in his size with the Chicago Bears emblem on it. What could he order, and about how much would this cost?

6. Will's community center has a football team called the Wildcats. About how much would it cost to buy all 25 members of the team turf shirts with Wildcats embroidered on them?

7. Will's grandma always gives him $100 for his birthday. Write up two estimated orders that Will might want to purchase.

8. Nicole came over to Will's house dressed in her favorite team clothing. She has on a home-and-away jacket (size S), a turf shirt, and a shadow cap. About how much did her ensemble cost?

9. Nicole told Will that her grandmother, who lives in Florida, bought her the outfit. About how much did the ensemble cost her grandmother?

Name

PUTTIN' ON THE DOG

Margie enjoys working with her three dogs to show at kennel club events. She has raised Beau, the beagle, from a pup and prefers to enter him in the obstacle course event. Simon, the Scottie, has a gentle temperament and minds well. He excels in the discipline events. Connie, the cocker spaniel, has personality and loves to show off. She performs well in the show dog classes. Help Margie solve the following problems to successfully prepare and compete in the dog show. (See if you can find out what the expression used in the title of this page means.)

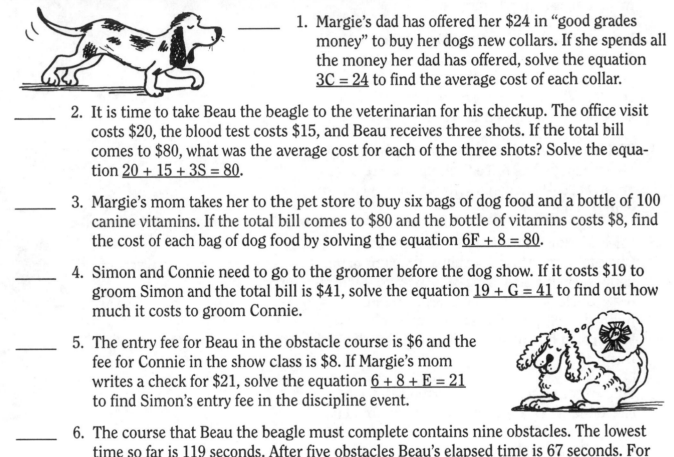

_____ 1. Margie's dad has offered her $24 in "good grades money" to buy her dogs new collars. If she spends all the money her dad has offered, solve the equation $3C = 24$ to find the average cost of each collar.

_____ 2. It is time to take Beau the beagle to the veterinarian for his checkup. The office visit costs $20, the blood test costs $15, and Beau receives three shots. If the total bill comes to $80, what was the average cost for each of the three shots? Solve the equation $20 + 15 + 3S = 80$.

_____ 3. Margie's mom takes her to the pet store to buy six bags of dog food and a bottle of 100 canine vitamins. If the total bill comes to $80 and the bottle of vitamins costs $8, find the cost of each bag of dog food by solving the equation $6F + 8 = 80$.

_____ 4. Simon and Connie need to go to the groomer before the dog show. If it costs $19 to groom Simon and the total bill is $41, solve the equation $19 + G = 41$ to find out how much it costs to groom Connie.

_____ 5. The entry fee for Beau in the obstacle course is $6 and the fee for Connie in the show class is $8. If Margie's mom writes a check for $21, solve the equation $6 + 8 + E = 21$ to find Simon's entry fee in the discipline event.

_____ 6. The course that Beau the beagle must complete contains nine obstacles. The lowest time so far is 119 seconds. After five obstacles Beau's elapsed time is 67 seconds. For Beau to tie the leader, solve the equation $119 = (9 - 5)T + 67$ to find out how many seconds per obstacle Beau can spend on the rest of the course.

_____ 7. Simon the Scottie received seven scores of eight and three scores of six from the ten judges at the discipline event. If the top dog got a score of 93, solve the equation $93 = (7 \times 8) + (3 \times 6) + D$ to find out how many points out of first place Simon fell.

_____ 8. In the spaniel class there were 36 entries. If the total number of spaniels in the class was nine times as many as the number of dogs that placed better than Connie (in the judge's opinion), solve the equation $36 = 9 (P - 1)$ to find out what place Connie took in the competition.

Name _____

GO FLY A KITE

Jessica and Gina find that kite flying is great exercise. They've decided to build their own kite. They have instructions for building the following types of kites: a three-foot box kite, a six-foot delta wing kite, and a two-foot traditional kite.

_____ 1. Jessica's brother gives the girls three yards of kite-making material, but they need seven yards total. Write an equation to find "M," the material they will need to buy.

_____ 2. If Jessica and Gina decide to buy four yards of material and spend $24, write an equation to find "P," the price per yard of the kite-making material.

_____ 3. The girls saved $60 to spend on their kite project. After spending $24 on material, write an equation to find "L," the money they have left to finish the project.

4. The hobby store sells the special wooden dowels for making kites at $2 per four-foot dowel. Gina has determined that they will need 48 feet of wood to make their three kites.

_____ a. Write an equation to find "D," the number of four-foot wooden dowels needed.

_____ b. Write an equation to find "W," the cost of the wood.

_____ 5. Jessica calculates that 300 feet of kite string will be needed. Write an equation to find "B," how many balls of string should be purchased if each ball contains 75 feet of string.

_____ 6. Jessica's mom says that "twice the height of the kite minus 100 is equal to the length of string that is let out" is an equation that can be used to calculate the approximate height of the kite. Write an equation to calculate the kite's maximum height "H" if all 300 feet of kite string are let out.

_____ 7. A traditional kite should have a tail that is twice as long as its length. If Gina has a kite tail that is six feet long, write an equation to find "K," the maximum length of the traditional kite with which it could be used.

_____ 8. Jessica thinks the delta wing kite flies best when the wind blows at least 15 miles per hour. Write an equation to calculate "R," the speed at which Jessica should run if the wind is blowing at 11 mph.

Name _____

THE BIG GUYS OF THE NBA

Not only are they tall—really tall—but their scores are tall as well. Here are some of the leading scorers in the NBA, and some of their scores from one basketball season.
Use the information on the chart to answer the questions below.

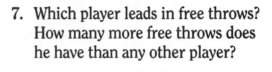

	Field Goals	Free Throws	Points	Average Points
michael Jordan	916	548	2,491	30
H. Olajuwon	768	397	1,936	27
SHAQUILLE O'NEAL	592	249	1,434	27
Karl Malone	789	512	2,106	26
David Robinson	711	626	2,051	25
Charles Barkley	580	440	1,649	23
Patrick Ewing	678	351	1,711	23
Grant Hill	564	485	1,618	20
Scottie Pippin	563	220	1,496	19
A. Hardaway	623	445	1,780	22

1. To determine how many more field goals Michael Jordan has than any other player, would you add, subtract, multiply, or divide? _____

2. To total up the number of points earned by Jordan, O'Neal, and Barkley, would you add, subtract, multiply, or divide?
   _____

3. A statistician determined the number of points each player averaged per game. How do you think the statistician was able to determine the average points of the players?
   _____

4. How many more points must Grant Hill score to catch up with Michael Jordan? _____

5. Scottie Pippin and Michael Jordan play for Chicago. Shaquille O'Neal and A. Hardaway used to play for Orlando. If both players on both teams had played an average game and they were the only players to score, would Chicago or Orlando have won? What would be the final score? _____

6. Which player leads in field goals? How many more field goals does he have than any other player? _____

7. Which player leads in free throws? How many more free throws does he have than any other player?
   _____
   _____

8. Which player leads in points? How many more points does he have than any other player?
   _____
   _____

9. If you wanted to determine how many points were earned by all the players in the chart, would you add, subtract, multiply, or divide?
   _____

10. Write three story problems that could be solved by using the chart of basketball statistics.

Name _____

FOLLOW THE CLUES

Follow the clues to find the name of the answer that matches each description (1–8). Pay attention to the integers written next to each athlete's name on the chart.

	Integer	Athlete
A.	–16	Kerri Strug
B.	8	Evander Holyfield
C.	–6	Shaquille O'Neal
D.	0	Penny Hardaway

	Integer	Athlete
E.	–2	Cigar
F.	4	Joe Montana
G.	–8	Emmit Smith
H.	10	Juwan Howard

_____ 1. This integer is greater than –20 but less than –12.
The athlete it represents is a famous gymnast that completed a final vault with a wrenched ankle to assist her team in winning a gold medal.

_____ 2. This integer is positive and is less than 7.
The athlete it represents was named Most Valuable Player in Super Bowls XVI, XIX, and XXIV.

_____ 3. This integer is greater than 9 and less than 15.
The athlete is 6'8" and received $105 million to play professional basketball.

_____ 4. This integer is greater than –2 but less than 1.
The athlete is an NBA player who drives a white Ferrari with a small "¢" embedded in gold on the hood.

_____ 5. This integer is greater than –3 but less than –1.
This is a horse that won 16 consecutive victories from October 1994 to August 1996.

_____ 6. This integer is greater than 4 but less than 9.
This athlete beat Mike Tyson in 1996.

_____ 7. This integer is greater than –9 but less than –6.
This athlete rushed 1,563 yards for the Dallas Cowboys.

_____ 8. This integer is greater than –7 but less than –4.
This athlete made a deal with the L.A. Lakers to earn $121 million over 7 years.

Name

PRESIDENTIAL GOLF

Many doctors and other experts agree that participating in sports is a great way to reduce stress. Lots of folks also agree that the most stressful job in the United States is that of President. Of the 16 Presidents between William Taft and Bill Clinton, only three did not play golf (Hoover, Truman, and Carter). Below is the scorecard from a fictional golf game the Presidents played against three leading golf pros. Review their scores, and then answer the questions on the next page (page 51).

Golf Scoring

- To play at par is to use the same number of strokes as the assigned par value and is scored as a 0.
- If a golfer uses 2 strokes more than the assigned par, the score is +2.
- Good golfers can use fewer strokes than the assigned par value. To play 1 stroke under par is scored −1.

President	Score	Par	+ or − Par
John F. Kennedy	80	72	+ 8
D. Eisenhower	79	72	+ 7
Gerald Ford	81	72	+ 9
Franklin Roosevelt	89	72	+17
Ronald Reagan	90	72	+18
Richard Nixon	92	72	+20
George Bush	81	72	+ 9
Bill Clinton	90	72	+18
William Taft	69	72	− 3
Warren Harding	100	72	+28
Woodrow Wilson	115	72	+43
Lyndon Johnson	101	72	+29
Calvin Coolidge	120	72	+48

Professional Golfers	Score	Par	+ or − Par
Tiger Woods	65	72	−7
Greg Norman	64	72	−8
Tom Watson	68	72	−4

TAKE COVER, IKE. I'M PLAYING THROUGH!

RIGHT-O, TAFT.

Use with page 51.

Name

PRESIDENTIAL GOLF, CONTINUED

Use with page 50.

1. On the number line plot the strokes of Gerald Ford, William Taft, Dwight Eisenhower, Bill Clinton, Tiger Woods, Greg Norman, and Tom Watson above (+) or below (−) par.

Score	62	64	66	68	70	72	74	76	78	80	82	84	86	88	90	92
+ or − Par	−10	−8	−6	−4	−2	0	2	4	6	8	10	12	14	16	18	20

2. Plot the scores of Tiger Woods and John F. Kennedy in relation to par 72 at 0 on the number line below.

Score	62	64	66	68	70	72	74	76	78	80	82	84	86	88	90	92
+ or − Par	−10	−8	−6	−4	−2	0	2	4	6	8	10	12	14	16	18	20

3. Calvin Coolidge was the least competent of all presidential golfers. On one hole he took 11 strokes to complete a par 3. Plot his strokes above par for this hole on the number line below. How many strokes above par was President Coolidge?

Score		1	2	3	4	5	6	7	8	9	10	11	12	13
+ or − Par			−2	−1	0	1	2	3	4	5	6	7	8	9	10

4. Woodrow and Edith Wilson often golfed together between 5 and 6 A.M. On a par 5, Edith's score was 4 and Woodrow's score was 7. Plot each of their scores in relation to par at zero.

Score	1	2	3	4	5	6	7	8	9	10
+ or − Par	−4	−3	−2	−1	0	1	2	3	4	5

5. President Clinton is known for taking mulligans. A mulligan is a golf shot that you get to "do over." By liberally using mulligans, Clinton scored an 80 one day when playing with Tom Watson. Tom Watson scored a 68. Plot each of their scores in relation to a par 72 at 0. How many shots separated the two golfers?

Score	62	64	66	68	70	72	74	76	78	80	82	84	86	88	90	92
+ or − Par	−10	−8	−6	−4	−2	0	2	4	6	8	10	12	14	16	18	20

- George Bush liked to play rapidly. He played 18 holes with a foursome in 1 hour and 42 minutes.

Did You Know?....

- William H. Taft weighed 355 pounds, but was a respectable golfer.
- Warren G. Harding spent Election Day in 1920 golfing in knickers and an old red sweater at Scioto Country Club in Columbus, Ohio.
- It was said that Lyndon B. Johnson "went to the ball as though he were killing a snake."

Name

DO YOU KNOW YOUR VENUES?

A **venue** is a location where something takes place. This word is used to describe the setting for Olympic events. The puzzle below will reveal venues of the Olympic Games in 1904, 1920, and 1932. First, you need to solve the integer problems to find the number that fits each letter. Then, write the letter on the line to match each letter in the puzzle.

Solve the problems below to find which letter is paired with each answer.

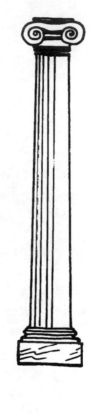

[A] $-8 - (-9) =$ _____

[B] $+5 + (+4) =$ _____

[C] $+(-6) - (+9) =$ _____

[D] $+12 + (-9) =$ _____

[E] $(-3) + (-5) =$ _____

[F] $(+23) - (+9) =$ _____

[G] $-(+13) - (-7) =$ _____

[H] $+(-11) - (+5) =$ _____

[I] $-(-2) + (-7) =$ _____

[J] $-11 + (+7) =$ _____

[K] $-5 + (-7) =$ _____

[L] $+13 + (-8) =$ _____

[M] $-(-3) + (+14) =$ _____

[N] $-6 + (+22) =$ _____

[O] $(-9) - (+8) =$ _____

[P] $-(-14) + (-17) =$ _____

[Q] $+(+4) - (-8) =$ _____

[R] $-(+18) + (+4) =$ _____

[S] $-1 + (+7) =$ _____

[T] $-9 - (+12) =$ _____

[U] $-(-15) - (+8) =$ _____

[V] $+6 + (-24) =$ _____

[W] $(+6) + (+9) =$ _____

[X] $-(+25) + (+12) =$ _____

[Y] $+(+18) - (+5) =$ _____

[Z] $-(-6) - (-12) =$ _____

[Blank] $(-4) + (-7) =$ _____

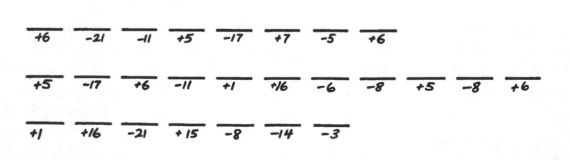

$\overline{}_{+6}$ $\overline{}_{-21}$ $\overline{}_{-11}$ $\overline{}_{+5}$ $\overline{}_{-17}$ $\overline{}_{+7}$ $\overline{}_{-5}$ $\overline{}_{+6}$

$\overline{}_{+5}$ $\overline{}_{-17}$ $\overline{}_{+6}$ $\overline{}_{-11}$ $\overline{}_{+1}$ $\overline{}_{+16}$ $\overline{}_{-6}$ $\overline{}_{-8}$ $\overline{}_{+5}$ $\overline{}_{-8}$ $\overline{}_{+6}$

$\overline{}_{+1}$ $\overline{}_{+16}$ $\overline{}_{-21}$ $\overline{}_{+15}$ $\overline{}_{-8}$ $\overline{}_{-14}$ $\overline{}_{-3}$

Name _____

IT HELPS TO SPEAK LATIN

Although the ancient Greeks held Olympic games every four years beginning around 776 B.C., the modern Olympic games have been around only since A.D.1896. At that time a French educator decided to invite young athletes from around the world to Athens to begin the modern Olympic games. While the Summer Olympics are now held in the years divisible by four and the Winter Olympics are held in even numbered years not divisible by four, the Olympic motto is still the same. The motto in Latin is "Citius, Altius, Fortius." Use the integer problems and alphabet key below to find (1) the last name of the French educator Baron Pierre de _____ , who began the modern Olympic games, and (2) the English translation for the Olympic motto.

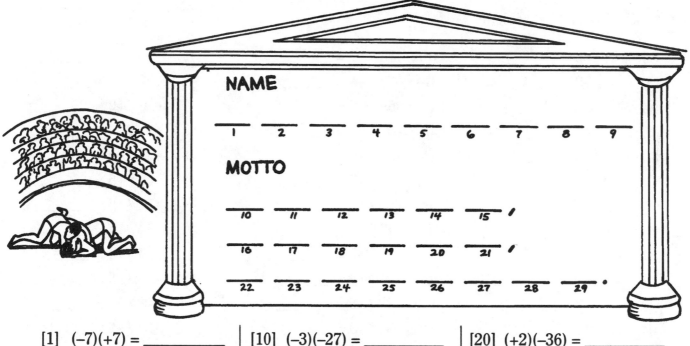

[1] $(-7)(+7)$ = _____

[2] $(+6)(-6)$ = _____

[3] $(-5)(-13)$ = _____

[4] $(-4)(-9)$ = _____

[5] $(-8)(+9)$ = _____

[6] $(+8)(-7)$ = _____

[7] $(+8)(+6)$ = _____

[8] $(-9)(+6)$ = _____

[9] $(-4)(-5)$ = _____

[10] $(-3)(-27)$ = _____

[11] $(-3)(+14)$ = _____

[12] $(-3)(-24)$ = _____

[13] $(+3)(+16)$ = _____

[14] $(+12)(-6)$ = _____

[15] $(-4)(+14)$ = _____

[16] $(-6)(-7)$ = _____

[17] $(+3)(-18)$ = _____

[18] $(-15)(0)$ = _____

[19] $(+2)(+21)$ = _____

[20] $(+2)(-36)$ = _____

[21] $(-2)(+28)$ = _____

[22] $(-6)(-12)$ = _____

[23] $(-8)(-6)$ = _____

[24] $(-8)(+7)$ = _____

[25] $(+12)(-3)$ = _____

[26] $(-2)(-10)$ = _____

[27] $(+16)(0)$ = _____

[28] $(-18)(+4)$ = _____

[29] $(-14)(+4)$ = _____

Alphabet for Matching Answers to Letters

A = −42	B = +36	C = −49	D = −65	E = −72	F = +81	G = 0	H = +42	I = −54
J = −81	K = +24	L = −50	M = −64	N = +20	O = −36	P = +32	Q = −18	R = −56
S = +72	T = +48	U = +65	V = −32	W = −24	X = +18	Y = +64	Z = −45	

Name

MYSTERY NAME

? This mystery athlete turned professional as a twenty-year-old. In his first year as a pro he earned $60 million in endorsements. Besides being named the top amateur in his sport for three years in a row, he won two professional tournaments in the first seven that he entered, beating both Payne Stewart and Davis Love III. Although he did not win the first Skins Game he played as a professional, he did prove that he could drive the ball as far as John Daly. Many predict that he will win a green jacket before Greg Norman. The letters of this athlete's name are scrambled in the grid below. Follow the directions in this worksheet to find out how to reveal the name.

FIRST, work the problems.

(a) $-36 / -6 =$ _____

(b) $0 / +9 =$ _____

(c) $-64 / +8 =$ _____

(d) $+28 / +7 =$ _____

(e) $-45 / -5 =$ _____

(f) $+54 / -9 =$ _____

(g) $+42 / +6 =$ _____

(h) $-56 / -7 =$ _____

(i) $+32 / -8 =$ _____

(j) $+63 / +9 =$ _____

(k) $-35 / -7 =$ _____

(l) $-81 / +9 =$ _____

(m) $-18 / +3 =$ _____

(n) $+35 / -5 =$ _____

(o) $-63 / +7 =$ _____

(p) $-32 / -4 =$ _____

(q) $+56 / -8 =$ _____

(r) $-42 / +7 =$ _____

(s) $-54 / -6 =$ _____

(t) $+45 / +9 =$ _____

(u) $-28 / +7 =$ _____

(v) $+64 / +4 =$ _____

(w) $-72 / -8 =$ _____

(x) $+36 / -3 =$ _____

(y) $+24 / -4 =$ _____

(z) $-22 / -2 =$ _____

(?) $+50 / +2 =$ _____

(@) $-25 / -5 =$ _____

(#) $+30 / -6 =$ _____

($) $-40 / +5 =$ _____

(%) $+60 / -5 =$ _____

(&) $-30 / +3 =$ _____

(*) $+16 / +4 =$ _____

(>) $-50 / -5 =$ _____

(<) $0 / -3 =$ _____

(=) $-24 / -6 =$ _____

SECOND, circle all letters or symbols marking problems with answers between or including 0 to 6 and –25 to –7 on the number line.

THIRD, shade these symbols or letters in the grid below.

@ d x u p f c b z h a w = P n r x h # L % p > i % & b # t d L o $ e i b @ m h * L @ % ? $ o x t
a e g t v n ? Y k m d ? j u b f @ i < ? u k g X S e p u Y h = ? s w C S # q i k f s n y b V S f
= z i # h $ w > x g L s g # o v = z $ f s # r ? a m z g s j @ m g > % h Y L ? < o t * w d @ < z
b v # & r o e i % P $ v < m * Y t e d Z < o v r h * V P f m n r u m & j g = J C = v > g = r ? h
< > w q s L m u q V @ f = h c ? L P b j h t Y f w # c i w > a # Y V * ? u $ e a Y X z j k e w >
c k $ Y y z @ d # Y r k u & z > q g w = @ P e < n k > ? u e b f j z m d k w > & # f $ u % q & C

FOURTH, unscramble the letters to reveal the name of the mystery athlete described above.

____ ____ ____ ____ ____ ____ ____ ____ ____ ____ ____

Name

OLYMPIC MOMENTS, 1996

The 1996 Summer Olympics in Atlanta brought many memorable moments to sports fans around the world. Muhammad Ali's lighting of the flame at the Opening Ceremonies was one of the highlights for his many fans. For the United States, the thrill of watching the women's gymnastic team win gold was a highlight of the games. Although Shannon Miller ably captained the team, the most memorable gymnastic performance was on the vault by a tiny gymnast with a strained ankle. Solve the equations below to spell out the name of the athlete who had to be carried to the medal stand by her coach Bela Karolyi.

Solve these equations for x.

[1] $4 - x = 11$ _____

[2] $x - 12 = 4$ _____

[3] $3x = -18$ _____

[4] $54 = -9x$ _____

[5] $x + 9 = 1$ _____

[6] $5 - 3x = -31$ _____

[7] $-6x - 4 = -40$ _____

[8] $3 - 7x = 45$ _____

[9] $2(4 - x) = 14$ _____

[10] $-3(x + 5) = -45$ _____

Match the answer from each problem to a letter in the alphabet below. Then place that letter into the appropriate blank at the bottom of the page.

A	+8	J	+13	S	+12		
B	−11	K	−7	T	+6		
C	+3	L	−15	U	−3		
D	+9	M	−12	V	+14		
E	+16	N	+15	W	−16		
F	+5	O	−10	X	+11		
G	+10	P	+7	Y	+4		
H	−4	Q	−13	Z	−5		
I	−8	R	−6				

1. _____ 2. _____ 3. _____ 4. _____ 5. _____

6. _____ 7. _____ 8. _____ 9. _____ 10. _____

Name

WHOLE NUMBERS & INTEGERS
ASSESSMENT AND ANSWER KEYS

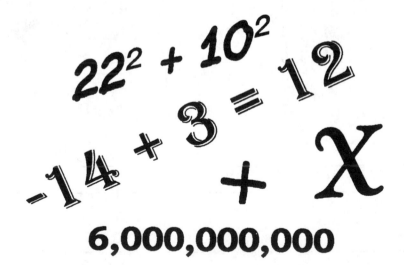

WHOLE NUMBERS & INTEGERS
SKILLS TEST

Each answer is worth 1 point, except questions 30–34 and 76–85, which are worth 2 points. Total possible score: 100 pts.

1–3: Write these numerals in words.

1. 2,304,611 _____

_____

2. 110,013 _____

_____

3. 5,000,010 _____

_____

4–6: Write the numerals represented by these words.

4. two hundred twenty-two thousand, seventeen

_____

5. four million, seven hundred, ten

_____

6. sixty-nine thousand, forty-three

_____

7–11: Tell the value of the place that is underlined.

7. 6̲05,319 _____

8. 2,0̲00,000 _____

9. 153,9̲66 _____

10. 200̲4 _____

11. 2̲6,917,211 _____

12–16: Put the following numerals in order from smallest to largest. Write them on the lines.

600,006   661,106   601,160   666,601   610,116

12. _____

13. _____

14. _____

15. _____

16. _____

17–21: Put the following numerals in order from smallest to largest. Write them on the lines.

−17   21   −4   7   −6

17. _____

18. _____

19. _____

20. _____

21. _____

22. Which numbers below question 23 are PRIME numbers? _____

23. Which numbers below are COMPOSITE numbers? _____

20   7   3   6   19   8   23

24–29: Round these numbers according to directions.

24. 51,736 _____
Round to the nearest hundred.

25. 9,374,196 _____
Round to the nearest hundred.

26. 299,566 _____
Round to the nearest thousand.

27. 2,814,609 _____
Round to the nearest thousand.

28. 874,331 _____
Round to the nearest ten thousand.

29. 208,109 _____
Round to the nearest ten thousand.

Name _____

30–34: Write the letter that shows the property represented by each equation. Each answer is worth 2 points.

  A = Associative Property
  C = Commutative Property
  D = Distributive Property

_____ 30. $12 + 6 = 6 + 12$

_____ 31. $(4 + 3) + 8 = 4 + (3 + 8)$

_____ 32. $5(2 + 6) = 5 \times 2 + 5 \times 6$

_____ 33. $8(7 + 9) = 8 \times 16$

_____ 34. $20 \times 7 = 7 \times 20$

35. Which of these numbers are divisible by 3?

_____

  8   39   16   31   57   18

36. Which of these numbers are NOT divisible by 6?

_____

  9   18   21   22   15   30   24

37. Write the lowest common multiple of 9 and 18.

_____

38. Write the lowest common multiple of 4, 16, and 20. _____

39. What is the value of 100^3? _____

40. What is the value of 4^4? _____

41. What is the value of 6^3? _____

42. What is the value of 2×10^2? _____

43. What is the value of 3×10^3? _____

44. What is the value of $298{,}000 \div 10^2$? _____

45. What is the value of 5×10^4? _____

46. Give the opposite of –33. _____

47. Give the opposite of +16. _____

48–58: Solve these problems.

48. $21 + -21 =$ _____

49. $-11 + 7 + -12 + 9 =$ _____

50. $-14 - -26 =$ _____

51. $-16 - -3 + -4 =$ _____

52. $5 \times -3 =$ _____

53. $-4 \times -7 =$ _____

54. $-18 \times 5 =$ _____

55. $-12 \div 4 =$ _____

56. $-72 \div -8 =$ _____

57. $-80 \div 10 =$ _____

58. $95 \div -5 =$ _____

59–65: Solve for *n.*

59. $-3 + -2 = n$ _____

60. $-4 \times -7 = n \times -4$ _____

61. $4(93 + 67) = n$ _____

62. $n + 88 = 199$ _____

63. $210 = 15n$ _____

64. $4n = 180$ _____

65. $n - 7116 = 861$ _____

66–75: Solve these.

66. $47 \times 10^2 =$ _____

67. $369 \times 111 =$ _____

68. $280 \div 20 =$ _____

69. $10^4 \times 20 =$ _____

70. $10^6 \div 10^2 =$ _____

71. $400{,}000 \div 100 =$ _____

72. $(600 + 739) - 400 =$ _____

73. $(-5 \times -5) + (-6 \times 3) =$ _____

74. $10^8 \div 10 =$ _____

75. $2400 \div 600 =$ _____

Name _____

76–85: Solve these word problems.
Each answer is worth 2 points.

_____ 76. Basketball Player Q earns $470,000 a year. Player B has a 3-year contract for $1,200,000 total. In three years, which player will earn more?

_____ How much more?

_____ 77. An arena for a diving championship holds 7000 people. It is at full capacity for 17 competitions. How many people attended in all 17 meets?

_____ 78. The temperature on the day of the ski race was –17° F at 6 A.M. in the morning. By 4 in the afternoon, it had risen 52° F. What was the temperature at 4 P.M.?

_____ 79. The high school booster club sold 1456 tickets to the Homecoming Game. This was twice as many as they had sold to the last game. How many did they sell for the last game?

_____ 80. Suzanne spent half her savings on new soccer shoes. After that, she bought a sweatsuit for $35 and new ski poles for $45. She had $10 left. How much did she spend on the soccer shoes?

_____ 81. Samantha and Sam jogged together every day for 5 weeks. Their total mileage was 140 miles each. If they each jogged the same distance each day, how far did each one jog each day?

_____ 82. The day of the outdoor skating competition, the temperature dropped 17° F before 8 A.M. It dropped another 22° F by noon. In the afternoon, the temperature increased 5° F by 2 P.M. If the temperature was –4° F at 2 P.M., what was it before 8 A.M.?

_____ 83. Wrestler Tom weighs 128 pounds, which is 37 pounds less than wrestler Jake, who weighs 14 pounds more than wrestler Bill. How much does Bill weigh?

_____ 84. Each member of a 16-person soccer team owns 7 pairs of soccer shoes. How many total shoes is that?

_____ 85. A basketball team scores 1485 points in a season. If 15 different players get equal playing time, what is the average number of points scored per player?

SCORE: Total Points _____ out of a possible 100 points

Name

WHOLE NUMBERS & INTEGERS
SKILLS TEST ANSWER KEY

Each answer is worth 1 point, except questions 30–34 and 76–85, which are worth 2 points.

1. two million, three hundred four thousand, six hundred eleven
2. one hundred ten thousand, thirteen
3. five million, ten
4. 222,017
5. 4,000,710
6. 69,043
7. 6 hundred thousands
8. 0 ten thousands
9. 9 hundreds
10. 0 tens
11. 2 ten millions (or 20 millions)
12. 600,006
13. 601,160
14. 610,116
15. 661,106
16. 666,601
17. –17
18. –6
19. –4
20. 7
21. 21
22. 3, 7, 19, 23
23. 6, 8, 20
24. 51,700
25. 9,374,200
26. 300,000
27. 2,815,000

28. 870,000
29. 210,000
30. C
31. A
32. D
33. D
34. C
35. 39, 57, 18
36. 9, 21, 22, 15
37. 18
38. 80
39. 1,000,000
40. 256
41. 216
42. 200
43. 3000
44. 2980
45. 50,000
46. +33
47. –16
48. 0
49. –7
50. +12
51. –17
52. –15
53. +28
54. –90
55. –3
56. +9

57. –8
58. –19
59. –5
60. –7
61. 640
62. 111
63. 14
64. 45
65. 7977
66. 4700
67. 40,959
68. 14
69. 200,000
70. 10,000
71. 4000
72. 939
73. 7
74. 100,000,010
75. 4
76. Q; $210,000
77. 119,000
78. 35° F
79. 728
80. $90
81. 2 miles
82. + 30°
83. 151 pounds
84. 224 shoes (112 pairs)
85. 99 points

ANSWERS

page 18

1. two million, seven hundred eighty-three thousand, seven hundred twenty-six
2. seven million, three hundred twenty-two thousand, five hundred sixty-four
3. one million, five hundred eighty-five thousand, five hundred eighty-seven
4. 2,833,511
5. 1,744,124
6. 3,711,043
7. 8,863,164
8. two million, three hundred eighty-two thousand, one hundred seventy-two
9. one million, eight hundred thirty-one thousand, one hundred twenty-two
10. four million, three hundred eighty-two thousand, two hundred ninety-seven
11. one million, six hundred seven thousand, one hundred eighty-three
12. 1,566,280
13. 372,242
14. 1,972,961

page 19

1. $9,000,000
2. five million
3. ten millions
4. ten thousands
5. 400,000
6. $600
7. 100,000,000 (one hundred million)
8. 2
9. 100,000 (one hundred thousand)
10. 800,000 (eight hundred thousand)

page 20

1. 3000 + 900 + 60 + 6
2. 1000 + 900 + 40 + 5
3. 700,000 + 60, 000 + 7,000 + 200
4. 100 + 60 + 2
5. 4000 + 900 + 60 + 2
6. 50,000 + 1,000 + 10 + 1
7. 2,000 + 900 + 60 + 2
8. 1,000 + 900 + 10 + 3
9. 200,000,000
10. 6,000 + 900 + 40 + 2
11. 3,000 + 600
12. 1,000 + 300 + 30 + 6

page 21

1. NY Knicks—$1000
   LA Lakers—$600
   Chicago Bulls—$400
   Houston Rockets—$375
   LA Clippers—$275
   Charlotte Hornets—$180
   Minnesota Timberwolves—$174
2. 3 tickets to Chicago Bulls—$300
3. 5 tickets to Chicago Bulls—$800
4. 3 tickets to LA Clippers—$105

5. 5 tickets to Houston Rockets—$675
6. Minnesota, Charlotte, LA Clippers, Houston, Chicago
7. Answers will vary.

page 22

1.	530	21.	3,000
2.	790	22.	3,000
3.	1,250	23.	5,000
4.	6,870	24.	9,000
5.	800	25.	2,000
6.	40	26.	5,000
7.	10	27.	8,000
8.	60	28.	55,000
9.	570	29.	544,000
10.	2,270	30.	7,000
11.	600	31.	40,000
12.	1,200	32.	260,000
13.	600	33.	90,000
14.	800	34.	210,000
15.	1,100	35.	460,000
16.	400	36.	790,000
17.	600	37.	90,000
18.	4,000	38.	760,000
19.	4,200	39.	10,000
20.	900	40.	50,000

page 23

A = 18	1. wildcats
B = 22	2. bengals
C = 27	
D = 12	3. lions
E = 23	4. panthers
G = 28	
H = 35	5. tigers
I = 60	
J = 33	6. bobcats
L = 29	7. cougars
N = 26	
O = 11	8. jaguars
P = 13	
R = 44	
S = 49	
T = 24	
U = 15	
W = 9	
Y = 17	

pages 24–25

1. frame 1 = 9
   frame 2 = 16
2. a. frame 1 = 16
   b. frame 2 = 24
3. spare
   frame 1 = 19
   frame 2 = 28
4. a. 13
   b. 17
   c. 3
   d. 7

5. Scores in frames 1–2–3–4–5:
   Sylvia : 6–15–35–53–62
   Mark: 8–25–32–48–56
   Jana: 8–28–46–54–62
   Jay: 19–28–46–55–64

page 26

1. a. 3
   b. 8
2. a. 7
   b. 7
3. a. C
   b. A
   c. C
   d. A
   e. C
   f. A
4. a. 7, 7
   b. 5
5. a. (12 + 7) +3   (May vary.)
   b. (6 x 8) x 2   (May vary.)
   c. 9 + (5 + 11)   (May vary.)
   d. (10 x 4) + (10 x 3)
   e. 6(5 + 2)
   f. (1 + 9) + 5   (May vary.)
   g. (7 x 4) x 12   (May vary.)
   h. 11 x (2 x 7)   (May vary.)
   i. 8 x (10 x 2)   (May vary.)
   j. 14 + (3 + 8)   (May vary.)

page 27

1. a. 0	c. 0	e. 4
b. 2	d. ⅓	f. 9

2. a. inverse	d. identity	g. zero
b. zero	e. identity	h. identity
c. identity	f. inverse	i. identity

3. 1. E	4. B	7. A
2. C	5. F	8. A
3. D	6. E	

page 28

1. 3, 6, 9, 12, 15, 18, 21, 24, 27, 30
2. 6, 12, 18, 24, 30, 36, 42, 48, 54, 60
3. 7, 14, 21, 28, 35, 42, 49, 56, 63, 70
4. 2, 4, 6, 8, 10, 12, 14, 16, 18, 20
5. a. Cougars 36; Panthers 34
   b. Bobcats 94; Wildcats 90
   c. Lions 36; Tigers 37
   d. Cougars 110; Jaguars 97

page 29

1. 42–42	13. 45
2. 24 baseballs	14. 300
3. 60 pounds	15. 30
4. yes	16. 252
5–10. Answers will vary.	17. 60
11. 154	18. 624
12. 60	19. 750

pages 30–31

1. I. 14 mi
   II. 15 mi
   III. 12 mi

2. I. 98 min
   II. 105 min
   III. 84 min

3. I. 20 mi
   II. 18 mi
   III. 19 mi

4. I. 120 min
   II. 108 min
   III. 114 min

5. I. A-B-E-H-L-O-S
   II. 21 mi

6. 105 min

7. 20 mi

page 32

1. 5-$10
   3-$27
   7-$28   Total = $205
   4-$92
   8-$48

2. 9-$108
   6-$174
   7-$35   Total = $446
   27-$108
   3-$21

3. 5-$15
   3-$42
   7-$42   Total = $233
   2-$116
   9-$18

page 33

1. $25 million
2. $8 million
3. $16 million
4. $7,142,857
5. $35 million
6. $15 million
7. $10 million
8. $400,000
9. a. $250,000
   b. $10,000

page 34

C = 90	R = 632
T = 700	P = 774
O = 3	U = 29
N = 8	L = 12
A = 4	B = 31
Y = 9	E = 22
H = 6	

Answer: Coach Paul "Bear" Bryant

page 35

1. yes   2. no   3. yes   4. yes   5. yes

	58	153	228	523	80	104	180	89	532	90
2	x		x		x	x	x		x	x
3		x	x				x			x
4			x		x	x	x		x	
5					x		x			x
6			x				x			x
10					x		x			x

page 36

Answer reads: GO TEAM

page 37

1. D	5. H	9. F	13. 1,000,000	17. 196	21. 5000
2. A	6. J	10. I	14. 1,080,000	18. 25	22. 1600
3. G	7. C	11. 392	15. 576	19. 2916	
4. B	8. E	12. 43,200	16. 1,250,000	20. 1440	

page 38

1. 2×10^2 m; 4×10^2 m
2. 5×10^2 ft; 6×10^3 in
3. 1×10^5 mm
4. 60 m or 60,000 mm
5. 2390 mm or 890 cm
6. 8×10^3 sec
7. 5×10^4 yd
8. a. 1.2×10^2 sec   b. $2.3 \ 10^3$ yd
9. 9×10^3 mm
10. 95,000 mm

page 39

1. 920 yds
2. 680 yds
3. 890 yds
4. 730 yds
5. 9500 yds
6. 1400 yds
7. 2700 yds
8. 3100 yds
9. 8700 yds
10. 10,600 yds
11. C-S-G-V-R-D-C or C-D-R-V-G-S-C
12. 23,870 yds

page 40

1. 298 kph
2. 97 kph
3. 3529.56 kph
4. 206 kph
5. 556 kph
6. 45 kph
7. 230 kph
8. 1224 kph
9. 86 kph
10. 4 = parachutist
7 = racing pigeon
1 = jet plane
6 = water skier
3 = hydroplane
9 = board sailor
5 = ice yacht
2 = jet vehicle
8 = skateboarder

page 41

1. 10,000
2. Answers will vary according to the year.
3. About 22 mph
4. $430
5. $145
6. $225
7. $390; $130 each installment
8. $200

pages 42–43

1. $5
2. $9
3. Total: $261; each boy's share: $87
4. Mountain Biking $12; Picnic $14; Water Slide $18; Jet Ski $100; Video Games $9; Dinner $25; Bowling $27; Movies $5; Total $210. Each boy's share: $70
5. Total $104; Change $16
6. Total $42; $21 each
7. Total:$54; $18 each
8. $8
9. Total 18 hours or 6 hours per boy.
10. (a) 648; (b) approx. 23 cents

pages 44–45

Estimates will vary somewhat.
1. $210
2. Answers will vary.
3. about $420–$450
4. a shadow cap
5. turf shirt: $30; pro jersey: $200; shadow cap: $20; Shipping $10 Total about $250
6. $750–$760
7. Answers will vary.
8. $170
9. $180–$190

page 46

1. C = 8
2. S = 15
3. F = 12
4. G = 22
5. E = 7
6. T = 13
7. D = 19
8. P = 5

page 47

1. $M + 3 = 7$ or $M = 7 - 3$
2. $4P = 24$ or $P = \frac{24}{4}$
3. $L + 24 = 60$ or $L = 60 - 24$
4. a. $4D = 48$ or $D = \frac{48}{4}$
   b. $2D = W$
5. $75B = 300$ or $B = \frac{300}{75}$
6. $2H - 100 = 300$
7. $2K = 6$ or $K = \frac{6}{2}$
8. $R + 11 = 15$ or $R = 15 - 11$

page 48

1. subtract
2. add
3. divided the number of points by the number of games
4. 873
5. Neither would win; it would be a 49–49 tie
6. M Jordan; 127
7. D Robinson; 78
8. M Jordan; 385
9. add
10. Answers will vary.

page 49

1. A—Kerri Strug
2. F—Joe Montana
3. H—Juwan Howard
4. D—Penny Hardaway
5. E—Cigar
6. B—Evander Holyfield
7. G—Emmit Smith
8. C—Shaquille O'Neal

pages 50–51

You will need to look at students' papers to see if points are located correctly on the number lines.

page 52

St. Louis – Los Angeles – Antwerp

A = +1	O = –17
B = +9	P = –3
C = –15	Q = +12
D = +3	R = –14
E = –8	S = +6
F = +14	T = –21
G = –6	U = +7
H = –16	V = –18
I = –5	W = +15
J = –4	X = –13
K = –12	Y = +13
L = +5	Z = +18
M = +17	Blank = –11
N = +16	

page 53

Name: Coubertin
Motto: Faster, Higher, Stronger
1. –49
2. –36
3. +65
4. +36
5. –72
6. –56
7. +48
8. –54
9. +20
10. +81
11. –42
12. +72
13. +48
14. –72
15. –56
16. +42
17. –54
18. 0
19. +42
20. –72
21. –56
22. +72
23. +48
24. –56
25. –36
26. +20
27. 0
28. –72
29. –56

page 54

a. +6
b. 0
c. –8
d. +4
e. +9
f. –6
g. +7
h. +8
i. –4
j. +7
k. +5
l. –9
m. –6
n. –7
o. –9
p. +8
q. –7
r. –6
s. +9
t. +5
u. –4
v. +16
w. +9
x. –12
y. –6
z. +11
?. +25
@. +5
#. –5
$. –8
%. –12
&. –10
*. +4
>. +10
<. 0
=. +4

Answer: Tiger Woods

page 55

1. –7
2. +16
3. –6
4. –6
5. –8
6. +12
7. +6
8. –6
9. –3
10. +10

Answer: Kerri Strug

GEOMETRY & MEASUREMENT

Skills Exercises

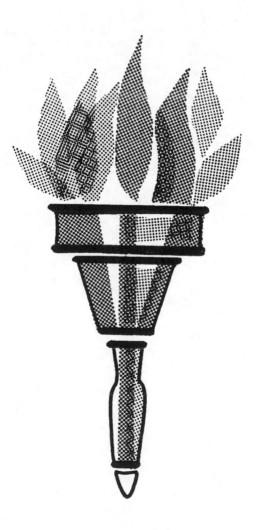

SKILLS CHECKLIST FOR GEOMETRY & MEASUREMENT

✔	SKILL	PAGE(S)
	Identify and describe points, lines, and planes	66
	Identify kinds of angles	67, 83, 99
	Identify kinds of lines	66, 68, 69
	Identify and define kinds of triangles	72
	Identify and define different polygons	70–72
	Identify, define, and distinguish among quadrilaterals	73, 79, 81
	Define and determine perimeter	74, 75, 96
	Identify properties and parts of a circle	76
	Determine the circumference of circles	77
	Identify similar and congruent figures	78, 84
	Use formulas to determine the area of quadrilaterals	79, 96
	Use a formula to determine the area of triangles	80, 96
	Use a formula to determine the area of trapezoids	81, 96
	Use a formula to determine the area of circles	82
	Identify congruent angles	83
	Identify congruent triangles and other polygons	84
	Recognize and define different space figures	85
	Use formulas to determine volume of space figures	85–87, 98
	Use formulas to determine the volume of prisms and pyramids	86, 87, 98
	Identify and use various metric units for measuring	88, 89
	Convert among metric measurements	89
	Identify and use various U.S. customary units for measuring	90–92
	Convert among U.S. measurements	90–92
	Determine the appropriate unit for a measurement task	90, 93
	Measure length	94, 95
	Measure and find area	96
	Find weight	97
	Measure and find volume	98
	Measure angles	99
	Estimate measurements	100–101
	Convert U.S. customary units to metric units	90, 102
	Determine measurements of temperature	103
	Solve problems with time measurements	104

FLYING FEATHERS

There is an Olympic legend that Hercules, an archer, founded the Olympic games. Instead of shooting arrows into a target, ancient archers used live tethered doves as their targets. Using birds as targets gave birth to the saying, "Now the feathers are really flying!" Check your aim with the following problems.

Study the diagram and answer the questions below.

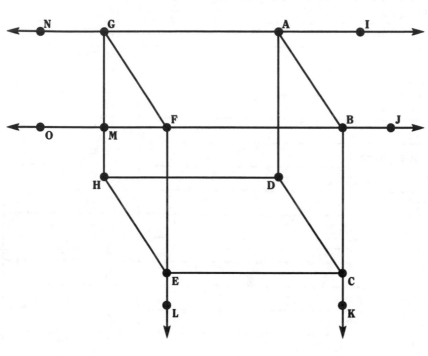

1. Name 10 points. _____

2. Name 2 lines. _____

   _____

3. Name 10 line segments. _____

   _____

4. Name 4 pairs of parallel line segments. _____

5. Name 2 pairs of perpendicular line segments. _____

6. Name 6 rays. _____

7. Planes are named by giving the vertices of a face of a figure. Name 5 planes. _____

   _____

   _____

Name _____

SOME SPECTACULAR ANGLES

Gymnasts get their bodies into the most spectacular positions. If you watch them, you'll see all kinds of angles represented in their maneuvers.

A. Identify the numbered angle of each gymnast's body as **acute, obtuse,** or **right**.

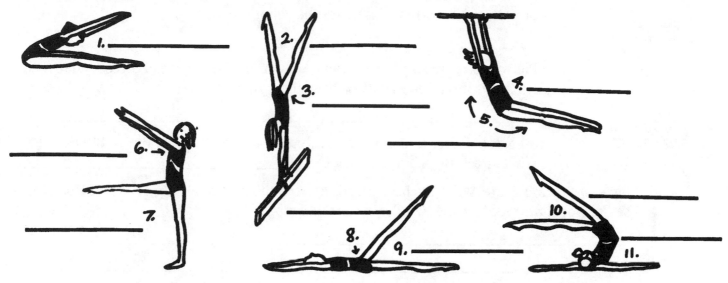

B. Identify these angles as either **complementary** or **supplementary** angles. Then find the measure of each numbered angle.

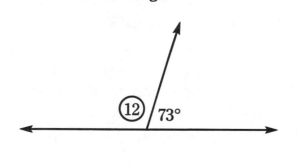

⑫ 73°

_____ _____°

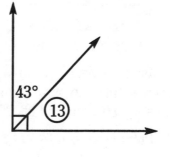

43° ⑬

_____ _____°

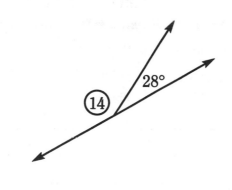

28°

⑭

_____ _____°

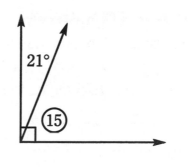

21° ⑮

_____ _____°

Name _____

CONFUSION IN THE VILLAGE

Pierre could not find his way around the Olympic Village so he asked for directions. Use the map to determine where Pierre will be if he follows these directions.

1. Pierre left his room in International Dorm A through the front door on a street that runs parallel to 3rd Avenue. He turned at the intersection of 1st Street and Elm Street. Where was he going?

   _____

2. Pierre was exercising at the Training Gym. He was on Broad Street and turned left at the intersection of Broad and 5th. Where did he go?

   _____

3. Siam told Pierre that the ATM machine was on a street parallel to 8th Street. What street was Siam referring to? _____

4. Pierre was running late. Write the best directions from International Dorm A to the Bus Stop. Use the words *intersection* and *parallel* in your directions.

   _____

   _____

   _____

   _____

5. If Pierre was at the Track and Field area and he exited at the 8th Street exit and turned at the intersection of 8th and N. West Boulevard, where would he be? _____

6. Pierre attended morning worship at the church. He walked on Church Street and turned right on a street that ran parallel to 8th Street. Then he went approximately two blocks and entered an establishment and bought a soft drink. Where was he? _____

7. Andrea told Pierre that 8th Street runs perpendicular to N. West Boulevard. Is that true or false? _____

8. Romana told Pierre that the laundry is just past the intersection of 1st Street and Broad Street. Is that true or false? _____

9. Pierre told Mary Ann that the Oak Street and Annex do not intersect. Is this true or false? __

10. Pierre needed to go from the pool to the training gym. Write directions below. Be certain to use words like *perpendicular, parallel,* and *intersecting* in your directions.

    _____

    _____

    _____

Use with map on page 69.

Name _____

CONFUSION IN THE VILLAGE, CONTINUED

Use with page 68.

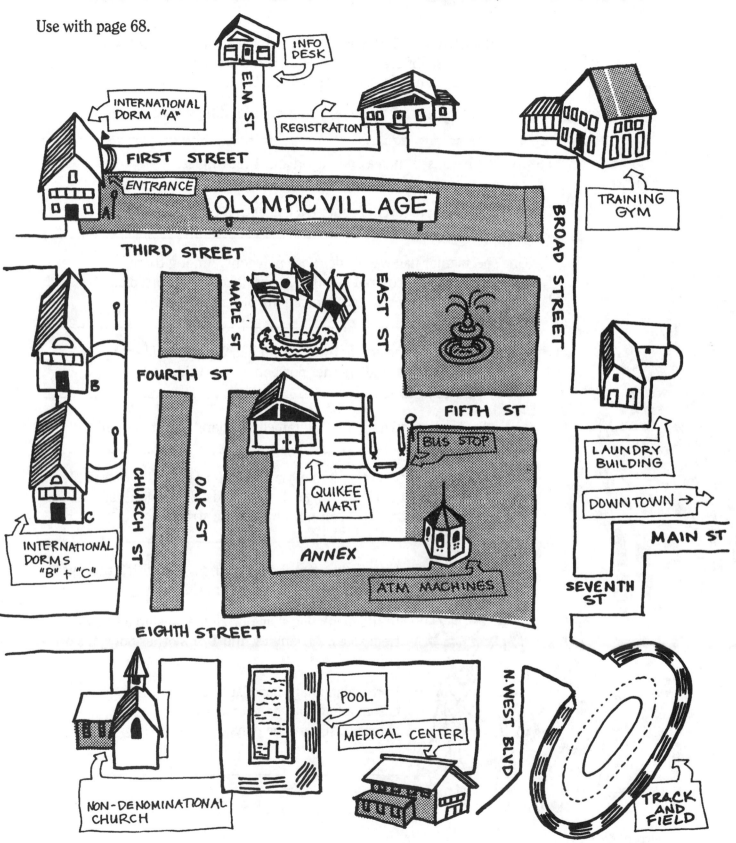

Name

THE COLORS OF THE OLYMPICS

At the opening ceremonies of the Olympics, Tasha was awed by the beautiful, colorful flags. She had never guessed that flags could be so different! Match her written descriptions of the flags to the drawings on the next page. Write the name of the country's flag after each description.

1. One strikingly beautiful flag contained 1 triangle, 2 trapezoids of different colors, and 1 pentagon. Country _____

2. Another one caught my eye because it had a dodecagon and 4 rectangles. Country _____

3. Near the Olympic torch, I spotted a flag with 3 trapezoids and 1 rectangle. Country _____

4. One spectacular flag was loaded with polygons. Among them were 8 triangles, 2 colored parallelograms, 2 colored trapezoids, and one large colored dodecagon, among other figures. Country _____

5. A beautiful flag at the end of the stadium had 2 equilateral triangles, 2 isosceles triangles, and another polygon with 16 sides. Country _____

6. Another striking flag contained 12 triangles surrounding a circle. Country _____

7. This flag was very simple, yet I couldn't take my eyes off it. It held 1 equilateral triangle, 2 trapezoids, 2 hexagons, and 1 decagon that is surrounded by a white stripe. Country _____

8. I saw a young athlete carrying a flag with 2 triangles, 2 trapezoids, and 1 pentagon. Country _____

9. In the blank flag shape labeled A, design a flag with 2 trapezoids, 2 triangles, and 1 or 2 other polygons of your choice.

10. In the blank flag shape labeled B, design a flag with polygons of your choice. List here the polygons you used: _____

_____

_____

Use with page 71.

Name _____

THE COLORS OF THE OLYMPICS, CONTINUED

Use with page 70.

TAIWAN

SWEDEN

TANZANIA

JAMAICA

UNITED KINGDOM

SUDAN

SOUTH AFRICA

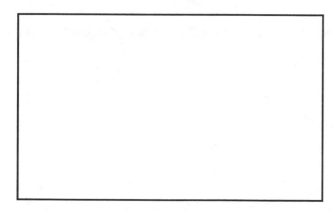

KUWAIT

A

B

Name

POOLSIDE GEOMETRY

One of the Olympic Pools that Kendall used in competition had an unusual and spectacular tile mosaic bottom. Identify the triangles and other figures by coloring them according to the key below.

blue = scalene triangles
red = equilateral triangles
green = isosceles triangles
black = right triangles
yellow = other shapes

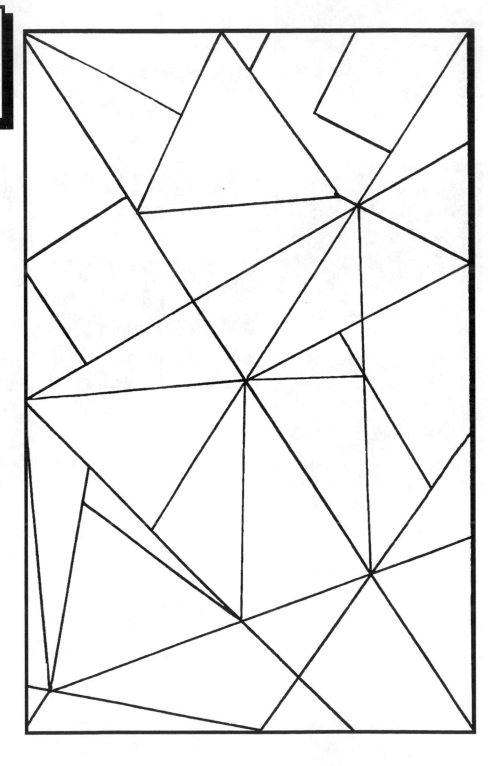

Name

DIFFERENT—YET THE SAME

The Olympic Games capture attention like no other sporting event. An estimated 35 billion people watch this international competition. The Olympics bring together people from almost 200 different countries. The athletes and fans share the common interest in the sports contests, but they represent widely diverse backgrounds. The shapes you run into at the Olympics are just as diverse, even if they share common characteristics. Many of them are quadrilaterals (4-sided polygons) yet the quadrilaterals differ.

A.

Match these different quadrilaterals with their correct definitions.

_____ 1. parallelogram   A. a parallelogram with all sides and angles congruent

_____ 2. trapezoid   B. a quadrilateral with exactly one pair of parallel sides

_____ 3. rectangle   C. a parallelogram with all angles congruent

_____ 4. rhombus   D. a parallelogram with all sides congruent

_____ 5. square   E. a quadrilateral with two pairs of parallel sides

B. Color each Olympic-related quadrilateral in this picture according to the key at the right. If one falls into 2 or more categories, color it partially with each color that applies.

trapezoids—blue
parallelograms—red
rectangles—green, white
squares—purple
rhombuses—yellow
triangles—black

Name _____

TRACKING DOWN DISTANCES

Athletes at the Summer Olympics run, ride, practice, and compete on many different tracks, surfaces, and courses. Calculate how far it is around the outside edge (perimeter) of each of these sports surfaces.

Use with page 75.

Name

TRACKING DOWN DISTANCES, CONTINUED

Use with page 74.

Rectangle .... $P = 2 (l + w)$
Square, rhombus .... $P = 4 s$
Triangle .... $P = s + s + s$
Circle .... $P = \pi d$
Other Polygons .... $P = $ sum of sides

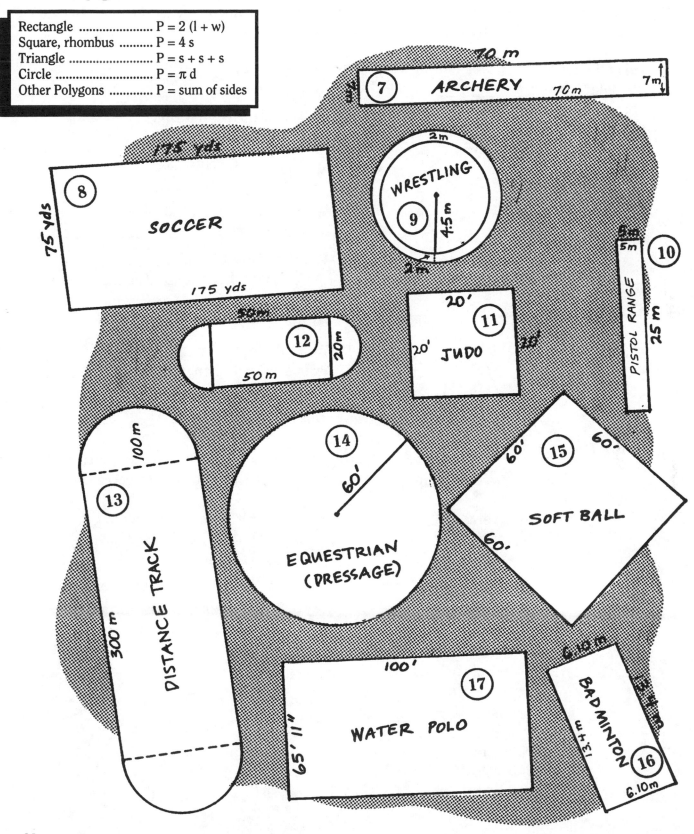

Name

NO HORSING AROUND

When Stephanie trains her horse for dressage, she spends many hours requiring the horse to do precise movements. Use the circle diagram to answer the questions about each command.

1. Stand at the center.
   (What point is this?) _____

2. Walk both diameters.
   (Name the line segments.) _____

3. Walk the radii.
   (Name the segments.) _____

4. Walk an acute central angle.
   (Name the angle.) _____

5. Walk an obtuse central angle.
   (Name the angle.) _____

6. Walk all intersecting chords.
   (Name the chords.) _____

7. Walk 3 chords.
   (Name 3 chords.) _____

8. Walk 5 arcs.
   (Name 5 arcs.) _____

9. Walk all central angles.
   (Name all central angles.) _____

10. The horse walks $\overline{MN}$.
    This is 12 feet. How long is $\overline{MK}$? _____

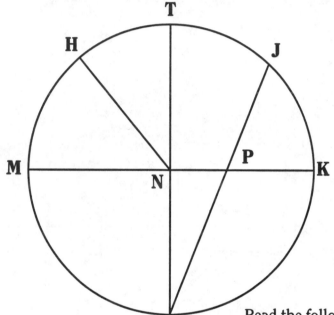

Read the following statements concerning circles. Determine if each statement is **always** true (A), **sometimes** true (S), or **never** true (N).

_____ 11. Some arcs are line segments.

_____ 12. Chords are diameters.

_____ 13. All radii in a cirle are the same length.

_____ 14. All diameters in a circle are the same length.

_____ 15. A central angle has its vertex on the circle.

_____ 16. Small circles measure less than 360 degrees. Larger circles measure more than 360 degrees.

_____ 17. Circles are congruent.

_____ 18. Circles are regular polygons.

_____ 19. All radii are half the length of all diameters of a particular circle.

_____ 20. All diameters pass through the center of the circle.

Name _____

CIRCULAR REASONING

A circle is a common sight at the Olympic Games, starting with the rings in the Olympic symbol. Many of the sports contain elements that are circular or spherical in shape. Use the formula for circumference (C = πd) to answer these questions about circles found around the Olympic venues.

1. One of the 5 Olympic Rings on the front of the Olympic Village sign has a diameter of 3 meters. What is the circumference of one of the rings?

2. In mountain biking, an "endo" is a "graceful" maneuver that occurs when a rider is catapulted from the bike as the rear wheel lifts off the ground. This is an easy move if the tire has a diameter of 20 inches. What is the circumference of such a tire?

3.

4. A softball is larger than a baseball. The official size is 12⅛ inches in diameter. What is the circumference of a softball?

5. The table tennis ball is made of celluloid and is approximately 1.5 inches in diameter. What is the circumference of a table tennis ball?

6. Team handball combines the skills of running, jumping, catching, and throwing. The men's handball is 60 centimeters in circumference. What is its diameter?

3. Leon Flameng, the first Olympic cyclist to win gold, circled a 333.33 m cement track 300 times to beat out his competition. What was the diameter of that track?

7. Tennis balls are made from rubber molded into two cups. The cups are cemented together and covered with wool felt. The tennis ball is approximately 2.5 inches in diameter. What is its circumference?

8. Today's discus is make from wood and metal and has the shape of a flying saucer. The athlete must stand in a throwing circle that has a diameter of 2.5 meters. What is the circumference of the throwing circle?

9. In volleyball, the ball is slightly smaller than a basketball. The ball's circumference is about 27 inches. What is its diameter?

10. In the hammer throw, the throwing circle is 7 feet in diameter. What is the circumference of the throwing circle?

Name

SEEING DOUBLE

Synchronized swimming was added to the Summer Olympic Games in 1984. When watching duet synchronized swimming, you think you are seeing double! Look at the geometric figures below and decide if you are seeing double (or congruent shapes) or just two shapes that are similar!

Congruent polygons are exactly the same. **Similar polygons** have the same shape. Their corresponding angles are congruent and their corresponding sides are proportional.

Place the letters after each correct answer on the corresponding blanks below to discover the only American in 20 years to win all 3 synchronized swimming events at a World Championship.

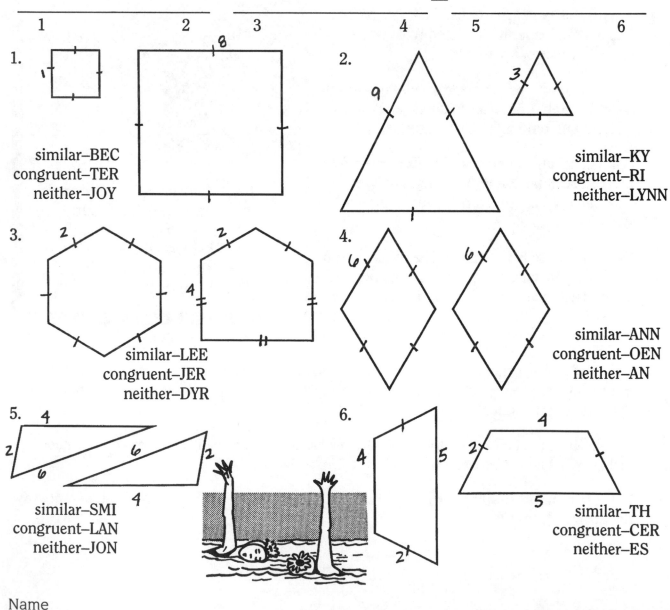

1   2   3   4   5   6

1.
similar–BEC
congruent–TER
neither–JOY

2.
similar–KY
congruent–RI
neither–LYNN

3.
similar–LEE
congruent–JER
neither–DYR

4.
similar–ANN
congruent–OEN
neither–AN

5.
similar–SMI
congruent–LAN
neither–JON

6.
similar–TH
congruent–CER
neither–ES

Name

PLACES AND SPACES

The settings where Olympic athletes compete include places and spaces of all sizes and shapes. Many of them are quadrilaterals (4-sided figures). You can learn something about these spaces by solving the following problems about their areas.

1. The wrestling mat is a 21-foot square. What is the area of the wrestling mat?

2. The platform where weight lifting occurs is 5 feet x 6 feet. What is the area of the platform?

3. The pool used for water polo must be 100 feet by 65 feet. What is the area of the pool?

4. The indoor volleyball court is 18 meters by 9 meters. What is the area of the court?

5. An Olympic tennis court measures 78 feet by 36 feet when designed for doubles play. The width of the tennis court must be reduced to 27 feet when a singles match is being played. What is the difference in the area of the court between doubles and singles play?

6. The table tennis table is 9 feet in length and 5 feet in width. What is the total area of the table?

7. The lanes in Olympic-sized swimming pools can vary. Some pools' lanes are 50 meters long and have a lane width of 3 meters. Other pools have the same length but only a lane width of 2 meters. What is the difference in the area of these lanes?

Name

SMOOTH SAILING

In the early days of yachting, the sails were no more than bedspreads that were attached by clothesline. Now the main type of sail on yachting vessels is triangular. Look at the sails below and determine the area of each.

$$A = \tfrac{1}{2}bh$$

1. _____   3. _____   5. _____   7. _____

2. _____   4. _____   6. _____   8. _____

Name

HOMEWORK FROM HOME

Friends back home decided to surprise Eric with some homework from his school. They decided he shouldn't get behind on the math they were doing in class. So they sent him postcards at the Olympic Village. These postcards asked him to find the area of trapezoids. But, in choosing the correct answer for each problem, he was also solving a puzzle that sent him a message. Can you figure out the message his friends sent?

1.
F 200 in²
G 30 in²
A 60 in²

(figure: trapezoid with 5", 4", 10")

5.
B 177,422.4 m²
L 3492.8 m²
F 6985.6 m²

(figure: trapezoid with 37 m, 59.2 m, 81 m)

2.
O 144 ft²
D 1,260 ft²
E 288 ft

(figure: trapezoid with 9', 12', 15')

6.
O 912 in²
R 456 in²
U 81 in²

(figure: trapezoid with 8", 6", 19")

3.
T 396 cm²
O 67.5 cm²
P 198 cm²

(figure: trapezoid with 11 cm, 9 cm, 4 cm)

7.
C 75 in²
D 913.5 in²
E 456.75 in²

(figure: trapezoid with 14½", 6", 10½")

4.
D 19.2 cm²
X 153.2 cm²
W 76.61 cm²

(figure: trapezoid with 8.4 cm, 2.4 cm, 7.6 cm)

8.
K 11.97 ft²
L 23.94 ft²
M 51.21 ft²

(figure: trapezoid with 3½', 2¾', 5½')

___ ___ ___ ___ ___ ___ ___ ___
1   2   3   4   5   6   7   8

Name _____

SIZABLE DIFFERENCES

When a group of athletes got together for lunch, they were all wearing T-shirts with pictures of the balls used in their sports. They got into a grand discussion about whether or not the size of the ball made the sport harder or easier. The final consensus was that size had nothing to do with difficulty—all their sports took great skill! But, just to satisfy their curiosity, they measured the pictures on their T-shirts and ranked the areas from largest to smallest.

I. Complete the chart.

Sport	Diameter	Radius	Area
1. soccer ball	d = 8.5 in.		
2. women's softball	d = 3.82 in.		
3. table tennis ball	d = 1.5 in.		
4. men's team handball	d = 2.31 in.		
5. women's team handball	d = 2.23 in.		
6. tennis ball	d = 2.5 in.		
7. basketball	d = 9 in.		
8. volleyball	d = 8 in.		
9. baseball	d = 3 in.		

II. Rank the balls in order from largest to smallest.

1. _____
2. _____
3. _____
4. _____
5. _____
6. _____
7. _____
8. _____
9. _____

Name _____

ON TARGET

In the sport of archery, archers shoot 72 arrows at the target. A score of 720 is a perfect score. See if you can get a score this high by identifying congruent angles in the figures below and answering questions about the angles. Each correct answer is worth 60 points.

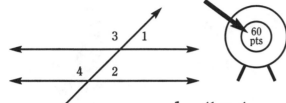

1. ∠1 ≅ ∠ ___

2. ∠3 ≅ ∠ ___

75°

3. If ∠8 measures 75°, what other angle measures 75°?

_____

4. What does ∠6 measure? _____

5. List all angles that are congruent to ∠10.

_____

_____

6. List all angles congruent to ∠13.

_____

7. List all angles congruent to ∠15.

_____

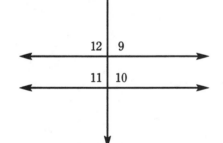

9. If ∠21 measures 60°, what does ∠31 measure? _____

10. If ∠25 measures 60°, what does ∠22 measure?

_____

8. If ∠25 and ∠26 measure 60°, what does ∠27 measure?

_____

11. List all angles congruent to ∠26.

_____

_____

12. List all angles congruent to ∠28.

_____

_____

Name _____

FLIPPED FIGURES

Divers and gymnasts do plenty of flips and turns. Geometric figures can be flipped and turned, too. But if the measurements of the sides and angles stay the same, a figure will not change. When a polygon has the same numbers of sides and angles, with the same measurements as another figure, the figures are **congruent**, even if the figures are in a different position.

Match each polygon in Column A with its congruent polygon in Column B.

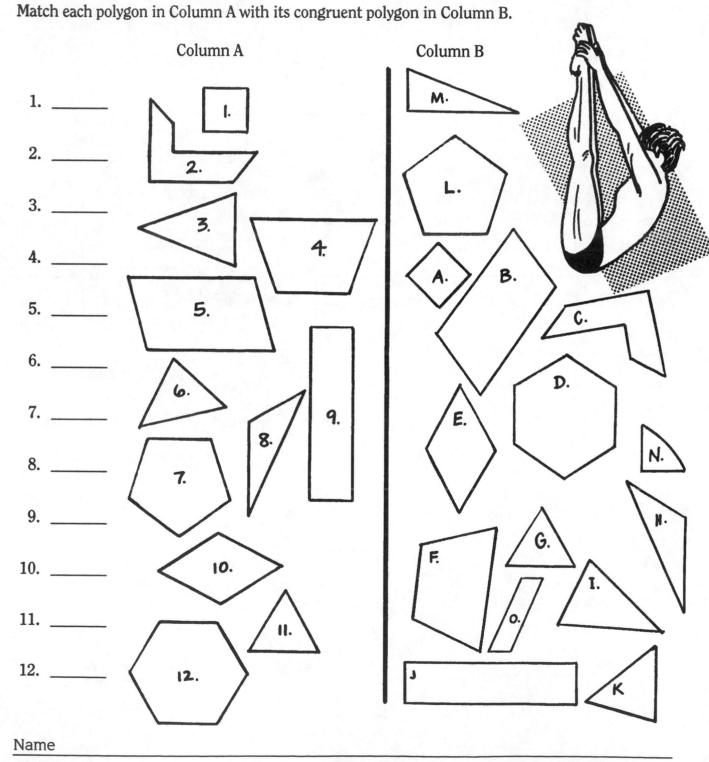

Column A   Column B

1. _____
2. _____
3. _____
4. _____
5. _____
6. _____
7. _____
8. _____
9. _____
10. _____
11. _____
12. _____

Name _____

DUFFEL BAG MATH

If you snooped inside the duffel bag of this Olympic athlete, you would find some containers that are space figures. Identify each space figure by name, then find its volume. (Round each answer to the nearest hundredth.)

Which container has the greatest volume?

Prism	$V = Bh$
Sphere	$V = \frac{4}{3}\pi r^3$
Cone	$V = \pi r^2 h \frac{1}{3}$
Cylinder	$V = \pi r^2 h$
r = radius	
h = height	
B = area of base	

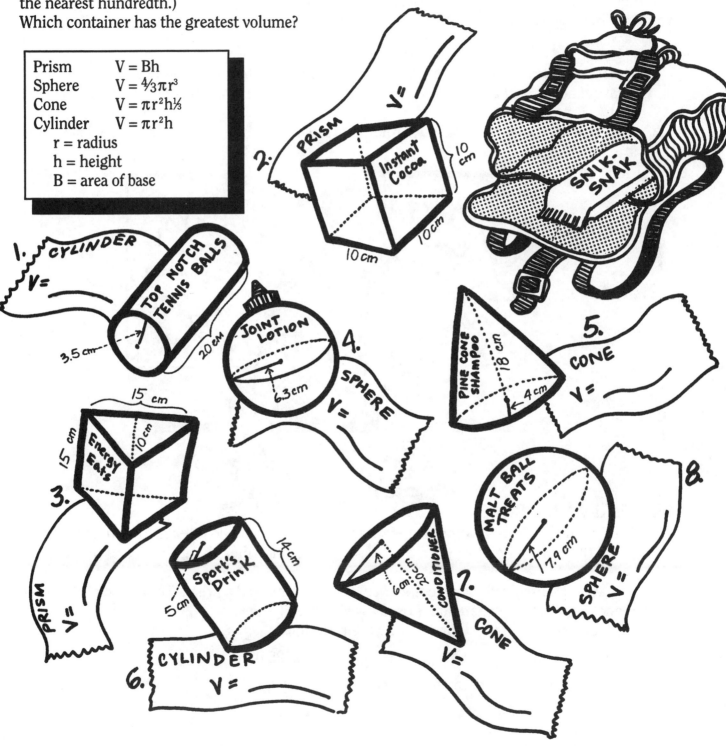

2. PRISM V =
Instant Cocoa
10 cm
10 cm
10 cm

SNIK-SNAK

1. CYLINDER V =
TOP NOTCH TENNIS BALLS
3.5 cm
20 cm

4. JOINT LOTION
6.3 cm
SPHERE V =

5. PINE CONE SHAMPOO
18 cm
4 cm
CONE V =

3. PRISM V =
15 cm
15 cm
10 cm
Energy Eats

6. CYLINDER V =
Sport's Drink
14 cm
5 cm

7. CONDITIONER
20 cm
6 cm
CONE V =

8. MALT BALL TREATS
7.9 cm
SPHERE V =

Name

PRISM & PYRAMID CALCULATIONS

One night after the games the athletes from Egypt and Mexico were discussing the unique land-marks in their countries. They quickly realized that both groups had pyramids in their homeland. Read about the pyramids below and determine their volume. Using the formula V= ⅓ Bh, find the volume of each pyramid.

EGYPT

1. The Pyramid at Madydun is 93 m high. The Egyptian athletes weren't sure of the other measurements, so they estimated. They believed that the pyramid had a square base that was about 75 m on each side.
2. The largest pyramid in the world is Khufu. Its square base measures 230 m on each side, and it is 147 m high.

CENTRAL AMERICA

3. The Pyramid of the Sun is the largest pyramid in Mexico. It is 66 m high. The athletes esti-mated that the base of the pyramid was a square that measures about 45 m on each side.

Later, the athletes discussed the difference between a pyramid and a prism. They remembered that the volume formula for a rectangular prism was $V = Bh$ or $V = lwh$.
Match the following rectangular prisms with their volumes.

_____ 4. l = 15 in., w = 13 in., h = 17 in   a. 13.125 in³

_____ 5. l = 2.5 in., w = 1.5 in., h = 3.5 in   b. 3315 in³

_____ 6. l = 1.2 in., w = 1.2 in., h = 1.2 in   c. 1.728 cm³

Use with page 87.

Name

PRISM & PYRAMID CALCULATIONS, CONTINUED

Use with page 86.

Match the following triangular prisms with their volumes. Don't forget how to measure a triangular base! Find the area of the triangular base and then multiply that number by the height of the prism.

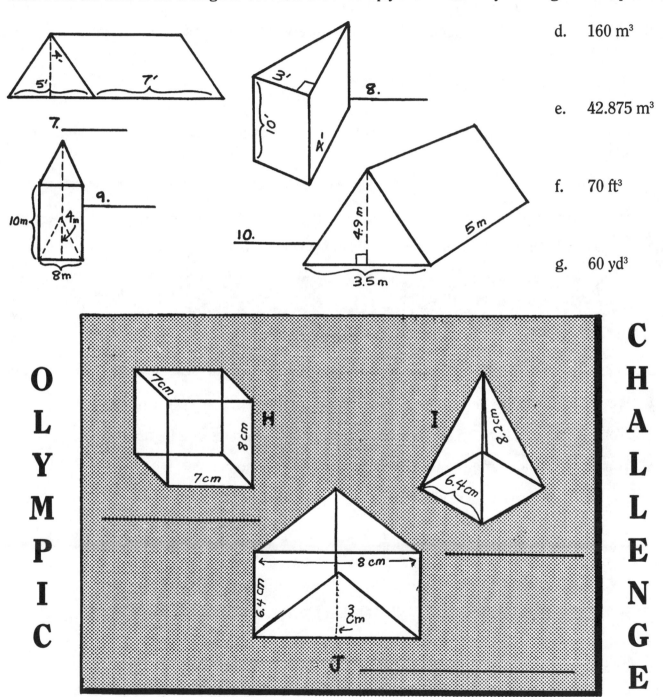

d.   160 m³

e.   42.875 m³

f.   70 ft³

g.   60 yd³

Which has the greatest volume? _____

Name

DO YOU SPEAK METRIC?

Most measurements found at the Olympics are metric. This is because the metric system is one that is used and understood all over the world, no matter what the language is. Show how well you understand the different units of metric measurement by answering these questions about Olympic measurements.

1. If in the long jump two opponents were very close, would you measure their jumps in centimeters or meters?

2. To mark off the running track for the relay race, would you measure the track in centimeters or meters?

3. If a thirsty biker were buying a water bottle for his bike, would he want a liter or a kiloliter of water?

4. To set up the distance between the hurdles would you measure in meters or millimeters?

5. Are marathon races usually measured in meters or kilometers?

6. Would it make sense to measure the diameter of a softball in meters of centimeters?

7. Would the weights that weight lifters use be measured in grams or kilograms?

8. Would a tall swimmer give his height in centimeters or kilometers?

9. Would the gold in a gold medal be weighed in grams or decagrams?

10. Would the length of the blade on a fencing sword be measured in millimeters or centimeters?

11. If you needed to know how many soccer balls would fit into a large bag, would you calculate the bag's volume using cubic millimeters or cubic centimeters?

12. Would the amount of water in a diving pool be measured in milliliters or kiloliters?

13. Which unit is more likely to be used to measure the height of a pole vaulter's jump: grams, liters, meters, or kilometers?

14. Is it likely that an athlete could throw the javelin 30 kilometers?

15. Do you think an Olympic basketball player might weigh about 50 grams?

Name

IT TAKES TEAMWORK

Basketball team members must work together very effectively to have a chance of winning. Teamwork can help you solve math problems, too. Here are some measurements showing how far the ball moved forward in different situations. Work with a partner to change these linear metric measurements into different units.

Use this sentence to help you remember the order of size of metric units.

Kids	Have	Done	Metrics	During	Cooperative	Math Lessons
Kilo-	*Hecto-*	*Deka-*	*Meters*	*Deci-*	*Centi-*	*Milli-*
1000	100	10	1	0.1	0.01	0.001

1. 10 m   = _____ mm

2. 3.54 m   = _____ cm

3. 137 m   = _____ km

4. 1 km   = _____ cm

5. 12.34 m   = _____ cm

6. 10 cm   = _____ mm

7. 124.5 km   = _____ cm

8. 1.2 mm   = _____ cm

9. 45.67 m   = _____ mm

10. 0.99 km   = _____ m

11. 56.72 m   = _____ km

12. 45.67 cm   = _____ m

13. 569 mm   = _____ m

14. 98.43 cm   = _____ m

15. 900 mm   = _____ cm

16. 456 mm   = _____ m

17. 27 km   = _____ cm

18. 876.1 mm   = _____ cm

19. 0.851 km   = _____ m

20. 567 mm   = _____ km

Name

THE GREAT MEASUREMENT SWITCH

The metric system is used for measurements at the Olympics. But many U.S. citizens understand their customary system better. How good are you at knowing which metric unit corresponds best to which U.S. measurement unit? Find out by answering these questions with either: inches, feet, yards, miles, pints, quarts, ounces, or pounds.

1. The badminton courts are 13.4 meters.
   The best U.S. customary unit of measure to convert this to would be _____ .

2. To score 3 points in Olympic basketball, the player must be 6.25 meters away from the goal.
   The best U.S. customary unit of measure to convert this to would be _____ .

3. A flyweight in boxing weighs 51 kg.
   The best U.S. customary unit of measure to convert this to would be _____ .

4. In cycling, the course is measured in kilometers.
   The best U.S. customary unit of measure to convert this to would be _____ .

5. The men's platform in diving is 10 meters high.
   The best U.S. customary unit of measure to convert this to would be

   _____ .

6. In fencing, the foil can be 1100 millimeters in length.
   The best U.S. customary unit of measure to convert this to would be

   _____ .

7. In rowing, the course is 2000 meters.
   The best U.S. customary unit of measure to convert this to would be _____ .

8. The sprint race in swimming is 50 meters long.
   The U.S. best customary unit of measure to convert this to would be _____ .

9. The ball used in table tennis weighs 2.5 grams.
   The best U.S. customary unit of measure to convert this to would be _____ .

10. The handball is 60 centimeters in circumference.
    The best U.S. customary unit of measure to convert this to would be _____ .

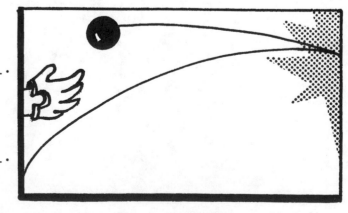

Use with page 91.

Name

THE GREAT MEASUREMENT SWITCH, CONTINUED

Use with page 90.

11. The take-off board in the long jump is 20 centimeters wide.
The best U.S. customary unit of measure to convert this to would be _____ .

12. The discus weighs 2 kilograms.
The best U.S. customary unit of measure to convert this to would be _____ .

13. The men's javelin must weigh at least 800 grams.
The best U.S. customary unit of measure to convert this to would be _____ .

14. The volleyball court measures 18 meters.
The best U.S. customary unit of measure to convert this to would be _____ .

15. Each time a weight lifter makes a lift attempt, the weight lifted must be increased by at least 2.5 kilograms. *The best U.S. customary unit of measure to convert this to would be* _____ .

16. The men's biathalon has a 30-kilometer relay.
The best U.S. customary unit of measure to convert this to would be _____ .

17. One track and field event for women is a 1500 meter run.
The best U.S. customary unit of measure to convert this to would be _____ .

18. Divers leaving the 10-meter platform can travel up to 48 kilometers per hour into the water.
The best U.S. customary unit of measure to convert this to would be _____ .

19. The smallest gymnast at the 1996 Summer Olympics weighed about 36 kilograms.
The best U.S. customary unit of measure to convert this to would be _____ .

20. A singles tennis court measures 23.8 m x 8.2 m.
The best U.S. customary unit of measure to convert this to would be _____ .

21. A tennis ball weighs less than 500 grams.
The best U.S. customary unit of measure to convert this to would be _____ .

22. The winner of the pole vault at the 1996 Summer Olympics cleared a bar that was over 579 centimeters from the ground.
The best U.S. customary unit of measure to convert this to would be _____ .

23. A runner drank 8 liters of water on one hot day at the Olympics.
The best U.S. customary unit of measure to convert this to would be _____ .

24. Many of the race courses for women kayakers are 500 meters long.
The best U.S. customary unit of measure to convert this to would be _____ .

Name _____

MIXED-UP MEASURES

Sometimes Olympic judges and officials get into some sticky predicaments. The mix-ups here have to do with measurements given in the wrong units. Help them make sense out of the mixed-up measures.

1. Art the Archer hit a bulls-eye from 105 feet. Convert 105 feet to yards. _____

2. The workers were trying to mark off the length of the badminton court.
   Someone told them it was 528 inches long. How many feet is that? _____

3. Babyface Nelson said he weighed 2352 ounces. What is his weight in pounds? _____

4. The timekeeper for field hockey was confused. The umpire told him each half of the game lasted 2100 seconds. His scoreboard needs the time in minutes. How long is a half? _____

5. Julie Jumper wasn't sure how wide the balance beam was. The only measurement she had was that it was $\frac{1}{3}$ of a foot. How many inches wide is that? _____

6. The workers were installing the outfield fence at the softball field. The only measurement they had was that the fence needed to be 2400 inches from home plate. How many yards from home plate should they install the fence? _____

7. The tennis net fell down. The referee came out to fix it.
   It needed to be at a height of 36 inches. How many feet high is that? _____

8. Daddy Longlegs once jumped 660 inches in the triple jump. How many feet did Daddy jump? _____

9. The 10K run was completed in 1620 seconds by Speedy Sam. How many minutes is that? _____

10. The hammer used in the hammer throw weighs 256 ounces. How many pounds does it weigh? _____

Name _____

92

MEASUREMENT MATTERS

Knowing how to measure and knowing what unit to use are critical skills for anyone who is involved in sports. Answer the following questions about measurements by circling the correct measurements.

1. Which unit of measure would be appropriate to use to describe the length of a badminton court? (feet, pounds, or inches)

2. In boxing, the athlete gets a 60 (second or hour) break between rounds.

3. In mountain biking, the course is between 4 and 20 (inches, feet, yards, or miles) long.

4. In the Tantrum race, cyclist are riding at approximately 50 (miles, feet, or yards) per hour.

5. The platform diving board is 33 (feet, inches, or yards) high.

6. In 1968, Marion Coakes won the show jumping silver medal with her pony Stroller. The pony was only 57 (inches, feet, or yards) tall.

7. The foil is the sword of choice in fencing. It may be as long as 43.307 (inches, feet, or yards) in length.

8. In field hockey, it is possible for the ball to travel 100 (miles, inches, or feet) an hour.

9. In gymnastics, the balance beam is only a slim 4 (inches, feet, or yards) wide.

10. A softball weighs about 7 (pounds, ounces, or tons).

11. In softball, the pitcher's mound is 40 (feet, inches, miles) from home plate.

12. In the high jump, Dick Browning somersaulted over a bar set at 7 (feet, inches, or yards).

Name

AN OLYMPIC TRADITION

If you follow these directions carefully, you'll create a drawing of a symbol that has represented the Olympics for hundreds of years. Use the next page for your drawing.

1. Beginning at point A draw an equilateral triangle. Label the triangle ABC. Point B is on the left side of the paper and Point C is on the right side of the paper. Each side of the triangle must measure 4 inches.

2. From Point B draw a straight line (toward the top of the paper) that measures 3¾ inches. Label this line segment $\overline{BE}$.

3. Using point E as the vertex of the angle, draw ∠ BEF. It must measure 40°. (Point F should be to the right of point E.) The length of $\overline{EF}$ must measure 1 inch.

4. Find the midpoint of $\overline{BC}$ and label it point J. From point J, measure (towards the top of the paper) 5¼ inches and draw a point. Label it point G.

5. From point C draw a staight line (toward the top of the paper) that measures 5½ inches. Label this segment $\overline{CI}$.

6. Find the midpoint of $\overline{JC}$. Label this point K.

7. Place point H 4½ inches above point K.

8. Using point F as the vertex of the angle, draw ∠ EFG. It must measure 75°. The length of $\overline{FG}$ must measure 2½ inches. Point G is near the top of the paper.

9. Using point H as the vertex, draw ∠ GHI. It must measure 80°. The length of $\overline{GH}$ must measure 1 inch and $\overline{HI}$ must measure 1½ inches.

10. What Olympic symbol did you create? _____

Use page 95 for your drawing.

Name _____

AN OLYMPIC TRADITION, CONTINUED

Use with page 94.

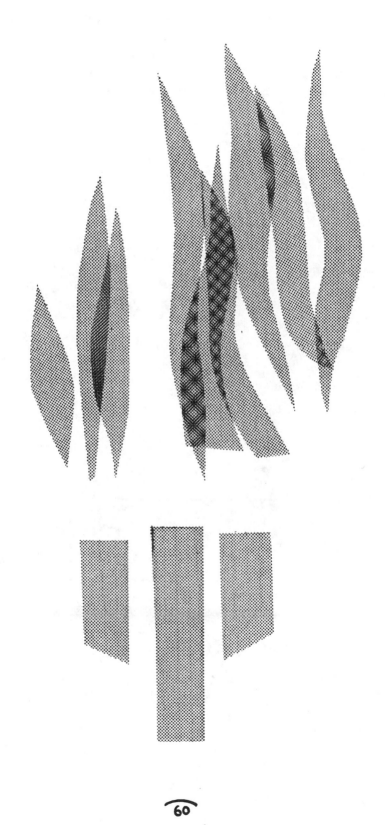

60

• A

Name

WHOSE ROOM IS ROOMIER?

When the U.S. Team arrived at the Olympic Village, they were surprised by their accommodations. Some of the rooms were very large and roomy. Others seemed really small. Below are scale drawings of their rooms. You can compare the sizes of the rooms by doing some measuring. Note the scale: 1 cm = 2 ft. Then measure and find the area and perimeter of each room. *(Note: the rooms are slightly irregular, so your measurements may be approximate.)*

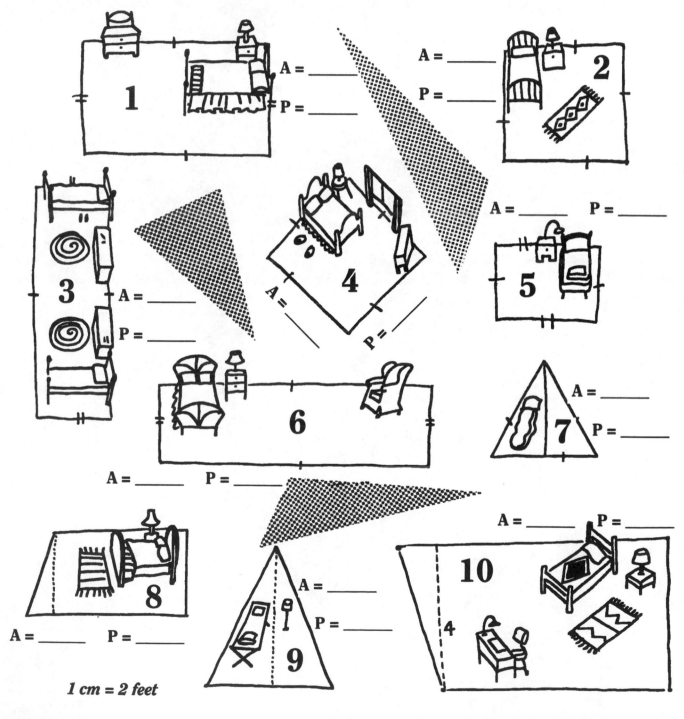

1 cm = 2 feet

Name

The BASIC/Not Boring Middle Grades Math Book

EMPIRICAL, SPHERICAL FACTS

The sports in the Summer Olympics use balls of many different kinds. The shape rarely varies—because most balls are spheres. But they differ greatly in size and weight. This chart shows the size and weight of some of the balls you'd expect to find at the Olympics. Use the statistics on the chart to answer the questions. (You'll need to use a dictionary or math glossary to refresh your knowledge about the statistical concepts of **mean, median,** and **range.**)

Type of Ball	Circumference	Weight
Baseball	9.25 inches	5.25 ounces
Basketball	30 inches	22 ounces
Soccer	28 inches	16 ounces
Tennis	8.25 inches	2.062 ounces
Volleyball	26 inches	9.25 ounces
Polo	11 inches	4.5 ounces
Ping-Pong	4.7 inches	0.091 ounces

1. Which type of ball is the closest in circumference to the volleyball? _____
2. Which type of ball is the closest in circumference to the basketball? _____
3. What is the range of the circumferences of the balls? _____
4. What is the mean of the circumferences of the ball? _____
5. What is the median of the circumferences of the balls? _____
6. Which of the balls are the closest in weight? _____
7. Which ball is the heaviest? _____
8. What is the mean weight of the balls in the chart? _____
9. What is the median weight of the balls in the chart? _____
10. What is the range of the weight of the balls in the chart? _____
11. Rank order the balls from lightest to heaviest. _____

_____

Name _____

MIDNIGHT SNACKS

Some members of the U.S. swim team paid a midnight visit to the vending machines for snacks. They were astounded by the prices! Which snacks should they buy to get the most for their money? If all the snacks below cost the same, figure out which one holds the greatest volume of food. Measure and calculate the volume for each. Measure in centimeters, and note the scale: 1 cm =10 cm. (Note: Figures may be slightly irregular so your answers may be approximate.)

Name

98

WRESTLING WITH ANGLES

Wrestling matches are won by receiving points for performing certain moves or techniques. One way to score points is called **exposure**. A wrestler gets points for exposure when he turns his opponent's shoulders to the mat. Points are awarded when the opponent's back is less than 90° from the mat. (His back is forming an acute angle with the mat!)

Score your own points by using a protractor to correctly measure these angles.

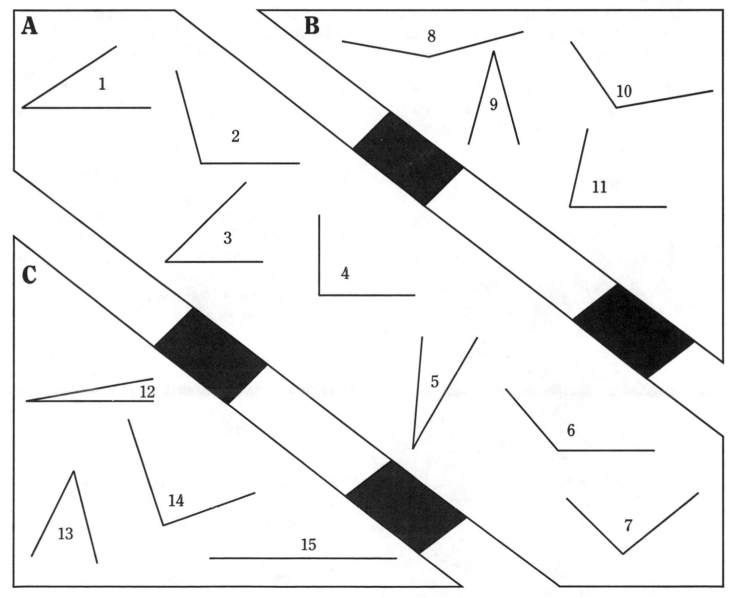

Name

ABOUT HOW MUCH?

Hundreds of measurements are needed to plan and run the Olympic Games. Not all of these measurements can be exact; many of them must be estimated. Here are some Olympic problems that need estimates.

1. The Olympics began around 900 BC. Approximately how many years ago did the Olympics begin?
   - A. 1000 years ago
   - B. 2000 years ago
   - C. 3000 years ago

2. In 1900, 1319 men and 11 women were involved in the games. About how many participants were there?
   - A. 1000 athletes
   - B. 1350 athletes
   - C. 1400 athletes

3. The TV rights for the 1968 Olympics were sold for $4.5 million. This included 44 hours of broadcasting. Approximately how much per hour did the TV rights cost?
   - A. $100,000 per hour
   - B. $10,000 per hour
   - C. $1,000,000 per hour

4. In Olympic basketball the three-point shot distance is not the same as the NBA three-point distance. The NBA distance is 22 feet. In the Olympics, it is about 20.5 feet. What is the approximate difference, in inches, of these two measurements?
   - A. About 30 inches
   - B. Around 20 inches
   - C. 10 inches

5. There are 12 weight classes in boxing at the Olympics. The light featherweight weighs up to 112 pounds and the super heavyweight may weigh up to 201 pounds. About how many pounds separate these two weight classes?
   - A. A little over 100 pounds
   - B. A little under 100 pounds
   - C. About 200 pounds

6. Leon Flameng, the first Olympic cyclist to win gold, circled a 333.33 m track 300 times. Altogether he cycled about
   - A. 100,000 meters
   - B. 1000 meters
   - C. 1,000,000 meters

7. In the equestrian three-day event, a horse is expected to jump a 3'11" obstacle. About how many inches high is this obstacle?
   - A. 40 inches
   - B. 48 inches
   - C. 60 inches

Use with page 101.

Name

ABOUT HOW MUCH?, CONTINUED

Use with page 100.

8. The foil is the sword that the majority of fencers use in the Olympics. It is about 44 inches long. About how many feet long is a foil?
   A. 5 feet
   B. 3 feet
   C. 4 feet

9. If you are a gymnast in college, according to NCAA guidelines you are allowed to practice no more than 20 hours a week. If a college gymnast kept to this training schedule for 4 years, about how many hours would the gymnast practice during his or her college career?
   A. 4000 hours
   B. 2000 hours
   C. 80 hours

10. Judo is performed on a 20 foot–square mat. About how many yards wide is the judo mat?
    A. 8 yards   B. 9 yards   C. 7 yards

11. The softball used in the Olympics is between 11⅞ and 12⅛ inches in diameter. It weighs 6¼ ounces to 7 ounces. If you were telling a friend about the Olympic softball, which statement reflects the best estimate?
    A. The softball is about 12 inches in diameter and weighs about 6 ounces.
    B. The softball is about 12 inches in diameter and weighs about 7 ounces.
    C. The softball is about 7 inches in diameter and weighs about 12 ounces.

12. Carl Lewis's best jump in Barcelona was 8.67 feet. What it the best estimate of this gold medal jump?
    A. 10 feet   B. 8.5 feet   C. 5 feet

13. Mary Decker Slaney was the first woman to run 880 yards in less than 2 minutes. About how many yards is she running a minute?
    A. 400 yards   B. 450 yards   C. 500 yards

14. Imagine that you were planning to spend 5 days at the Olympics. Use the numbers below to determine about how much money you should take with you to the games.
    (Don't forget to leave a little room in your budget for souvenirs!)

    Motel Room .... $170.00 a night   Event Tickets .... $100.00 a day
    Food .... $30.00 a day   Transportation .... $15.95 a day

    A. About $2000   B. About $500   C. About $4000

Name

WEIGHTY ISSUES

Weight lifting was part of the regimen of classic Greek athletes. They used stones that were held in one hand. These weights were later referred to as dumbbells. In 1928, one-handed weight lifting was abolished. The competition now consists of the "press," the "snatch," and the "jerk." Medals are awarded in each of the following ten different body weight classifications. Convert each of the weight classifications into pounds.

Use the following formula:

$$1 \text{ kg} = 2.203 \text{ lb}$$

and then round your answer to the nearest pound.

Metric Measures   **U.S. Customary Measures**

1. 54 kg   _____

2. 59 kg   _____

3. 64 kg   _____

4. 70 kg   _____

5. 76 kg   _____

6. 83 kg   _____

7. 91 kg   _____

8. 99 kg   _____

9. 108 kg   _____

10. Determine the final body classification by working backwards. The International Olympic Committee has imposed a 250-pound limit. Approximately how many kilograms would be the most an athlete in this event could weigh? _____

Name _____

THE HEAT IS ON

At the 1996 Summer Olympics in Atlanta, Georgia, one of the greatest concerns was the heat. Officials kept a close watch on the temperatures. Athletes had to drink plenty of fluids to avoid dehydration.

Record the temperature shown on each thermometer below.

 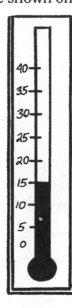   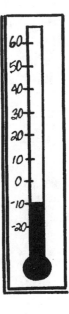

1. _____   2. _____   3. _____   4. _____   5. _____

Use a red pencil or marker to indicate on each thermometer the temperature written below it.

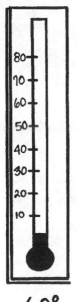 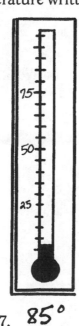 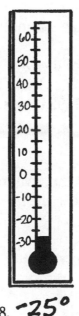 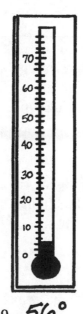 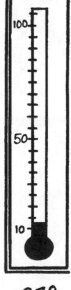

6. _60°_   7. _85°_   8. _-25°_   9. _56°_   10. _93°_

Name _____

TIME FLIES, AND SO DOES MICHAEL JOHNSON!

Michael Johnson is the only person ever to have run the 400 meter race in less than 44 seconds and the 200 meter distance in less than 20 seconds.

1. Using the formula
   $r \times t = d$,
   determine how
   fast Michael
   Johnson ran the
   400 meter race.

   _____
   meters per second

2. Using the formula
   $r \times t = d$,
   determine how
   fast Michael
   Johnson ran the
   200 meter race.

   _____
   meters per second

Bob Kennedy carried the United States hopes for the gold in the 1996 Summer Olympic games. His personal records include running the 5,000 meter race in a little over 13 minutes and the 3000 meter race in about 8 minutes.

3. Using the formula $r \times t = d$, determine how fast Bob Kennedy ran the 5000 meter race.

   _____ meters per minute

4. Using the formula $r \times t = d$, determine how fast Bob Kennedy ran the 3000 meter race.

   _____ meters per minute

5. Gail Devers has won gold medals in the Olympics and in the World Championships. In the space below, draw a $2\frac{1}{2}$ inch line. That's how much distance separated Gail from runner-up Juliet Cuthbert in the 1992 games.

6. Mary Decker Slaney is a middle distance running legend. She was the first woman to run 880 yards in less than 2 minutes. Use the formula $r \times t = d$ to determine how fast Mary Slaney was running.

   _____ yards per minute

7. Compare Michael Johnson's speed with Bob Kennedy's speed. Who is faster? _____

Name _____

GEOMETRY & MEASUREMENT ASSESSMENT AND ANSWER KEYS

GEOMETRY & MEASUREMENT
SKILLS TEST

Each answer is worth 1 point. Total possible score: 100 pts.

Use this figure for questions 1-10.

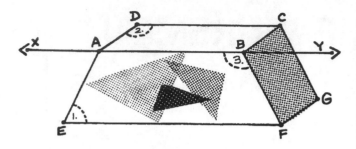

_____ 1. Name a line.

_____ 2. Name a line segment.

_____ 3. Name a ray.

_____ 4. Name 4 points on line $\overleftrightarrow{xy}$.

_____ 5. Name a pair of parallel line segments.

_____ 6. Name 2 non-parallel line segments.

_____ 7. Is this figure a pyramid?

_____ 8. Name a plane.

_____ 9. Name an obtuse angle.

_____ 10. Name an acute angle.

Use these figures for questions 11-18.

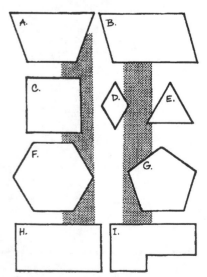

_____ 11. Name 2 rectangles.

_____ 12. Name a square.

_____ 13. Name 2 rhombuses.

_____ 14. Name 2 parallelograms.

_____ 15. Name a pentagon.

_____ 16. Name a hexagon.

_____ 17. Name a trapezoid.

_____ 18. Name a triangle.

Use these figures for questions 19-22.

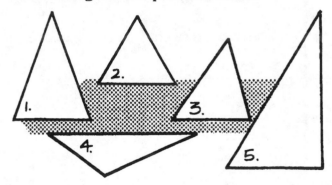

19. Which are scalene triangles? _____

20. Which are isosceles triangles? _____

21. Which are equilateral triangles? _____

22. Which are right triangles? _____

Use this figure for questions 23-27.

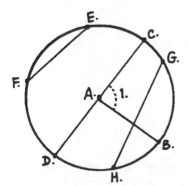

Name _____

_____ 23. Name 2 chords.

_____ 24. Name a diameter chord.

_____ 25. Name a radius.

_____ 26. Are there any intersecting chords?

_____ 27. Is angle 1 a central angle?

Give the perimeter (or circumference) of each of the figures below.

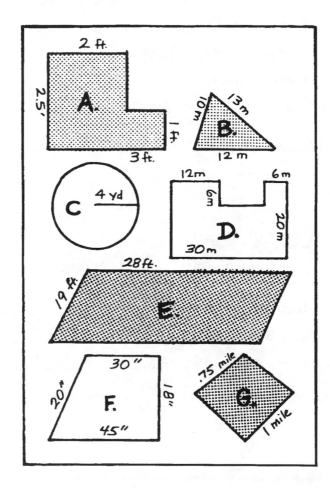

_____ 28. Figure A

_____ 29. Figure B

_____ 30. Figure C

_____ 31. Figure D

_____ 32. Figure E

_____ 33. Figure F

_____ 34. Figure G

Use these figures for questions 35-39.

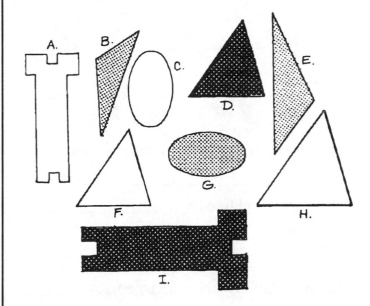

35. C is congruent to _____

36. F is similar to _____

37. D is congruent to _____

38. B is similar to _____

39. A is similar to _____

Find the area of each figure below.

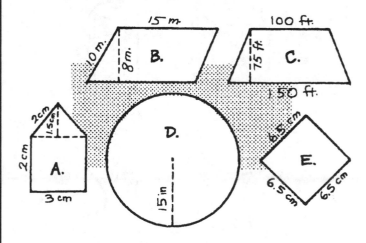

40. Figure A _____

41. Figure B _____

42. Figure C _____

43. Figure D _____

44. Figure E _____

Name

Use this figure for questions 45-52

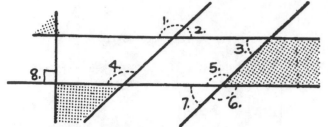

45. Name a pair of corresponding angles.

_____

46. Name an obtuse angle. _____

47. Name a pair of vertical angles.

_____

48. Are 4 and 5 supplementary angles? _____

49. Are 4 and 5 congruent? _____

50. Name a right angle. _____

51. Is 3 congruent to 7? _____

52. Name a pair of supplementary angles.

_____

Use these figures for questions 53-64.

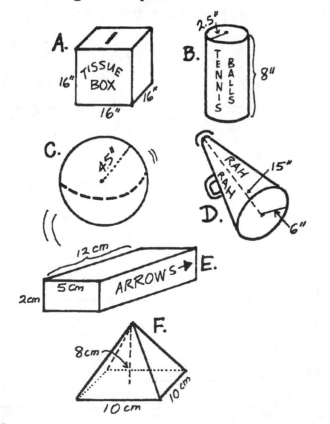

53. Name figure A. _____

54. Give the volume of figure A. _____

55. Name figure B. _____

56. Give the volume of figure B. _____

57. Name figure C. _____

58. Give the volume of figure C. _____

59. Name figure D. _____

60. Give the volume of figure D. _____

61. Name figure E. _____

62. Give the volume of figure E. _____

63. Name Figure F. _____

64. Give the volume of figure F. _____

Use centimeters to measure figures S, T, X, and Y

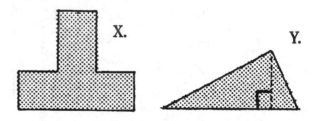

65. Give the perimeter of figure X. _____

66. Give the perimeter of figure Y. _____

67. Give the area of figure X. _____

68. Give the area of figure Y. _____

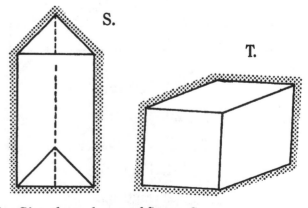

69. Give the volume of figure S. _____

70. Give the volume of figure T. _____

Name

Tell what each of these definitions describes.

71. An angle less than 90° _____

72. An angle greater than 90° _____

73. A triangle with 3 equal sides _____

74. A triangle with no equal sides _____

75. A triangle with 2 equal sides _____

Choose the correct answer for each question.

___ 76. 2 lines that intersect each other at right angles are
  a. parallel   b. perpendicular   c. line segments   d. planes

___ 77. 2 angles whose combined measures equal 90° are
  a. right angles   b. congruent angles   c. vertical angles   d. complementary angles

___ 78. 2 angles whose combined measures equal 180° are
  a. supplementary angles b. vertical angles   c. obtuse angles   d. complementary angles

___ 79. a quadrilateral with all angles (but not necessarily all sides) congruent is called a
  a. trapezoid   b. rhombus   c. rectangle   d. parallelogram

___ 80. The area of a trapezoid with bases 4 feet and 5 feet and a height of 6.5 feet is
  a. 130 ft²   b. 15.5 ft²   c. 29.25 ft²   d. 16.25 ft²

___ 81. The circumference of a circle with a radius of 9 inches is
  a. 28.26 in²   b. 56.52 in²   c. 254.34 in²   d. 1017.36 in²

___ 82. The volume of a cube with a side of 1.5 meters is
  a. 3.38 m³   b. 2.25 m³   c. 121.5 m³   d. 6 m³

___ 83. The best metric measure to convert gallons of milk into would be
  a. pints   b. milliliters   c. grams   d. liters

___ 84. The best unit for measuring the depth of a swimming pool would be
  a. centimeters   b. meters   c. kilometers   d. liters

___ 85. The volume of a pyramid with a square base (each side 12 cm) and a height of 8 cm is
  a. 384 cm³   b. 1152 cm³   c. 144 cm³   d. 576 cm³

___ 86. Which would be the best metric unit for measuring the weight of a soccer ball?
  a. kilograms   b. liters   c. square centimeters d. grams

___ 87. Which metric unit would be best for finding the amount of water in an Olympic diving pool?
  a. square meters   b. quarts   c. liters   d. metric tons

___ 88. 10,000 centimeters would convert to
  a. 10 meters   b. 100 meters   c. 1000 meters   d. .1 meters

___ 89. 4 gallons would convert to
  a. 8 quarts   b. 256 fluid ounces   c. 32 cups   d. 32 pints

___ 90. An athlete who has run a 3000 meter run in 47 races has run approximately
  a. 14 kilometers   b. 1,410 kilometers   c. 141 kilometers   d. 14,100 kilometers

91. A line segment having endpoints on a circle is a _____ .

92. 120 lbs is about _____ kg.

93. A 10-sided figure is a _____ .

94. A 19-ft pole vault is _____ meters.

95. A four-sided polygon is a _____ .

96. 24 quarts = _____ gallons

97. 1.75 meters = _____ millimeters

98. 1700 milliliters = _____ liters

99. 48 feet is about _____ meters

100. Volume of a sphere with a radius of 7 cm is _____ .

SCORE: Total Points _____ out of a possible 100 points

Name _____

GEOMETRY & MEASUREMENT
SKILLS TEST ANSWER KEY

Questions are worth 1 point each.

1. $\overleftrightarrow{XY}$
2. any of these answers: $\overline{AB}$, $\overline{AE}$, $\overline{AD}$, $\overline{BC}$, $\overline{BF}$, $\overline{CG}$, $\overline{FG}$, $\overline{EF}$, $\overline{DC}$
3. $\overrightarrow{AX}$, $\overrightarrow{BY}$, $\overrightarrow{BX}$, $\overrightarrow{AY}$
4. X, A, B, Y
5. $\overline{EF}$ & $\overline{AB}$, $\overline{AB}$ & $\overline{CD}$, $\overline{AD}$ & $\overline{BC}$, $\overline{BF}$ & $\overline{CG}$, or $\overline{BC}$ & $\overline{FG}$
6. numerous combinations
7. no
8. ABFE or ABCD or BCGF
9. 2
10. 1
11. C, H
12. C
13. C, D
14. B, D
15. G
16. F
17. A
18. E
19. 3, 4, 5
20. 1
21. 2
22. 5
23. Any 2 of these: $\overline{EF}$, $\overline{CD}$, $\overline{GH}$
24. CD
25. AB
26. no
27. yes
28. 8.5
29. 35 m
30. 25.12 yd
31. 112 m
32. 94 ft

33. 113 in
34. 4 mi
35. G
36. H
37. F
38. E
39. I
40. 8.25 cm²
41. 120 ft²
42. 9375 ft²
43. 706.5 in²
44. 42.25 cm²
45. 3 & 7, 4 & 5, 4 & 1
46. 1, 4, 5, or 6
47. 5 & 6
48. no
49. yes
50. 8
51. yes
52. 1 & 2 or 6 & 7
53. cube
54. 4096 m³
55. cylinder
56. 157 in³
57. sphere
58. 381.5 in³
59. cone
60. 565.2 in³
61. prism
62. 120 cm³
63. pyramid
64. 266.67 m³
65. 11 cm
66. 8 cm

67. 4.5 cm²
68. 2.625 cm²
69. 3.5 cm³
70. 8 cm³
71. acute
72. obtuse
73. equilateral
74. scalene
75. isosceles
76. b
77. d
78. a
79. c
80. c
81. b
82. a
83. d
84. b
85. a
86. d
87. c
88. b
89. d
90. c
91. chord
92. 54.48 kg
93. decagon
94. 5.79 m
95. quadrilateral
96. 6
97. 1750
98. 1.7
99. 16
100. 1436.03 cm³

ANSWERS

p. 66

Answers will vary somewhat, as there are many choices for each.
1. Points: A, B, C, D, E, F, G, H, I, J, K, L, M, N, O
2. NI and OJ
3-6. There are several correct answers for each of these.
7. Planes: ABFG, ABCD, CDHE, GFEH, BCEF, GADH

p. 67

1. acute
2. acute
3. obtuse
4. obtuse
5. obtuse
6. obtuse
7. right
8. obtuse
9. acute
10. acute
11. acute
12. supplementary, 107
13. complementary, 47
14. supplementary, 152
15. complementary, 69

pp. 68-69

1. Information Desk
2. Laundry Building
3. Annex
4. Answers will vary.
5. Medical Center
6. Market
7. True
8. False
9. True
10. Answers will vary.

pp. 70-71

1. Sudan
2. Sweden
3. Kuwait
4. United Kingdom
5. Jamaica
6. Taiwan
7. South Africa
8. Tanzania
9–10. Student designs will vary.

p. 73

A. 1. E
   2. B
   3. C
   4. D
   5. A

B. Check student drawings for accuracy.

pp. 74-75

1. 635.5 m
2. 54 m
3. 84 ft
4. 140 ft
5. 200 m
6. 393 ft
7. 154 m
8. 500 yds
9. 40.82 m
10. 60 m
11. 80 ft
12. 162.8 m
13. 914 m
14. 376.8 ft
15. 240 ft
16. 39 m
17. 331 ft, 10 in

p. 72

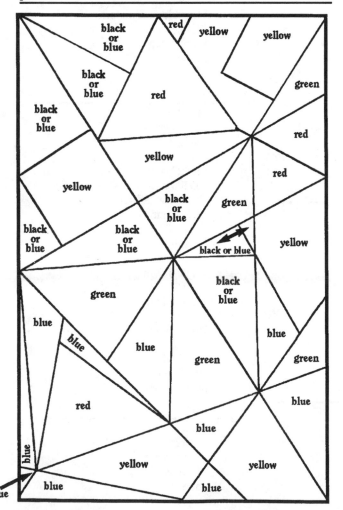

p. 76

1. Point N
2. $\overline{TQ}$ and $\overline{MK}$
3. NT, NK, NQ, NM
4. $\angle$ MNH or $\angle$ HNT
5. $\angle$ HNK
6. $\overline{MK}$ and $\overline{TQ}$, $\overline{MK}$ and $\overline{JQ}$
7. $\overline{TQ}$, $\overline{JQ}$, $\overline{MK}$
8. MH, HT, TJ, JK, KQ, QM
9. $\angle$ MNH, $\angle$ MNT, $\angle$ TNK, $\angle$ MNQ, $\angle$ QNK, $\angle$ HNT
10. 24 feet
11. N
12. S
13. A
14. A
15. N
16. N
17. S
18. N
19. A
20. A

p. 77

1. 9.42 m
2. 62.8 in
3. 106.156 m
4. 38.07 in
5. 4.71 in
6. 19.108 cm
7. 7.85 in
8. 7.85 m
9. 8.59 in
10. 21.98 ft

p. 78

1. similar
2. similar
3. neither
4. congruent
5. congruent
6. congruent

Athlete's name: Becky Dyroen-Lancer

p. 79

1. 441 ft²
2. 30 ft²
3. 6500 ft²
4. 162 ft²
5. 702 ft²
6. 45 ft²
7. 50 m²

p. 80

1. 17ft²
2. 12m²
3. 43.4 ft²
4. 3.08 m²
5. 24 ft²
6. 1.35 yd²

7. 60 yd²
8. 90 ft²

p. 81

Message is: GOOD LUCK

p. 82

I. 1. r = 4.25 in, A = 56.72 in²
2. r = 1.91 in, A = 11.46 in²
3. r = .75 in, A = 1.77 in²
4. r = 1.16 in, A = 4.23 in²
5. r = 1.12 in, A = 3.93 in²
6. r = 1.25 in, A = 4.91 in²
7. r = 4.5 in, A = 63.59 in²
8. r = 4 in, A = 50.24 in²
9. r = 1.5 in, A = 7.07 in²

II. 1. basketball
2. soccer ball
3. volleyball
4. women's softball
5. baseball
6. tennis ball
7. men's team handball
8. women's team handball
9. table tennis ball

p. 83

1. 2
2. 4
3. 7
4. 105
5. 9, 11, 12
6. 14, 16, 17
7. 18
8. 60
9. 60
10. 120
11. 19, 20, 21, 23, 25, 27, 29, 31, 32
12. 22, 24, 30

p. 84

1. A
2. C
3. I
4. F
5. B
6. K
7. L
8. H
9. J
10. E
11. G
12. D

p. 85

1. 769.3 cm³
2. 1000 cm³
3. 1125 cm³
4. 1046.86 cm³
5. 301.44 cm³
6. 1099 cm³

7. 753.6 cm³
8. 2064.19 cm³
Figure # 3 has the largest capacity.

pp. 86-87

1. 174,375 m³
2. 2,592,100 m³
3. 44,550 m³
4. b
5. a
6. c
7. 70 ft³
8. 60 yd³
9. 160 m³
10. 42.875 m³
11. H

p. 88

1. centimeters
2. meters
3. liter
4. meters
5. kilometers
6. centimeters
7. kilograms
8. centimeters
9. grams
10. centimeters
11. cubic centimeters
12. kiloliters
13. meters
14. no
15. no

p. 89

1. 10,000 mm
2. 354 cm
3. 0.137 km
4. 10,000 cm
5. 1234 cm
6. 100 mm
7. 12,450,000 cm
8. 0.12 cm
9. 45,670 mm
10. 990 m
11. 0.0567 km
12. 0.4567 m
13. 0.569 m
14. 0.9843 m
15. 90 cm
16. 0.456 m
17. 0.00027 cm
18. 87.61 cm
19. 851 m
20. 0.000567 km

pp. 90-91

1. feet
2. feet
3. pounds
4. miles
5. feet

6. inches
7. miles
8. yards
9. ounces
10. inches
11. inches
12. pounds
13. pounds
14. feet or yards
15. pounds
16. miles
17. yards
18. miles
19. pounds
20. feet
21. ounces
22. feet
23. quarts
24. feet or yards

p. 92

1. 35 yards
2. 44 feet
3. 147 pounds
4. 35 minutes
5. 4 inches
6. about 66 ⅔ yards
7. 3 feet
8. 55 feet
9. 27 minutes
10. 16 pounds

p. 93

1. feet
2. second
3. miles
4. miles
5. feet
6. inches
7. inches
8. miles
9. inches
10. ounces
11. feet
12. feet

pp. 94-95

Finished figure should look like this:

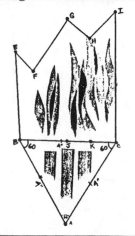

p. 96

Measurements will be approximate. Give credit for answers close to these:

1. A = 60 ft²   P = 32 ft
2. A = 36 ft²   P = 24 ft
3. A = 48 ft²   P = 32 ft
4. A = 36 ft²   P = 24 ft
5. A = 24 ft²   P = 20 ft
6. A = 56 ft²   P = 28 ft
7. A = 15 ft²   P = 18 ft
8. A = 32 ft²   P = 25 ft
9. A = 28 ft²   P = 23 ft
10. A = 104 ft²   P = 42 ft

Roomiest Room is # 10

p. 97

1. soccer
2. soccer
3. 25.3 inches
4. about 16.74 inches
5. 11 inches
6. baseball and polo ball
7. basketball
8. about 8.45 ounces
9. 5.25 ounces
10. 21.909 ounces
11.   1. ping pong
      2. tennis
      3. polo
      4. baseball
      5. volleyball
      6. soccer
      7. basketball

p. 98

Answers will be approximate. Give credit for answers close to these measurements.

1. 8400 cm³
2. 9750 cm³
3. 8670 cm³
4. 9000 cm³
5. 7280 cm³
6. 15,000 cm³
7. 9375 cm³
8. 18,630 cm³
9. 10,000 cm³

8 has greatest volume

p. 99

A   1 = 33°
     2 = 105°
     3 = 45°
     4 = 90°
     5 = 25°
     6 = 130°
     7 = 95°
B   8 = 155°
     9 = 30°
     10 = 115°
     11 = 77°
C   12 = 10°
     13 = 40°

14 = 88°
15 = 180°

pp. 100-101

1. C
2. B
3. A
4. B
5. B
6. A
7. B
8. C
9. A
10. C
11. B
12. B
13. B
14. A

p. 102

1. 119 lb
2. 130 lb
3. 141 lb
4. 154 lb
5. 167 lb
6. 183 lb
7. 200 lb
8. 218 lb
9. 238 lb
10. 113 kg approx.

p. 103

1. 40° 3F
2. 15° F
3. 48° F
4. 25° F
5. −10° F

p. 104

1. 9.09
2. 10
3. 384
4. 375
5. Make sure student has drawn a 2 ½ inch line.
6. 440
7. Michael Johnson

FRACTIONS & DECIMALS

Skills Exercises

12¾ yds.   33¼ yds.

2½ yds.

SKILLS CHECKLIST FOR FRACTIONS & DECIMALS

✔	SKILL	PAGE(S)
	Name fractional parts of a whole or set	116
	Read and write fractional numbers and mixed numerals	116, 117
	Compare and order fractions	118
	Write mixed numerals as fractions	119
	Identify factors, prime factors, and composite factors and multiples	120–122
	Identify common factors and greatest common factors	121
	Identify multiples and least common multiples	122
	Identify equivalent fractions	123, 124
	Identify and write fractions in lowest terms	125
	Add and subtract fractions with like denominators	126–128
	Add and subtract fractions with unlike denominators	126–128
	Add and subtract mixed numerals	129
	Multiply fractions	130
	Multiply mixed numerals	131, 132
	Divide fractions	133
	Read and write decimals and mixed numerals	134–136
	Compare and order decimals and mixed numerals	136
	Identify place value in decimals	137
	Round decimals	138
	Add and subtract decimals	139
	Multiply decimals	140
	Divide decimals	141, 154
	Convert fractions to decimals	142
	Convert decimals to fractions	143
	Understand, read, and write percents	144
	Write decimals as percents and percents as decimals	144, 145, 154, 156
	Write fractions as percents	145, 146
	Solve problems to find percents	147, 148, 156
	Find the original number when the percent is known	148
	Compare numbers or quantities by writing ratios	149, 150, 156
	Define and determine rate and write rates as ratios	150
	Understand and write proportions	151–153
	Use cross multiplication to solve proportions	151–153
	Solve problems with fractions and decimals	154–156

IT'S A DOG'S LIFE

The International Sled Dog Racing Association calls dogsledding the "world's fastest growing winter sport." Dog teams generally consist of 14 dogs, but can include as many as 20 dogs. Not every dog on the team is a husky. Many other breeds are used. Labradors, hounds, Irish setters, Alaskan malamutes, and non-purebred mixes are popular choices. Examine the dog teams below and answer the following questions.

Dog Team 1	Dog Team 2	Dog Team 3	Dog Team 4	Dog Team 5
4 Labradors	1 Labrador	8 Labradors	2 Labradors	1 Labrador
4 Alaskan malamutes	3 Alaskan malamutes	4 Alaskan malamutes	10 Alaskan malamutes	4 Alaskan malamutes
1 hound	1 hound	1 hound	2 huskies	2 huskies
1 Irish setter	2 Irish setters	1 Irish setter		5 non-purebred mixes
2 huskies	3 huskies			
2 non-purebred mixes	4 non-purebred mixes			

1. Team 1 has 14 dogs. Write a fraction that represents the ratio of the number of Labradors to the number of dogs on the whole team. _____

2. Team 1 has 14 dogs. Write a fraction that represents the number of Alaskan malamutes and huskies compared to the number of dogs on the whole team. _____

3. Team 2 has 14 dogs. Write a fraction that compares the number of Irish setters and huskies to the number of dogs on the whole team. _____

4. Team 2 has 14 dogs. Write a fraction that compares the number of huskies to the number of dogs on the whole team. _____

5. Team 3 has 14 dogs. Write a fraction that compares the number of Labradors and Alaskan malamutes to the number of dogs on the whole team. _____

6. In Teams 4 and 5 there are 26 dogs. Write a fraction that compares the number of Alaskan malamutes in both teams to the total number of dogs in both teams. _____

7. The number of dogs on all teams combined is 68. Complete the chart below to show how many of each breed are on the teams. Write a fraction for each breed.

Type of dog	Labrador	Alaskan malamute	Hound	Irish setter	Husky	Non-purebred
Fraction (Number in That Breed / Total Number of Dogs)						

Name _____

WHICH WINTER WEAR?

Maria is making choices about clothing for winter skiing and mountain-climbing adventures. She's comparing winter gear in several catalogs. Read and answer the questions below about the clothing she is considering buying.

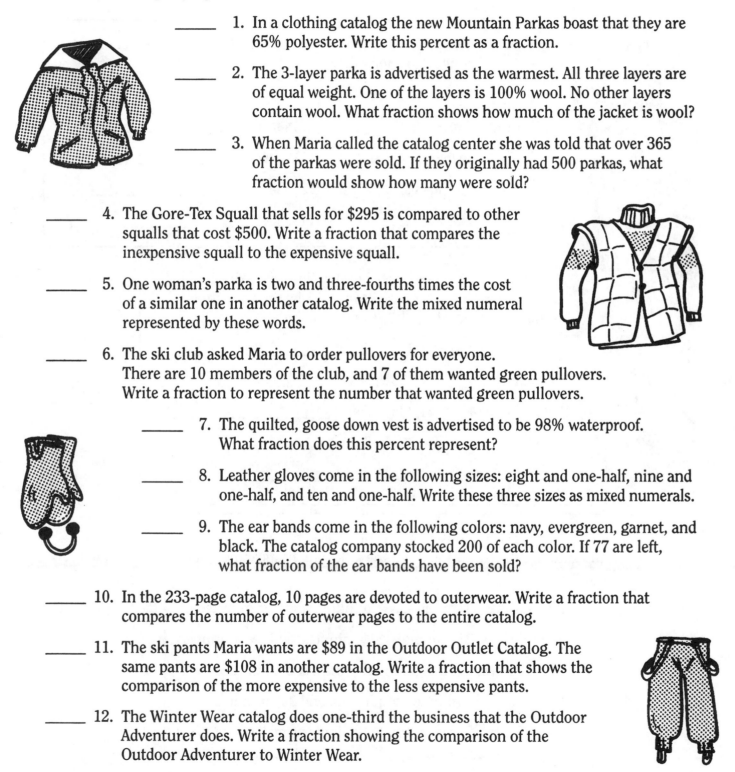

_____ 1. In a clothing catalog the new Mountain Parkas boast that they are 65% polyester. Write this percent as a fraction.

_____ 2. The 3-layer parka is advertised as the warmest. All three layers are of equal weight. One of the layers is 100% wool. No other layers contain wool. What fraction shows how much of the jacket is wool?

_____ 3. When Maria called the catalog center she was told that over 365 of the parkas were sold. If they originally had 500 parkas, what fraction would show how many were sold?

_____ 4. The Gore-Tex Squall that sells for $295 is compared to other squalls that cost $500. Write a fraction that compares the inexpensive squall to the expensive squall.

_____ 5. One woman's parka is two and three-fourths times the cost of a similar one in another catalog. Write the mixed numeral represented by these words.

_____ 6. The ski club asked Maria to order pullovers for everyone. There are 10 members of the club, and 7 of them wanted green pullovers. Write a fraction to represent the number that wanted green pullovers.

_____ 7. The quilted, goose down vest is advertised to be 98% waterproof. What fraction does this percent represent?

_____ 8. Leather gloves come in the following sizes: eight and one-half, nine and one-half, and ten and one-half. Write these three sizes as mixed numerals.

_____ 9. The ear bands come in the following colors: navy, evergreen, garnet, and black. The catalog company stocked 200 of each color. If 77 are left, what fraction of the ear bands have been sold?

_____ 10. In the 233-page catalog, 10 pages are devoted to outerwear. Write a fraction that compares the number of outerwear pages to the entire catalog.

_____ 11. The ski pants Maria wants are $89 in the Outdoor Outlet Catalog. The same pants are $108 in another catalog. Write a fraction that shows the comparison of the more expensive to the less expensive pants.

_____ 12. The Winter Wear catalog does one-third the business that the Outdoor Adventurer does. Write a fraction showing the comparison of the Outdoor Adventurer to Winter Wear.

Name

HIGH-SPEED SPORTING

Bobsledding is a fast and dangerous winter sport. It's also one of the most thrilling. The sleds are made of aluminum and steel, and they travel up to 90 miles per hour. The length of each sled cannot exceed $12\frac{1}{2}$ feet.

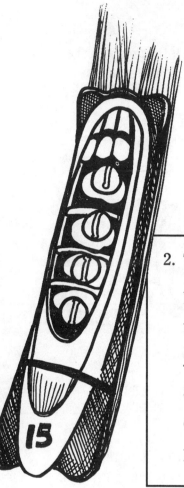

1. Place the sleds in order by their length. List these sleds from longest to shortest.

   United States' sled $11\frac{7}{8}$ feet   _____

   Jamaica's sled $12\frac{1}{3}$ feet   _____

   Switzerland's sled $11\frac{8}{9}$ feet   _____

   Canada's sled $12\frac{1}{2}$ feet   _____

   Russia's sled $11\frac{1}{4}$ feet   _____

2. The total weight allowed on a bobsled (including the crew) is 1,389 pounds. Place these sleds in order by their weight, listing them from the lightest to the heaviest.

   United States $1,333\frac{1}{2}$ lbs.   _____

   Jamaica $1,386\frac{1}{3}$ lbs.   _____

   Switzerland $1,386\frac{3}{4}$ lbs.   _____

   Canada $1,386\frac{1}{8}$ lbs.   _____

   Russia $1,333\frac{3}{4}$ lbs.   _____

3. Championship bobsled races consist of four heats. The team with the lowest composite (total) score wins. Total the following heats and circle the winning team.

   United States $2\frac{1}{2}$ minutes, 3 minutes, $3\frac{1}{2}$ minutes, and $2\frac{1}{2}$ minutes

   Jamaica $2\frac{1}{2}$ minutes, $2\frac{1}{2}$ minutes, $3\frac{1}{2}$ minutes, and $2\frac{1}{2}$ minutes

   Switzerland $2\frac{1}{3}$ minutes, 2 minutes, $2\frac{1}{2}$ minutes, and 3 minutes

   Canada   2 minutes, $2\frac{1}{2}$ minutes, 2 minutes, and $2\frac{1}{3}$ minutes

   Russia $2\frac{3}{4}$ minutes, $2\frac{1}{2}$ minutes, $2\frac{1}{2}$ minutes, and 3 minutes

Name _____

HOMEWORK FIRST

You've got your roller blades over your shoulder and are ready to go out the door, when your mom yells, "You have to do your homework first." Quickly finish these fraction problems about skating time.

I. Each improper fraction gives a time that one skater spent on roller blades for the past 10 days. Rewrite each improper fraction as a whole number or a mixed numeral in simplest form.

1. $5/2$ hrs. ______________
2. $8/3$ hrs. ______________
3. $13/4$ hrs. ______________
4. $11/8$ hrs. ______________
5. $9/3$ hrs. ______________
6. $12/5$ hrs. ______________
7. $24/7$ hrs. ______________
8. $3/2$ hrs. ______________
9. $15/2$ hrs. ______________
10. $13/5$ hrs. ______________

II. Each mixed numeral gives an amount of time that you've spent skating in the last 10 days. Rewrite each mixed numeral as an improper fraction.

11. 1 and $1/4$ hrs. ______________
12. 1 and $3/4$ hrs. ______________
13. 2 and $1/4$ hrs. ______________
14. 2 and $1/5$ hrs. ______________
15. 2 and $4/5$ hrs. ______________
16. 4 and $1/5$ hrs. ______________
17. 1 and $1/10$ hrs. ______________
18. 1 and $5/10$ hrs. ______________
19. 3 and $1/10$ hrs. ______________
20. 2 and $7/8$ hrs. ______________

Name ______________________________

RED & WHITE OR BLACK & BLUE

Basketball players may get black and blue if they have mishaps or make mistakes on the court. But if they make mistakes in math class, their papers will look pretty red and white. Take a look at the math paper of star basketball player Shaundra. She's trying to sort out factors, prime factors, and composite factors.

I. First, practice these concepts yourself. If you see a prime number, circle it in red. If you see a composite number, circle it in blue.

1. $12 = 2 \times 6$
2. $24 = 2 \times 2 \times 6$
3. $13 = 1 \times 13$
4. $36 = 2 \times 2 \times 3 \times 3$
5. $21 = 3 \times 7$
6. $28 = 2 \times 2 \times 7$
7. $56 = 7 \times 8$
8. $63 = 3 \times 3 \times 7$
9. $48 = 2 \times 2 \times 12$

II. Now look at Shaundra's paper. Her assignment was to factor all these numbers down to prime factors. Circle in blue all the ones she did correctly. In red, correct all her mistakes.

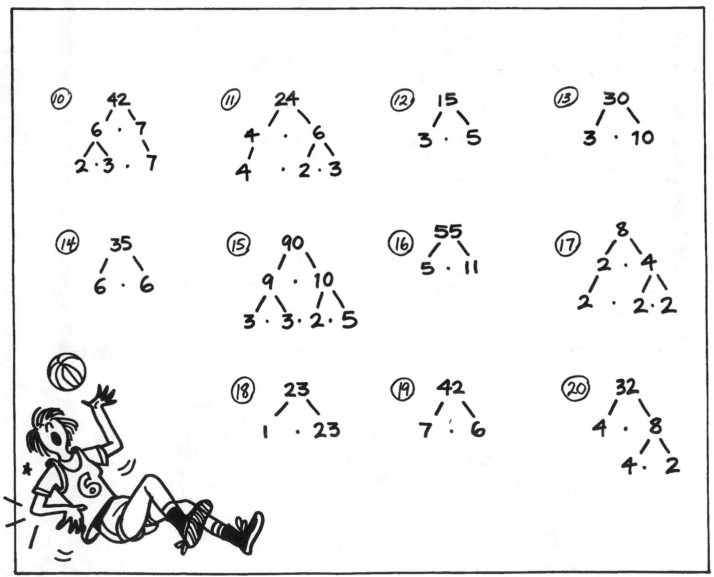

FOUL WEATHER OR FOWL WEATHER?

Whether you are an athlete engaged in an outdoor winter sport or just someone who spends a lot of time outside in the cold weather, you ought to know all about "cutis anserine." To determine what "cutis anserine" are, match the two numbers in the left column to their greatest common factor in the right column. (Remember: A common factor is a factor that two numbers share. A greatest common factor is the largest factor two numbers share!)

_____ 1. GCF of 12 and 24   O. 8

_____ 2. GCF of 8 and 36   E. 4

_____ 3. GCF of 8 and 16   G. 12

_____ 4. GCF of 13 and 39   P. 2

_____ 5. GCF of 4 and 16   O. 8

_____ 6. GCF of 10 and 25   B. 3

_____ 7. GCF of 21 and 36   S. 13

_____ 8. GCF of 5 and 15   U. 5

_____ 9. GCF of 11 and 33   S. 13

_____ 10. GCF of 8 and 30   #. 5

_____ 11. GCF of 39 and 52   M. 11

So what are "cutis anserine"? _____

Solve these problems in a SNAP! (A cold snap, that is!)

_____ 12. GCF of 6 and 21

_____ 13. GCF of 12 and 15

_____ 14. GCF of 12 and 20

_____ 15. GCF of 7 and 35

_____ 16. GCF of 16 and 24

_____ 17. GCF of 9 and 15

_____ 18. GCF of 9 and 18

_____ 19. GCF of 18 and 20

_____ 20. GCF of 5 and 50

Name _____

AT THE TOP

To be at the top of their sports, these champions have won multiple titles or records. Use the numbers on these top 10 lists to practice identifying multiples.

WOMEN'S TOP 10 GRAND SLAM SINGLES WINNERS

	# of titles
Margaret Court	24
Helen Wills-Moody	19
Chris Evert-Lloyd	18
Martina Navratilova	18
Steffi Graf	18
Billie Jean King	12
Maureen Connolly	9
Suzanne Lenglen	8
Molla Mallory	8
Monica Seles	8

TOP 10 WORLD GOLF WINNERS OF MAJORS

	# of wins
Jack Nicklaus	18
Walter Hagen	11
Ben Hogan	9
Gary Player	9
Tom Watson	8
Harry Varden	7
Gene Sarazen	7
Bobby Jones	7
Sam Snead	7
Arnold Palmer	7

TOP 10 WINNING GRAND PRIX DRIVERS

	# of wins
Alain Prost	51
Ayrton Senna	41
Nigel Mansell	31
Jackie Stewart	27
Jim Clark	25
Niki Lauda	25
Juan Fangio	24
Nelson Piquet	23
Michael Schumacher	18
Stirling Moss	16

TOP 10 MALE (singles) FIGURE SKATERS
(World & Olympic Titles)

Ulrich Salchow	11
Karl Schafer	9
Dick Button	7
Gillis Grafstrom	6
Hayes Jenkins	5
Scott Hamilton	5
Willy Bockl	4
David Jenkins	4
Ondrej Nepela	4
Kurt Browning	4

1. List the 3 lowest common multiples of the totals of the 10th athletes in tennis and skating. _____

2. What is the least common multiple of the top 3 figure skaters' number of titles? _____

3. List the 2 lowest common multiples of Steffi Graf, Gary Player, and Karl Schafer. _____

4. Margaret Court's total is a common multiple of which other players' totals?

   _____

5. What is the least common multiple of Scott Hamilton's, Jim Clark's, and Monica Seles' totals?

   _____

6. Chris Evert-Lloyd's total is the least common multiple of which players' totals?

   _____

Name _____

FAMOUS WORDS

Lawrence Peter "Yogi" Berra won the American Baseball League's Most Valuable Player Award three times—1951, 1954, and 1955. Most folks also remember him for his famous, unpredictable comments. To discover one of his most famous sayings, match each fraction above to an equivalent fraction below.

(Don't worry if you see an alphabet letter several times. That just means that the letter is used several different times in Mr. Berra's famous comment and that the fractions are equivalent, too.) Dots represent spaces between words.

$$\frac{1}{2} \quad \frac{1}{3} \quad \frac{1}{4} \quad \frac{1}{5} \quad \frac{1}{2} \quad \frac{1}{6} \quad \frac{1}{9} \quad \frac{1}{3} \quad \frac{1}{4} \quad \frac{1}{7} \quad \frac{2}{5} \quad \frac{3}{5} \quad \frac{5}{6} \quad \frac{1}{4}$$

$$\frac{1}{9} \quad \frac{1}{3} \quad \frac{1}{2} \quad \frac{4}{5} \quad \frac{1}{4} \quad \frac{1}{2} \quad \frac{1}{3} \quad \frac{1}{9} \quad \frac{2}{3} \quad \frac{1}{4} \quad \frac{1}{7} \quad \frac{2}{5} \quad \frac{3}{5} \quad \frac{5}{6} \; .$$

N = $\frac{2}{12}$	A = $\frac{2}{10}$	T = $\frac{4}{12}$	O = $\frac{2}{14}$	I = $\frac{5}{10}$	' = $\frac{3}{27}$	V = $\frac{6}{15}$
T = $\frac{8}{24}$	I = $\frac{4}{8}$	• = $\frac{2}{8}$	V = $\frac{10}{25}$	L = $\frac{8}{10}$	R = $\frac{10}{12}$	E = $\frac{9}{15}$
T = $\frac{2}{6}$	• = $\frac{4}{16}$	S = $\frac{4}{6}$	R = $\frac{15}{18}$	• = $\frac{10}{40}$	• = $\frac{12}{48}$	E = $\frac{6}{10}$
I = $\frac{3}{6}$	' = $\frac{2}{18}$	• = $\frac{6}{24}$	T = $\frac{6}{18}$	I = $\frac{6}{12}$	O = $\frac{3}{21}$	' = $\frac{4}{36}$

Little League Baseball..."it's wonderful, it keeps the kids out of the house."

A famous restaurant....."Nobody goes there anymore. It's too crowded."

A famous Opera House...."It was pretty good. Even the music was nice."

Name

TOP 10 QUESTIONS

Here are 10 top questions about some top 10 topics in sports. You'll need to be in top shape with your understanding of equivalent fractions to answer these correctly. Choose your answers from the fractions sprinkled around the page.

$\frac{1}{5}$

$\frac{25}{110}$

$\frac{12}{52}$

$\frac{5}{18}$

$\frac{45}{50}$

$\frac{19}{11}$

$\frac{14}{20}$

$\frac{25}{30}$

$\frac{9}{21}$

$\frac{19}{10}$

$\frac{6}{20}$

$\frac{3}{5}$

$\frac{11}{44}$

1. Of the 10 most common sports injuries, 6 are specific to legs and knees. What fraction is equivalent to this ratio of $^6/_{10}$? _____

2. 5 of the 10 highest-earning sports movies feature boxing. Which fraction is equivalent to this ratio? _____

3. Over 40 million households watched Super Bowl XVI, the biggest TV audience ever for a sports event through 1996. Of the top 10 most-watched sporting events, 8 others were Super Bowls. What fraction shows the ratio of Super Bowls to the total of 10? _____

4. Riots, stampedes, crushes, collapsed stands, and fires at soccer games make up 7 of the top 10 worst disasters at sports events in the 20th century. What fraction shows the ratio of non-soccer disasters to soccer disasters? _____

5. In the 10 worst disasters at sports events, about 1900 people were killed. Approximately 1000 of these deaths happened at soccer events. What fraction shows this ratio? _____

6. The top 10 Olympic medal–winning countries in bobsledding have won a total of 90 medals. Switzerland holds 25 of these. What fraction shows the ratio of Switzerland's medals to the total? _____

7. U.S. Figure skater Kristi Yamaguchi, one of the top 10 world and Olympic title holders for women, holds 3 titles. Katarina Witt holds 6. Sonja Heine is number one with 13.
   a. What fraction shows the ratio of Kristi's to Katarina's titles? _____
   b. What fraction shows the ratio of Kristi's to Sonja's? _____

8. In the list of top 10 winners of the World Series, the NY Yankees are first with 22 wins. The Boston Red Sox are #5 with 5 wins. What fraction shows the ratio of Boston to NY? _____

9. In the list of the top 10 Olympic medal–winning countries, the U.S. at # 1 has over 1900. The USSR/CIS has over 1100. What fraction shows the U.S. to USSR/CIS ratio? _____

10. Of the top 10 highest-paid sportsmen in the world in 1995, 2 were basketball players. What fraction shows the ratio of basketball players to non-basketball sportsmen? _____

Name _____

WEIGHING IN!

Many athletes have to pay attention to their weight to participate in athletics. Some athletes, such as football players, wrestlers, or fighters, may wish to increase weight. In many cases, athletes are trying to reduce their weight. These fractions are a bit "weighty." They need reducing. In each case, reduce them to their lowest terms.

1. $\frac{4}{8}$ _____

2. $\frac{12}{16}$ _____

3. $\frac{20}{25}$ _____

4. $\frac{15}{30}$ _____

5. $\frac{2}{6}$ _____

6. $\frac{3}{9}$ _____

7. $\frac{9}{27}$ _____

8. $\frac{12}{15}$ _____

9. $\frac{36}{42}$ _____

10. $\frac{2}{4}$ _____

11. $\frac{2}{8}$ _____

12. $\frac{6}{8}$ _____

13. $\frac{4}{8}$ _____

14. $\frac{2}{12}$ _____

15. $\frac{8}{20}$ _____

16. $\frac{10}{25}$ _____

17. $\frac{25}{35}$ _____

18. $\frac{32}{36}$ _____

19. $\frac{20}{55}$ _____

20. $\frac{12}{21}$ _____

21. $\frac{15}{18}$ _____

22. $\frac{6}{9}$ _____

23. $\frac{3}{12}$ _____

24. $\frac{25}{30}$ _____

25. $\frac{30}{48}$ _____

26. $\frac{50}{100}$ _____

27. $\frac{9}{24}$ _____

28. $\frac{13}{39}$ _____

29. $\frac{8}{16}$ _____

30. $\frac{4}{18}$ _____

Reduced or **Not Reduced?** That is the question.

Circle all the fractions that are reduced to lowest terms. If a fraction is not reduced to lowest terms, reduce it and write your answer beside the fraction.

31. $\frac{13}{26}$ 32. $\frac{14}{42}$ 33. $\frac{8}{56}$ 34. $\frac{21}{63}$ 35. $\frac{5}{23}$ 36. $\frac{4}{21}$ 37. $\frac{30}{45}$ 38. $\frac{6}{23}$

Name _____

125

FRIDAY NIGHT FOOTBALL

East Middle School's football team is getting beaten badly by Franklin Middle School. The score is 42 to 10. Sherry and Elizabeth are bored with the game, but they have to stay until their older brother comes to pick them up. Maybe the time will go faster if they try to figure out the answers to these dilemmas. (Use the sketch of a football field on page 127 to help you solve problems.) Give your answers in fractions, whole numbers, or mixed numerals.

_____ 1. The first field goal East Middle School makes is $2\frac{1}{4}$ minutes into the first quarter. If the clock starts counting down at 12 minutes, how much time is left on the clock when this field goal is scored?

_____ 2. The second quarter starts and the clock is reset to 12 minutes. Franklin's first touchdown is made $3\frac{1}{4}$ minutes into the quarter. Another touchdown is made $5\frac{3}{4}$ minutes later. How much time is left in the second quarter when the second touch down is scored?

_____ 3. East scores their final touchdown $1\frac{1}{2}$ minutes into the third quarter. If the clock is reset to 12 at the beginning of each quarter, how many minutes are left after the East touchdown?

_____ 4. Franklin Middle School gains the following yards during one of their periods of possession: $12\frac{1}{2}$ yards, $9\frac{1}{2}$ yards, $32\frac{1}{2}$ yards, 2 yards, and $25\frac{1}{2}$ yards. How many yards are gained by Franklin Middle School?

_____ 5. East Middle School has possession of the ball on the 50-yard line. The team gains $11\frac{1}{4}$ yards. In the next play the ball is intercepted by Franklin's team and they run the ball $33\frac{3}{4}$ yards towards their goal. Where is the ball placed for the next play? Is it closer to Franklin's or East's goal? (Use the football field sketch to help with this problem.)

6. The sportswriter for the East School newspaper is writing an article for the paper. He is highlighting the players listed below. To help the sportswriter, use the information in the chart below and total the players' yards gained.

Yards Gained

Lightning Larry	$12\frac{3}{4}$ yds.	$7\frac{1}{4}$ yds.	2 yds.	_____ total
Cool-Kick Kerry	7 yds.	$2\frac{1}{2}$ yds.	$4\frac{1}{2}$ yds.	_____ total
Jumpin' Joe	$33\frac{1}{4}$ yds.	$2\frac{3}{4}$ yds.	10 yds.	_____ total
Speedy Sam	23 yds.	$3\frac{1}{3}$ yds.	$4\frac{2}{3}$ yds.	_____ total

Use with page 127.

Name

Use with page 126.

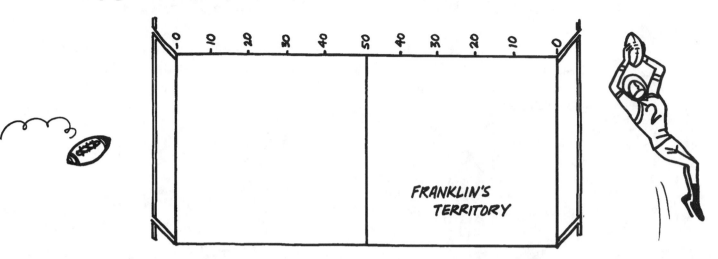

FRANKLIN'S
TERRITORY

_____ 7. Brad is over at the concession stand. He needs a hot dog, chips, and a drink; he has $3. Does Brad have enough money to buy a hot dog (a dollar and a half), a bag of chips (a half dollar), and a drink (three-quarters of a dollar)?

_____ 8. East is close to a touchdown in the first half. They have the ball 4½ yards back from their goal line. Franklin intercepts the ball and runs 43¾ yards in the other direction. How far back from East's goal line is the ball now?

_____ 9. Bored Elizabeth, watching the clock, notices that there are 3 minutes and 50 seconds left in the third quarter (3⅚ minutes). If each quarter is 12 minutes, how much time has already passed in the third quarter?

_____ 10. Sherry ate supper at 5:20. She looks at her watch and realizes that was 3 and ⅙ hours ago. What time is it now?

_____ 11. Elizabeth is so tired. She plans to be in bed in 2⅓ hours. That will be 11:30 P.M. What time is it now?

_____ 12. In the last quarter, Franklin runs the ball from East's 40 yard line to a position just 6⅓ yards back from their own goal line. How far do they move the ball on this play?

_____ 13. The biggest play of the game is a pass and a great run following it. James Johnston throws the ball from the 10 yard line of East. It is caught by Tom Jacobs at East's 32½ yard line. He then runs to Franklin's 13⅔ yard line. How far does the ball travel on that play?

_____ 14. Sherry and Elizabeth wait for their brother ¾ of an hour past the time when he was supposed to pick them up. If he was supposed to come at quarter past nine, when did he arrive?

Name _____

FRACTIONS IN A BACKPACK

Three friends are planning a backpacking trip to the Smoky Mountains. They can carry gear weighing up to one-fourth of their body weight. Study the information and answer the questions below:

Individual Camping Gear
sleeping bag 5 1/8 lb.
pack with frame 3 3/4 lb.
pocketknife 3/16 lb.
ground cloth 5/8 lb.
measuring drinking cup 1/8 lb.
silverware 7/16 lb.
mess kit with dip bag 15/16 lb.
full water bottle 1 1/2 lb.

Group Camping Gear
2 man tube tent 2 5/16 lb.
map 1/8 lb.
first aid kit 3 3/4 lb.
candles 7/16 lb.
camera 1 1/4 lb.
empty plastic water jug 3/8 lb.
water purification 11/16 lb.

Group Food
energy bars 1/4 lb.
2 breakfasts 7/8 lb.
2 lunches 1 3/16 lb.
2 dinners 1 5/8 lb.
hot chocolate 5/16 lb.
soups 7/16 lb.

Personal Gear
2 shirts 5/16 lb.
2 pr. pants 5/8 lb.
toiletries 1 7/8 lb.
bandanna 1/16 lb.
raincoat 1 5/16 lb.
underwear 7/8 lb.
hat 1/4 lb.
towel & washcloth 1/2 lb.
stuffed animal 11/16 lb.
reading book 7/16 lb.

Group Cooking Gear
pots & lids 2 1/8 lb.
portable grill 3/4 lb.
firestarters 1 1/16 lb.
matches 5/16 lb.
garbage bags 13/16 lb.

1. Find the total weight for each of these categories of backpacking gear.

   individual camping gear _____   group camping gear _____   group food _____

   personal gear _____   group cooking gear _____

2. The individual and personal gear weighs 19⅝ pounds. Complete the chart below by subtracting each individual gear weight from her pack allowance.

Girl's name	Girl's weight	Pack allowance	Individual gear	Group share
Sally	104	26	19⅝	
Mai	101	25¼	19⅝	
Tamika	98	24½	19⅝	

3. Add the group share for each of the three girls to get a total. _____

4. Total the weight of the group camping gear, group cooking gear, and group food from question 1. _____

5. Will the girls be able to carry all the group gear that they need? If yes, how much underweight is their group gear? If not, how much overweight is their group gear (subtract the answer in #4 minus the answer in #3)? _____

Name _____

DANGEROUS FRACTIONS

Snow-covered mountain peaks may look beautiful, but there are dangers lurking in those peaks for hikers, climbers, and skiers. To learn about safety in the great outdoors, solve the fraction problems in bold type in each statement below.

_____ 1. To avoid altitude sickness on your first day of mountain climbing, don't climb above **$4499\frac{2}{5} + 4500\frac{6}{10}$** feet.

_____ 2. To avoid windburn, you must cover **$\frac{4}{5} + \frac{3}{15}$** of your body.

_____ 3. You should be aware of not only the temperature, but also the wind chill factor. A wind speed of **$12\frac{1}{2}$ miles per hour + $17\frac{5}{10}$ miles per hour** can drive

_____ 5 degrees above zero to **minus $15\frac{1}{5} + 25\frac{8}{10}$** degrees.

_____ 4. Many weather factors affect the possibility of an avalanche: temperature, wind, storms, rate of snowfall, and type of snow. For example, a sustained wind of **$19\frac{3}{4} - 4\frac{6}{8}$** miles per hour increases the danger of an avalanche occurring.

_____ 5. Crevasses in glaciers can be extremely dangerous. One of these hidden gaps may be as deep as **$980\frac{2}{3} - 680\frac{6}{9}$** feet.

_____ 6. We think that hypothermia can occur only when the temperature is below 0°, but it can also occur when the temperature is as warm as **$43\frac{2}{5}° + 11\frac{6}{10}°$**.

_____ 7. Snow blindness occurs when the cornea and the conjunctiva of the eye are sunburned. Generally, snow blindness does not occur until you have been out-of-doors for **$3\frac{1}{3} + 4\frac{2}{6} + 2\frac{3}{9}$** hours.

_____ 8. When hiking in the mountains you can use an **$11\frac{3}{4} - 4\frac{2}{8}$** minute topological

_____ map. These maps have a scale of **$1\frac{3}{8} + 1\frac{4}{16}$** inches to a mile.

_____ 9. If you get lost while hiking in snow it is important to stay put. To enhance your chances of being found, tromp out a message in the snow. The letters need to be at least **$20\frac{1}{4} - 10\frac{3}{12}$** feet tall.

_____ 10. A climber spent **$2\frac{3}{4}$** hours going from point A toward point B, then found that point B was not reachable by this path, and returned to point A. The return took **$1\frac{2}{3}$** hours. Then she found another route to point B, which took **$3\frac{5}{6}$** hours. Altogether, how long did it take her to get from point A to point B?

Name _____

GREAT-TASTING AWARDS

Terry Castle won the Chess Master award for the Bobby Fisher League. The caterers for the awards banquet need to calculate how much food to serve the guests. There are two parts to the banquet—a reception for 160 and a luncheon for 48.

1. The reception is open to players, coaches, and parents. The proposed menu items with the amount planned per person is given below. Multiply each amount by the 160 persons expected to find the total amount of food for the caterers to order.

Food Item	Amount per person	Total amount to order
Mints	$\frac{1}{32}$ pound	_____
Pizza	$\frac{1}{8}$ pie	_____
Nuts	$\frac{3}{40}$ pound	_____
Punch	$\frac{5}{48}$ gallon	_____
Cookies	$\frac{1}{16}$ pound	_____
Fudge	$\frac{3}{64}$ pound	_____

2. The luncheon is by invitation only and includes only the top players, their parents, and one coach per club. The luncheon menu items and the budgeted amount per person are listed below. Multiply each amount by 48 to provide the caterers with the total amount which should be ordered.

Food Item	Amount per person	Total amount to order
Hotdogs	$\frac{1}{10}$ pound	_____
Hotdog buns	$\frac{1}{12}$ dozen	_____
Mustard	$\frac{1}{4}$ ounce	_____
Ketchup	$\frac{1}{3}$ ounce	_____
Hamburger	$\frac{1}{5}$ pound	_____
Hamburger buns	$\frac{1}{12}$ dozen	_____
Potato chips	$\frac{3}{16}$ pound	_____
Baked beans	$\frac{3}{8}$ cup	_____
Jello	$\frac{1}{24}$ pan	_____
Ice cream	$\frac{3}{32}$ pound	_____

3. Terry Castle's parents are so proud of him that they want all the guests from the reception to stay for lunch. Since they are willing to pay for all the extra food that will be needed, recalculate the luncheon order to accommodate 160 guests.

Name _____

THAT FISH WAS HOW BIG?

Brianna, Nan, Simon, and Jason went on a fishing trip to Lake Pardenpu. While there they decided to keep a record of the biggest fish that they could catch. Since the four friends were not going to stuff, clean, or eat what they caught, they planned to measure the length of their catch, then return them to the lake. To determine the weight of the fish that they caught they asked a state naturalist to tell them how much the big fish would weigh on average in ounces per inch.

The state naturalist gave them the following information about the fish in Lake Pardenpu.

Name of fish	Typical lengths in inches	Weight in ounces per inch
Bass, Smallmouth	15 – 25	$5\frac{15}{16}$
Bluegill Sunfish	8 – 15	$4\frac{3}{4}$
Bowfin	15 – 32	$7\frac{5}{8}$
Catfish, flathead	15 – 35	$16\frac{11}{16}$
Crappie, white	10 – 20	$3\frac{3}{8}$
Walleye	18 – 36	$8\frac{4}{5}$

For example: If Brianna caught a $10\frac{1}{2}$ inch bluegill sunfish, she would calculate its weight as $10\frac{1}{2}$ inches times $4\frac{3}{4}$ ounces per inch = $49\frac{7}{8}$ ounces.

Using the information in the chart above, calculate the weight of each fish caught.

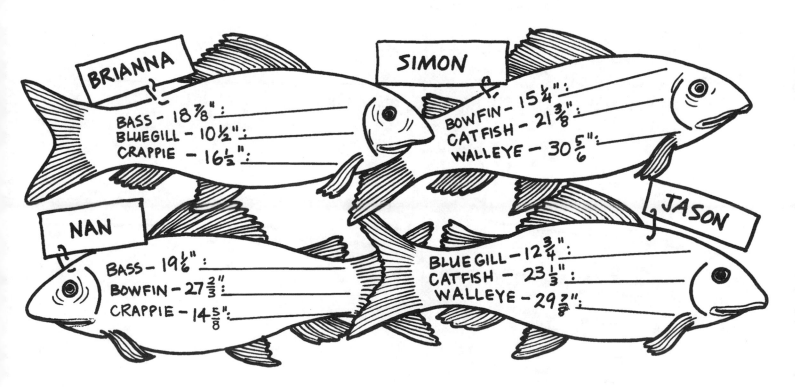

BRIANNA
BASS - $18\frac{3}{8}$":_____
BLUEGILL - $10\frac{1}{2}$":_____
CRAPPIE - $16\frac{1}{2}$":_____

SIMON
BOWFIN - $15\frac{3}{4}$":_____
CATFISH - $21\frac{3}{8}$":_____
WALLEYE - $30\frac{5}{6}$":_____

NAN
BASS - $19\frac{1}{6}$":_____
BOWFIN - $27\frac{2}{3}$":_____
CRAPPIE - $14\frac{5}{8}$":_____

JASON
BLUEGILL - $12\frac{3}{4}$":_____
CATFISH - $23\frac{1}{3}$":_____
WALLEYE - $29\frac{7}{8}$":_____

Name _____

WHAT'S COOKIN' ON THE CAMPFIRE?

A group of guys packed up for a weekend campout. They put Evan in charge of the food. He brought a recipe book that belonged to a cook at a camp. But there was a problem. The cook wrote these recipes when he was cooking in the military, so the recipes make enough food to feed an army. Reduce his recipes to the quantities listed. A group of only 10 campers will be going on the campout.

WARM YOU UP CHILI FOR 20
10 1/2 pound of hamburger
2 1/3 onions
3 1/2 green peppers
5 1/4 pound of tomatoes
6 3/4 T of chili powder
6 1/2 cans of tomato sauce
4 1/2 cans of beans

BACK WOODS POTATO SALAD FOR 30
9 1/2 lb. of potatoes
3 lb. of onions
2 1/2 lb. of celery
12 1/3 ounces of pickle relish
12 eggs
4 1/2 cups of mayonnaise
1/2 c. of mustard
2 1/2 T. of salt
1 3/4 T. of pepper
3/4 T of paprika

CRUNCHY APPLE CRISP FOR 20
12 lb. of apples
5 1/4 pound of brown sugar
8 1/3 cups of oatmeal
2 1/4 lb. of butter
2 1/2 T of cinnamon
1 3/4 t. of nutmeg

PEPPERMINT S'MORE BARS FOR 100
25 1/2 cups broken chocolate bars
55 cups crushed graham crackers
3 1/3 pounds marshmallows
3 3/4 cups crushed peppermint candy

Chili for Ten

Potato Salad for Ten

Apple Crisp for Ten

S'Mores for Ten

Name

CRASHING NOT INTENDED

Stock car races are great recreational fun for car owners and spectators alike. Owners fix up old cars with hot engines and try to win money, prizes, and prestige in races. No one intends to crash these cars! But crashes do occur quite often.

Twenty cars are in this race. Which ones will crash? It will be those that have problems with incorrect answers. You'll need skills at dividing fractions to figure out which ones those are. Write "crash" beside numbers of cars that *will* crash; put a check mark (✓) beside those that *will not* crash.

_____ 1. $\frac{5}{9} \div \frac{8}{15} = 1\frac{1}{24}$

_____ 2. $\frac{4}{9} \div \frac{3}{10} = 1\frac{13}{27}$

_____ 3. $\frac{5}{8} \div \frac{1}{2} = \frac{5}{16}$

_____ 4. $\frac{1}{2} \div \frac{5}{8} = \frac{1}{2}$

_____ 5. $\frac{1}{8} \div 8 = \frac{1}{64}$

_____ 6. $\frac{4}{3} \div \frac{1}{3} = \frac{4}{3}$

_____ 7. $10 \div \frac{3}{8} = 35$

_____ 8. $\frac{7}{10} \div \frac{4}{6} = 1\frac{1}{20}$

_____ 9. $8 \div \frac{3}{10} = 26\frac{2}{3}$

_____ 10. $\frac{9}{20} \div 6 = \frac{3}{40}$

_____ 11. $\frac{2}{5} \div \frac{4}{5} = \frac{1}{2}$

_____ 12. $\frac{1}{3} \div \frac{1}{3} = \frac{3}{9}$

_____ 13. $\frac{1}{2} \div \frac{1}{4} = 2$

_____ 14. $\frac{9}{27} \div \frac{1}{3} = 1$

_____ 15. $\frac{2}{3} \div \frac{7}{9} = \frac{6}{7}$

_____ 16. $\frac{4}{7} \div 4 = \frac{16}{7}$

_____ 17. $\frac{5}{9} \div \frac{1}{9} = 5$

_____ 18. $\frac{7}{9} \div \frac{9}{7} = \frac{49}{81}$

_____ 19. $\frac{1}{10} \div \frac{1}{10} = \frac{1}{100}$

_____ 20. $\frac{3}{10} \div 18 = \frac{1}{6}$

_____ 21. $\frac{6}{5} \div 1 = \frac{5}{6}$

_____ 22. $\frac{7}{8} \div \frac{6}{9} = \frac{15}{16}$

_____ 23. $\frac{1}{2} \div \frac{2}{3} = \frac{1}{6}$

_____ 24. $\frac{11}{12} \div \frac{1}{2} = 1\frac{2}{3}$

_____ 25. $\frac{1}{3} \div \frac{2}{3} = \frac{1}{2}$

_____ 26. $\frac{12}{15} \div \frac{1}{2} = 1\frac{3}{5}$

_____ 27. $\frac{1}{3} \div \frac{13}{18} = \frac{6}{13}$

_____ 28. $\frac{9}{10} \div \frac{10}{9} = \frac{81}{100}$

_____ 29. $\frac{7}{8} \div \frac{1}{4} = \frac{7}{16}$

_____ 30. $\frac{5}{25} \div \frac{1}{5} = 1$

Name _____

READ IT RIGHT!

This old-fashioned game of memory will never be a choice for inclusion in the Olympics. But it's a great game to play in order to practice any kind of math fact. This version will help you practice reading decimals correctly.

Cut out the 32 cards on this and the next page (pages 134 & 135). Mix them up well and line them up facedown in an arrangement of 8 by 5 rows. Get a partner. Take turns turning over 2 cards. If your decimal number card matches your card with the decimal number written out, you have a pair. You get to try again to locate another pair. The player with the most pairs wins. If the two cards do not form a matching pair, the cards are turned back to the facedown position, and it's your opponent's turn. To keep going and win this game, you'll have to be able to read the decimals right!

thirty-three and five hundredths	four tenths	twelve hundredths	twenty and fifty-six thousandths
33.05	0.4	0.12	20.056
three and thirty-five hundredths	four and four tenths	forty-two hundredths	two and fourteen hundredths
3.35	4.4	0.42	2.14

Use with page 135.

Name

Use with page 134.

two hundred fourteen thousandths	four hundred eighty-seven ten thousandths	thirty-three and five hundred eighty-three thousandths	forty-four hundredths
0.214	0.0487	33.583	0.44
eight thousandths	three and three hundred five thousandths	thirty-three and five hundredths	eight hundredths
0.008	3.305	33.05	0.08
four hundred eighty-seven thousandths	four hundred forty-four thousandths	four and eighty-seven hundredths	eight tenths
0.487	0.444	4.87	0.8

Name

HIGH-SPEED RECORDS

Mile runners have recorded some incredibly fast speeds—and every year, they try to break the records with faster speeds. These are some of the times for the 1 mile race recorded between the years 1973 and 1981. Rank these times from the fastest to the slowest (fastest being 1, slowest being 9).

Date	Year	Time (minutes)	Place	Rank
31 Aug.	1979	3:49.5	Crystal Palace	_____
25 July	1973	4:00.0	Motspur Park	_____
26 Aug.	1979	3:49.57	Crystal Palace	_____
17 July	1974	3:59.4	Haringey	_____
1 July	1980	3:48.82	Oslo	_____
30 June	1975	3:57.001	Stockholm	_____
20 Sept.	1978	3:52.8	Oslo	_____
26 June	1977	3:54.69	Crystal Palace	_____
28 May	1977	3:56.201	Belfast	_____

In 1912, Hannes Kolehmainen set the first 5000 meter world record with a time of 14:36.6 minutes. On the graph below, plot the points for the following times and connect them for the men's 5000 meter race.

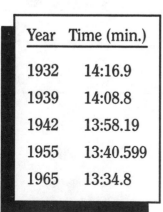

Year	Time (min.)
1932	14:16.9
1939	14:08.8
1942	13:58.19
1955	13:40.599
1965	13:34.8

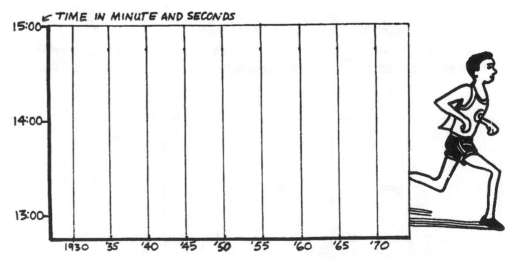

Name

AMAZING SPEED FACTS

You probably never timed a roller coaster, an elevator, or the hand on a wristwatch! But somebody has! Here are some surprising facts about the speed of things. The numbers are in miles per hour. Read the speeds of each of these unusual things and answer the questions about place value below each fact.

STATEMENT	SPEED (mph)

1. The tip of a ⅓ inch long hour hand on a wristwatch.
   a. What is the place-value position of the 2? _____
   b. What is the place-value position of the 7? _____
   c. What is the place-value position of the 5? _____
	0.00000275

2. The average ground speed of the three-toed sloth.
   a. What is the place-value position of the 8? _____
   b. What is the place-value position of the 9? _____
	0.098

3. A brisk walking pace for a human.
   a. What is the place-value position of the 5? _____
   b. What is the place-value position of the 7? _____
   c. What is the place-value position of the 3? _____
	3.75

4. The average speed of Roger Bannister during his 4-minute mile.
   a. What is the place-value position of the 1? _____
   b. What is the place-value position of the 5? _____
	15

5. The fastest passenger elevator. What is the place-value position of the 7? _____	**22.72**
6. The Beast roller coaster at King's Island. What is the place-value position of the 4? _____	**64.77**
7. The fastest bird in level flight, the white-throated spine-tailed swift. What is the place-value position of the 5? _____	**106.25**
8. Speed of ball in world's fastest recorded pitch by Nolan Ryan on August 20, 1974. What is the place-value position of the 9? _____	**100.9**
9. The speed reached by the space shuttle Columbia on its first flight approximately 9 minutes after takeoff. What is the place-value position of the 7? _____	**16,700**
10. The speed of light. What is the place-value position of the 7? _____	**670,251,600**

Name _____

WELL-ROUNDED ATHLETES

Many athletes are famous for one professional sport, such as baseball, football, or basketball, but they also participate in other sports. Read about these athletes and their other famous accomplishments.

_____ 1. Terry Bradshaw (professional football player) set a high-school javelin record of 74.64 meters in 1966. Round his javelin distance to the nearest tenth.

_____ 2. Herschel Walker (professional football player) was an outstanding sprinter. He sprinted 10.10 seconds for 100 m in 1982. Round his time to the nearest whole number.

_____

3. Gale Sayers (professional football player) was ranked third in the world junior long jump in 1961 with a jump of 7.58 m. Round his record to the nearest tenths place.

_____ 4. Jackie Robinson (professional baseball player) headed the world long jump ranking in 1938 with 7.78 m. Was his jump closer to 7 or 8 meters?

_____

5. Wilt Chamberlain (professional basketball player) was a successful high jumper. His best jump was 1.99 meters. Round his record to the nearest tenth.

Round the following decimals to the underlined place-value positions.

6. 7.3<u>5</u> _____   7. 5.9<u>8</u>6 _____   8. <u>8</u>.981 _____

9. 0.1<u>4</u> _____   10. 41.0<u>6</u>4 _____   11. 9.<u>6</u>5 _____

12. 400.0<u>5</u>8 _____   13. 0.1<u>7</u>1 _____   14. 2.6<u>5</u>43 _____

15. 1<u>7</u>.976 _____   16. 4.9<u>9</u>3 _____   17. 0.<u>0</u>181 _____

18. 45.<u>8</u>7 _____   19. 43<u>2</u>.987 _____   20. 87.1<u>2</u>45 _____

Name

TAKE TO THE SLOPES

Felipe, Raji, and Jim are taking to the ski slopes for the first time this year. Solve these problems to find out how much it costs to have fun in the snow. (Find the group's expenses.)

_____ 1. If ski boots cost $194.47, skis cost $327.28, and poles cost $65.79, how much is Felipe planning to spend if he purchases instead of rents his equipment?

_____ 2. Felipe's dad has given him $350 to spend on boots, skis, and poles. How much money will Felipe need to withdraw from his savings account to buy the equipment that he wants?

_____ 3. Raji is planning the transportation and lodging for the trip. If the round-trip airfare will be $341.93 each and three nights' stay at the motel will cost each boy $121.05, how much should each boy budget for his flight and motel room?

_____ 4. Jim is investigating renting his ski equipment. The first 2 days he is planning to ski, so he will need to rent boots for $10.87 and skis and poles for $15.46 a day. How much will his first 2 days' rental fees total?

_____ 5. The third day Jim plans to snow board. The boards rent for $8.25 an hour, and the boots rent for another $2.00 an hour. Lessons are $33.80 an hour. And he needs a lesson! He decides to snow board for 5 hours and, in that time, get a 1-hour lesson. He also must pay $35 for a lift ticket. How much will his third day on the slopes cost?

The boys plan to eat snacks at the lodge during the day to keep up their strength for skiing the slopes. Here are the prices on some typical snack foods at the lodge (tax is included).

MOUNTAIN VIEW LODGE MENU

PIZZA SLICE	$.2.73
SOFT DRINK	0.85
FRENCH FRIES	1.17
GRILLED CHEESE	1.72
BROWNIE	1.42
BAGEL	1.24
HOT CHOCOLATE	0.95

NACHOS	$1.06
PICKLE	0.88
COOKIES	0.95
HOT DOG	1.98
CHIPS	0.66
NOODLE SOUP	1.59
OATMEAL	1.31
SPRING WATER	1.08

_____ 6. Raji orders a pizza slice, nachos, cookies, and a soft drink. How much will his total be?
_____ If he pays with a $10 bill, how much will his change be?

_____ 7. Felipe orders hot chocolate, oatmeal, and a bagel. What does his
_____ order total and what will his change be if he pays with a $5 bill?

_____ 8. Jim decides to snack on a grilled cheese sandwich with noodle soup, spring water, pickle, chips, and a brownie. What is his total
_____ food bill and what is his change from a $20 bill?

Name _____

SPRINGBOARD TO DECIMALS

Melissa and Tom are on the diving team at Rocky Top School. They specialize in the 3-meter spring-board competitions. Today they will be competing against Tina and John of Challenger School. Their dives will be rated on a scale of 0 to 10 by a panel of five judges. The highest and lowest scores will be deleted. The sum of the three remaining scores will be multiplied by the degree of difficulty for the dive as assigned by FINA (Federation Internationale de Natation Amateur) diving rules and upheld by United States Diving, Inc. Find the divers' final scores using the information below.

Melissa — ROCKY TOP SCHOOL

Name of dive	Scores Used 1	2	3	Sum of 3 Scores	x	Degree of Difficulty =	Final Score
Back somersault (pike position)	8.1	7.9	8.3	_____		1.8	_____
Forward 1½ somersault (tuck)	8.7	8.8	8.5	_____		1.5	_____
Inward flying somersault (pike)	7.6	7.8	7.5	_____		1.9	_____

TOTAL SCORE = _____

TOM — ROCKY TOP SCHOOL

Name of dive	Scores Used 1	2	3	Sum of 3 Scores	x	Degree of Difficulty =	Final Score
Inward dive (straight position)	7.7	7.8	8.1	_____		1.7	_____
Forward double somersault (pike)	8.4	8.6	8.9	_____		2.1	_____
Reverse 1½ somersault (tuck)	7.4	7.9	7.6	_____		2.0	_____

TOTAL SCORE = _____

John — CHALLENGER SCHOOL

Dive name	Sum of 3 Scores	Degree of Difficulty	Final Score
Back double somersault (tuck)	22.6	2.0	____
Inward Flying somersault (pike)	24.7	1.9	____
Forward triple somersault (tuck)	21.9	2.5	____

TOTAL SCORE = _____

Tina — CHALLENGER SCHOOL

Dive name	Sum of 3 Scores	Degree of Difficulty	Final Score
Reverse flying somersault (tuck)	23.4	1.8	____
Forward double somersault (pike)	21.1	2.1	____
Inward double somersault (pike)	22.8	2.6	____

TOTAL SCORE = _____

Who had the highest final score? _____

Name

THREE TIMES THE WORK

Mitch and Debbie are preparing to compete in a triathlon. Participants are required to swim, bike, and run. It is considered a grueling test of fitness. Mitch has been jogging and Debbie has been swimming to stay in shape, but they have decided to train in all three events to prepare for the Cherokee Triathlon. Answer these questions about their training. (Remember: rate x time = distance; distance ÷ time = rate; and distance ÷ rate = time.) Round to the nearest hundred.

1. For their training ride, Debbie and Mitch decided to cycle the 12.8 mile course at the City Park. Calculate their rates in miles per hour. (First, change minutes to hours by dividing the minute time by 60. Then divide the distance by the time to find the rate.)

	Time	Time in Hours	Distance	=	Rate (mph)
a. Debbie	26.4 min.	_____	12.8 mi.		_____
b. Mitch	25.7 min.	_____	12.8 mi.		_____

2. Next they went to the pool to check on their swimming rates. They decided to swim 2000 m. (Change meters to miles by dividing by 1609.76.)

	Time	Time in Hours	Distance	=	Rate (mph)
a. Debbie	25.1 min.	_____	_____ mi.		_____
b. Mitch	26.9 min.	_____	_____ mi.		_____

3. The mini-marathon course in their city measures 13.4 miles. Calculate the rates for their running of this course based on their times.

	Time	Time in Hours	Distance	=	Rate (mph)
a. Debbie	66.4 min.	_____	13.4 mi.		_____
b. Mitch	59.8 min.	_____	13.4 mi.		_____

4. On the day of the big race Debbie and Mitch had calculated the rates that they needed to maintain in order to have what they felt was a respectable showing for their first triathlon. Based on their rates, calculate what their time goals will be in each of the three events. (Recall: Distance / Rate = Time)

Debbie's		Distance (mi.)	/	Rate (mph)	=	Time (hr.)
a.	Swim	2.4		14.7		_____
	Cycle	112.0		26.4		_____
	Run	26.2		9.9		_____

Mitch's		Distance (mi.)	/	Rate (mph)	=	Time (hr.)
b.	Swim	2.4		15.3		_____
	Cycle	112.0		24.8		_____
	Run	26.2		11.6		_____

Name

FACE OFF!

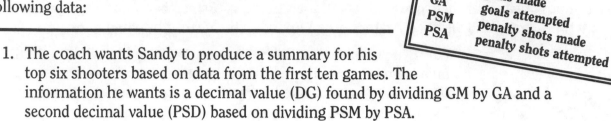

Initials	Meaning
G	games played
R	rebounds
P	total points
A	assists
GM	goals made
GA	goals attempted
PSM	penalty shots made
PSA	penalty shots attempted

Sandy Slapshot has been asked by the coach to update the statistics on the girls' and boys' Slippery Springs ice hockey teams. The coach has asked his assistants to track the following data:

1. The coach wants Sandy to produce a summary for his top six shooters based on data from the first ten games. The information he wants is a decimal value (DG) found by dividing GM by GA and a second decimal value (PSD) based on dividing PSM by PSA.

   Example: Sal Valenko had 14 goals made (GM) in 42 goals attempted (GA). So Sal's DG would be $^{14}/_{42} = 0.333$; Sal's PSM = 3 and his PSA = 12, so his PSD = $^{3}/_{12} = 0.250$.

Name	GM/GA	DG	PSM/PSA	PSD
Sal Valenko	$^{14}/_{42}$	0.333	$^{3}/_{12}$	0.250
Tseno Inqvest	$^{15}/_{40}$	_____	$^{6}/_{14}$	_____
Jeb Diskov	$^{18}/_{45}$	_____	$^{9}/_{32}$	_____
Tina Beaufort	$^{11}/_{55}$	_____	$^{7}/_{30}$	_____
Niki Tyler	$^{12}/_{72}$	_____	$^{5}/_{26}$	_____
Michelle Guilford	$^{13}/_{52}$	_____	$^{3}/_{27}$	_____

2. The coach would also like to know the following statistics on a per game basis: rebounds per game (R/G), total points per game (P/G), and assists per game (A/G). (Note: Total points are found by adding together goals made, penalty shots made, and assists.)

Name	G	R	P	A	R/G	P/G	A/G
S. Valenko	10	17	33	11	___	___	___
T. Inqvest	9	14	30	9	___	___	___
J. Diskov	10	11	39	12	___	___	___
T. Beaufort	9	9	25	8	___	___	___
N. Tyler	10	12	30	13	___	___	___
M. Guilford	9	13	26	10	___	___	___

3. Billy "the Puckman" Johnson is the team's starting goalie. In the 10 games he has played, he was able to stop 149 shots on goal, while allowing 38 goals to be scored. Calculate the following two statistics on Billy the Puckman.

   Saves per game = $^{149}/_{10}$ = _____ (decimal value)

   Goals allowed per game = $^{38}/_{10}$ = _____ (decimal value)

Name

A BOXING LEGEND SPEAKS

Muhammad Ali (formerly known as Cassius Clay) is considered by many to be the greatest heavyweight boxing champion of all time. He first came to prominence at the 1960 Rome Summer Olympics when he won a gold medal in boxing. You may have seen him lighting the flame at the opening ceremonies for the 1996 Summer Olympics in Atlanta.

The following is a famous quote by Muhammad Ali that refers to his boxing style. Change the decimals to fractions to reveal the letters in the quote.

___	___	___	___	___	___	___	___	___	___
0.105	0.55	0.75	0.08	0.555	0.55	0.38	0.15	0.625	0.08

___	___	___	___	___	___	___	___	___
0.972	0.425	0.555	0.555	0.625	0.58	0.105	0.55	0.3

___	___	___	___	___	___	___	___	___
0.548	0.555	0.38	0.4	0.855	0.55	0.38	0.15	0.625

___	___	___	___
0.08	0.972	0.625	0.625

I'm the greatest !!

ALPHABET OF FRACTIONS FOR DECIPHERING

A	$2/25$	H	$31/40$	O	$3/4$	V	$4/5$
B	$243/250$	I	$19/50$	P	$147/200$	W	$49/50$
C	$9/40$	J	$57/200$	Q	$13/40$	X	$149/200$
D	$1/5$	K	$3/20$	R	$29/50$	Y	$3/10$
E	$5/8$	L	$11/20$	S	$137/250$	Z	$3/50$
F	$21/200$	M	$203/250$	T	$111/200$		
G	$171/200$	N	$2/5$	U	$17/40$		

Name _____

BIRDS THAT COUNT

Marcia and Bradley helped with the Audubon Society's bird-counting project. They volunteered to be on a team that made the semiannual count of birds at the Municipal Park. After returning to the park shelter, a tabulation was made of all the birds that were sighted and the following statistics were compiled.

Example: Of the 1240 total birds sighted, 36 were cardinals. $^{36}/_{1240}$ = .029 = 2.9%

1. The decimal values in the chart below were found by dividing the count by 1240 which represents the total birds sighted this year. Find the equivalent percent of each.

	Name of bird	Count	Decimal Value	Percent
a.	Starling	556	0.448	_____
b.	Grackle	97	0.078	_____
c.	Cardinal	36	0.029	2.9%
d.	Bluebird	11	0.009	_____
e.	Wren	74	0.060	_____
f.	Chickadee	68	0.055	_____
g.	Sparrow	53	0.043	_____
h.	Finch	81	0.065	_____
i.	Woodpecker	51	0.041	_____
j.	Catbird	20	0.016	_____
k.	Mockingbird	35	0.028	_____
l.	Other birds	158	0.128	_____

2. The chart below shows the counts from this year and last year, and the percent change that occurred for each category. Use the percent change to find an equivalent decimal value.

	Name of bird	Count this year	Count last year	Percent change	Decimal value
a.	Starling	556	524	6.1%	0.061
b.	Grackle	97	84	15.5%	_____
c.	Cardinal	36	42	14.3%	_____
d.	Bluebird	11	50	78.0%	_____
e.	Wren	74	82	9.8%	_____
f.	Chickadee	68	75	9.3%	_____
g.	Sparrow	53	66	19.7%	_____
h.	Finch	81	78	3.8%	_____
i.	Woodpecker	51	71	28.2%	_____
j.	Catbird	20	39	48.7%	_____
k.	Mockingbird	35	47	25.5%	_____
l.	Other birds	158	103	53.4%	_____

Name

MUSICAL STATISTICS

Mario is curious about the types of music played by the top radio stations in his area. He has gotten together with some friends and started keeping track of music played. He wants his final statistics to be in the form of percentages, but he has been keeping track of his counts in the form of fractions. Use the charts to change his statistics into percentages.

1. In his first count, he listened to a popular radio station for one hour and counted twenty-five songs categorizing them by decade or as a current Top 40 Hit.

Category of song	Fraction (over 25)	Fraction (over 100)	Decimal	Percent
a. Decade - 50s, 60s	$^2/_{25}$	$^8/_{100}$	0.08	8%
b. Decade - 70s	$^4/_{25}$	_____	_____	_____
c. Decade - 80s	$^7/_{25}$	_____	_____	_____
d. Decade - 90s	$^3/_{25}$	_____	_____	_____
e. Current Top 40	$^9/_{25}$	_____	_____	_____

2. In a thirty-minute period he surfed as many stations as he could and counted fifty songs, arranging the count by category.

Music by category	Fraction (over 50)	Fraction (over 100)	Decimal	Percent
a. Pop/Rock	$^{14}/_{50}$	$^{28}/_{100}$	0.28	28%
b. Country	$^{11}/_{50}$	_____	_____	_____
c. R&B/Rap	$^9/_{50}$	_____	_____	_____
d. Christian	$^7/_{50}$	_____	_____	_____
e. Oldies	$^6/_{50}$	_____	_____	_____
f. Classical	$^3/_{50}$	_____	_____	_____

FREAKY FERGUS — DISC JOCKEY
K-NOIZ - 940 FM

Name _____

OFF THE TEE

Martina is going to play a round of golf at the Falling Waters Golf Course. She has heard that this new eighteen-hole course is one of the most unusual and challenging courses around. She and her friends will need a lot of golfing skill to do well on this course. You'll need to be skilled at changing fractions into percents to solve these golf problems.

_____ 1. The fees for the course and golf cart come to $159. Martina's share comes to $61. Change $^{61}/_{159}$ to a percent to find what percent of the fees she paid.

2. On the first hole Martina's score was an eight, which included two penalty strokes and three putts.

_____ a. Change $^2/_8$ to a percent to see what percent of her strokes were due to penalties.

_____ b. Change $^3/_8$ to a percent to see what percent of her strokes were putts.

3. Of the eighteen holes, three are par threes, five are par fives, and ten are par fours. What percent of the holes are:

_____ a. par threes?

_____ b. par fours?

_____ c. par fives?

_____ 4. Martina and her friends buy 40 golf tees for driving the golf balls. If Martina takes 12 of the tees, what percent of them should she pay for?

_____ 5. After playing nine holes, the golfing partners go into the clubhouse to eat a quick lunch. Martina's food and drink come to $7, and the total bill is $32. What percent of the lunch bill is Martina's?

6. To determine how long it takes to play each hole, Martina notices that par threes take 10 minutes to play, par fours take 12 minutes to play, and par fives take 15 minutes to play. If the total playing time of the eighteen holes is 225 minutes, then find what percent of golfing time is spent playing each.

_____ a. par three?

_____ b. par four?

_____ c. par five?

7. At the end of the round, Martina reflects on her score of 97 strokes. She adds up her strokes by category to see that she used 36 putts, 15 shots with woods, 20 iron shots, and 26 shots using wedges. Find the percent of her total score that can be attributed to:

_____ a. putts

_____ b. shots using woods

_____ c. iron shots

_____ d. shots using wedges

Name

CAN YOU CANOE?

Three friends have gone on a four-day canoe trip that will take them 42 miles down the Buffalo River. They have practiced their canoeing skills and boating safety on the lake and are ready to tackle a new challenge.

1. A normal 12-hour camping day consists of: 1 hour for breakfast and cleanup, 1 hour to load the canoes and take down the tents, 3 hours of morning paddling, 1 hour for swim break and lunch, 3 hours of afternoon paddling, 1 hour to unload canoes and set up camp, 2 hours for firebuilding, dinner, and cleanup.

   _____ a. What percent of the day is used for canoeing?

   _____ b. What percent of the day is used to swim and to prepare, eat, and clean up from meals?

   _____ c. What percent of the day is used to load and unload canoes and set up and take down the camp?

2. Their plan calls for the following miles to be canoed each day: day one 6 miles, day two 12 miles, day three 16 miles, and day four 8 miles.

   _____ a. What percent of the trip will be covered on the last day?

   _____ b. The first and second day taken together represent what portion of the trip?

   _____ c. Day three covers the most miles. What percent of the trip does this represent?

3. Sheila, Jamie, and Tony will be sharing a canoe. Each one will take turns bowing (paddling in the front of the boat), sterning (paddling and steering from the rear, and duffing (sitting in the middle resting). The chart below represents how many miles each paddler spent in each position in the canoe.

	Bowing	Sterning	Duffing
Sheila	10	18	14
Jamie	15	15	12
Tony	17	9	16

   _____ a. Who spent the largest portion of the trip in the bow?

   _____ What percent of his or her trip did this paddler spend in the bow?

   _____ b. Who spent the least amount of time duffing?

   _____ What percent of his or her trip was spent resting in the middle of the boat?

   _____ c. Who spent the most time sterning?

   _____ What percent of the trip did he or she spend steering the canoe?

   _____ d. Who paddled the most (spent the most miles bowing and sterning)?

   _____ What percent of the trip did he or she spend paddling?

Name _____

LOST: SOFTBALL STATS

Marlene is the manager of the Marvelous Mavens softball team. She has kept the statistics for the team throughout the season. Each page in her team notebook has been dedicated to a different type of softball statistic, but the page of TOTALS has slipped out. Help her to recreate this page in time for the team's end-of-the-season banquet and awards ceremony.

_____ 1. Jose's leading batting percentage is 43.23%. If he had 162 at-bats, how many times did he get a hit?

_____ 2. The Mavens' winning percentage was 55%. If they played 41 games in all, how many did they win?

_____ 3. Ralph, the Mavens' best pitcher, won 75% of the games that he pitched. If he pitched 11 games, how many did he win?

_____ 4. Tim, the shortest player on the team, walked the most number of times. If Tim came to bat 155 times and walked 11% of the these times, find the number of walks issued to Tim by opposing pitchers.

_____ 5. Solon is the team's top base stealer. 23% of the time he gets on base he gets a stolen base. If Solon got on base 76 times, how many times did he steal a base?

_____ 6. Ken is the most accurate pitcher on the team. 68% of his pitches are strikes. If the coach usually lets him pitch about 90 pitches per game, how many strikes does he throw per game?

_____ 7. Jonathan has the best slugging percentage of all the Mavens with 59%. (Slugging percentage is found by comparing total bases to total at bats.) If Jonathan had 124 at bats, how many total bases did he get this season?

_____ 8. Mitchell is the Mavens' home run king. He was able to hit a homer 8% of the time he was at bat. If Mitchell had 152 at bats, how many home runs did he hit?

_____ 9. Scott is the pitching staff's saves leader saving 72% of the games in which he pitched. If he pitched in 28 games, how many saves did he earn?

_____ 10. Josh is the Mavens' catcher. He threw to second base 137 times trying to catch base stealers. He was successful in cutting down 41% of the runners he attempted to throw out. How many opposing runners did he throw out at second?

Name _____

ON TO WIMBLEDON?

Jana and Cindy have been playing tennis in the hopes of making the high school team in the spring. Their most recent head to head match was won by Jana in three sets with scores of 6–1, 2–6, and 6–3. Here are the statistics of their most recent match. They each might learn something to improve their games if they examine these numbers carefully. You will need to write a ratio to analyze each statistic.

1. Since Jana's games won are listed first in the set scores, she won 14 of the 24 games that were played.

    _____ a. Write Jana's wins to total games played as a reduced ratio.

    _____ b. Find a reduced ratio for Jana's games won to Cindy's games won.

_____ 2. In the first set Jana served 36 points and got 16 first serves in bounds. State her first serves to points served as a reduced ratio.

_____ 3. Jana won 12 of the points in which she got her first serve in bounds. Write a reduced ratio to show these points compared to her first 16 good serves.

_____ 4. Jana served two aces (service winners) out of the 16 first serves that were good. Find a reduced ratio for Jana's service aces to good first serves.

The chart below gives an analysis of Cindy's shots for the match.

TYPE OF SHOT	WINNERS	GOOD SHOTS	UN-FORCED ERRORS	TOTAL
SERVES	12	32	44	88
GROUND STROKES	75	49	41	165
LOBS	8	10	4	22
VOLLEYS	9	3	12	24
OVERHEADS	2	4	10	16
TOTAL	106	98	111	315

5. Find reduced ratios for each of the following comparisons.

    _____ a. unforced errors that were volleys to total volleys

    _____ b. lobs that were good shots to lobs that were unforced errors

    _____ c. total overheads to overhead shots that were unforced errors

    _____ d. good shots that were ground strokes to total good shots

Name

AND THEY'RE OFF!

Sam is a runner. He can run the 1000 meters in 2.50 minutes. That is a ratio of 1000:2.50 or 4000:10 or 400:1 and can be stated as a rate of 400 meters per minute. Sam is interested in investigating the speeds achieved in other races.

1. The Kentucky Derby is a famous horse race in Louisville, Kentucky, that covers a distance of 1 mile 550 yards or 2110 meters. One horse ran the race in 2 minutes.

_____ a. Find the rate achieved by the race horse in meters per minute.

_____ b. Since 2 minutes is 120 seconds, find the rate of the race horse in meters per second.

_____ 2. Amy Van Dyken swam to a new American record in the 50 m freestyle at the 1996 Atlanta Olympic Games with a time of just under 25 seconds. Find her rate in meters per second.

_____ 3. Amateur cyclists racing from a standing start can cover 1000 meters in 62.5 seconds. Find the rate of these cyclists in meters per second.

4. Twelve dogs can pull a sled through the snow a distance of 3900 meters every 10 minutes.

_____ a. Give the sled dog's speed in meters per minute.

_____ b. Since 10 minutes is 600 seconds, find the dog's speed in meters per second.

5. Racing greyhounds can achieve speeds over 37 miles per hour. 37 miles is about 60,000 meters, and one hour is 3600 seconds.

_____ a. Calculate the greyhound's speed in meters per second.

_____ b. According to their speeds in m/s, which is faster: the horse in #1, the cyclist in #3, or the greyhound?

_____ 6. At the Barcelona Olympics the U.S. Men's 4 x 100 relay team of Marsh, Burrell, Mitchell, and Lewis covered the 400 meters in 37.4 seconds. Give this speed in m/s.

_____ 7. Dale Jarrett won the pole position for the Daytona 500 in 1995 with a speed of 193.5 mph. This is equivalent to 309,600 meters per 3600 seconds. What is this speed in meters per second?

_____ 8. The fastest Indianapolis 500 was won in 1990 by Arie Luyendyk when his car covered the 500 miles in 2.69 hours. Give this winning speed in miles per hour.

_____ 9. Kenny Bernstein set the Top Fuel Drag Racing speed in 1994 when his car covered the 1320 foot strip in 2.86 seconds. Find this speed in feet per second.

Name _____

ARE WE LOST—OR WHAT?

Irma and Ima are going to participate in their second State Orienteering Meet.
It is a 2-person novice team event to be held in the state park. Both girls are
confident of their compass skills and are anxious to try out their map reading
under competitive conditions. They will pick up their control card and map to
begin at 9:05 A.M. The map is drawn using a scale of 1 cm = 50 m. Let's hope
they don't get lost. Let's hope you remember how to solve proportions. You'll
need to write and solve proportions for several of these problems.

SHOULD WE TAKE THE DETOUR ?

_____ 1. Irma begins by measuring the distance between the start triangle
and the circle on the first control point while Ima sets the
compass to a bearing of 325°. Since the distance on the map is
7 cm, the competitors set up a proportion to calculate the actual
distance to the first control point. Write the proportion and solve
it to find the distance to the first control point. (You'll need to use
cross multiplication.)

2. The most direct route from the first to second control points is a train trestle, but it has
been marked out of bounds. Ima and Irma have measured and calculated the distances of
two alternate paths, but must determine which one is the quicker route.

_____ a. One path follows a winding fire road for 750 m. If 50 m of fire road takes 24 seconds to
travel, how long will this route take?

_____ b. The second route is 320 m and requires crossing a hilly forest and a stream. If the girls can
cover about 40 m in 48 seconds, how long will this take?

_____ c. Which was faster?

3. Irma notices that the process of taking six compass bearings has taken a total of 96 seconds.

_____ a. Solve the proportion $\frac{2}{?} = \frac{6}{96}$ to find out how long 2 compass bearings take.

_____ b. How long will it take to complete 5 compass bearings?

4. The competitors have to decide whether to go right or left around an irregularly shaped
field that says, "NO TRESPASSING." While the distance to the left will take 240 seconds to
travel, it will require stopping to take 5 compass bearings. The distance around the right
side will take 290 seconds but will require 2 compass bearings.

_____ a. How long will it take to go right?

_____ b. How long will it take to go left?

_____ c. Which is quicker according to your calculations, and by how many seconds?

_____ 5. The home leg shows a bearing of 120° to get to the two concentric circles marking the
finish area. If the final leg is 375 m, how long is the line on the map marking the home leg?

_____ 6. The total time for Irma and Ima was 42 minutes. Last year they finished in 16th place with
a time of 48 minutes. The ratio of their place to their total time is the same as last year's
ratio of place to total time. What will their finishing place be this year?

Name _____

UNDERGROUND EXPLORATIONS

Maria and six certified spelunking friends are going to explore Salamander Cave to collect samples for environmental testing. It has been reported that sewage thrown into sinkholes has polluted the underground stream which feeds the cave. The strenuous trip will take seven hours and will involve rope work for climbing and rappelling. Use proportions to solve these problems. Write the answers.

1. To get the exploration party from the cars to the mouth (entrance) of the cave involves following a map which has a scale of 3 cm to 1000 ft.

   a. The map shows that the distance from the road to the spring in the forest is a distance of 11 cm. Write a proportion to calculate the distance to the spring in feet. _____

   b. The distance from the spring to the cave is about 2500 ft. Write a proportion that will calculate how far apart the spring and the cave should be on the map. _____

2. Two lengths of rope will be necessary equipment for this excursion. One rope will be 350 ft. long to rappel into the cave and another rope will be used for scaling rock face. The specialty climbing rope being used weighs 2 lbs. for every 15 ft.

   a. Write a proportion to calculate the weight of the 350-ft. rope. _____

   b. If the second rope weighs 48 lbs., write a proportion to calculate its length. _____

3. To get into the cave, the spelunkers will rappel down a 315-ft. pit. This requires the use of carabiners on a rack so that the descent can be controlled. For each 75 lbs. of weight one carabiner is placed on the rack. Write a proportion to calculate how many carabiners are necessary to equip a rappeller that weighs 200 lbs. with his equipment. _____

4. The certified climber will scale an 85-ft. rock face. For safety he will install spring-loaded camming devices into creases in the rock every 15 ft., which will break his fall in the event that he should slip. Write a proportion that will help to calculate the number of spring-loaded camming devices necessary to make a safe climb.

5. The cave map is drawn to the scale of 2 cm = 75 ft.

   a. If the map shows the waterfall to be 9 cm from the mouth of the cave, write a proportion that will calculate how far into the cave the party must hike before reaching the waterfall.

   b. If the back of the cave is known to be 1200 ft. from the mouth of the cave, write a proportion to figure how many centimeters in length that the map of the cave should be.

Name

6. Every spelunker is responsible for bringing three sources of light that will each burn twice as long as the expected duration of the trip underground. Maria has chosen to bring a battery-operated headlamp, chemical light sticks, and candles. Since the trip is to last 7 hours, each of her light sources should burn 14 hours. Write a proportion to calculate the number of light sticks each spelunker would need
to bring if each light stick lasts 4 hours. _____

7. When the explorers reach the back of the cave, they will take water samples from Crystal Lake to test for pollution. The last time the lake water was tested it was determined that the lake contained no coliform bacteria.

   a. If a 1000 ml sample contains 0.1 ml of coliform pollution,
   write a proportion to calculate the gallons of coliform
   pollution in a 500,000-gallon lake. _____

   b. If 3 parts per million is the standard for water that can be made safe
   by boiling, write a proportion for calculating how many milliliters
   of coliform pollution must be found in a 1000 ml sample in order
   to declare Crystal Lake too polluted for drinking. _____

8. To climb out of the pit at the mouth of the cave, Maria has chosen to use prussic knots. If each turn in the knot is capable of handling 50 lbs. of weight, write a proportion to determine how many turns Maria should tie into each of her prussic knots if she estimates that her total weight will be 160 lbs. with clothing, equipment,
and mud as she prepares to make her ascent out of the cave. _____

9. The girls spent 5 minutes climbing for every 2 minutes they were involved in other exploring tasks. If they were in the cave for 420 minutes, how much of that time
did they spend climbing? (Set up a proportion to help solve this.) _____

10. Ima can carry 8 pounds of equipment for each 30 lbs. of her body weight. If she is carrying 30.4 lbs., how much does she weigh?
(Set up a proportion to help solve this.) _____

Name _____

HIGHS & LOWS

Skydivers and scuba divers share diving thrills—but at opposite extremes of location. Use their places, high in the sky or deep down under the ocean, for fun in this exercise. Examine each problem below. (The answers are given!) If the answer is correct, write the number of the problem in the box high in the sky. If the answer is wrong, write the number way down below near the scuba diver.

1. $13/52 = 1/3$

2. $6\frac{2}{3} + 9\frac{4}{7} = 16\frac{1}{4}$

3. $3.66 = .0366\%$

4. $8/11 = 0.727$

5. In $12/18 = x/126$, $x = 84$

6. 15% of $8400 = 1200$

7. $15/40 = 37.5\%$

8. $7/9 \times 4/5 = 28/45$

9. $7/2 = 4/2 = 51/2$

10. $0.89 = 8.9\%$

11. $9/7 \approx 12/10$

12. $0.428 = 3/7$

13. $60.32 + 9.9 = 70.31$

14. 55% of $212 = 116.6$

15. $147/49 = 3$

16. $4\frac{1}{2} \times 3\frac{1}{3} = 15$

17. 80% of $95 = 76$

18. $2.33 \times 6.11 = 14.44$

19. $9/10 \div 3/5 = 1\frac{1}{5}$

20. $1.06 \div 1.06 = 2.12$

21. $\frac{1}{2} \div \frac{1}{8} = \frac{1}{16}$

22. $7/10 \div 2/4 = 1\frac{1}{5}$

23. $8\frac{1}{3} - 7\frac{5}{6} = \frac{1}{2}$

24. $8/9 = 93\%$

Name

A MATTER OF SECONDS

In sporting events such as running, seconds—even fractions of seconds—make all the difference. Races are won or lost by tenths, hundredths, or thousandths of seconds. So decimals really matter. Here are some facts about winning times in the 1996 Summer Olympic Games. Use these facts to answer the questions below.

Donovan Bailey of Canada won the men's 100-meter race in 9.84 seconds.
Gail Devers of the U.S. won the women's 100-meter race in 10.94 seconds.
Michael Johnson of the U.S. won the men's 200-meter race in 19.32 seconds.
Marie-Jose Perec of France won the women's 200-meter race in 22.12 seconds.
Michael Johnson of the U.S. won the men's 400-meter race in 43.49 seconds.
Marie-Jose Perec of France won the women's 400-meter race in 48.25 seconds.
The Canadian team won the men's 400-meter relay race in 37.69 seconds.
The U.S. team won the women's 400-meter relay race in 41.95 seconds.
Allen Johnson of the U.S. won the men's 110-meter hurdle race in 12.95 seconds.
Ludmila Enquist of Sweden won the women's 100-meter hurdle race in 12.58 seconds.
Derrick Adkins of the U.S. won the men's 400-meter hurdle race in 47.95 seconds.
Deon Hemmings of Jamaica won the women's 400-meter hurdle race in 52.82 seconds.

_____ 1. What is the difference between the winning time of the men's and women's 400-m hurdles?

_____ 2. How much longer did Michael Johnson run for the 400 m than the 200 m?

_____ 3. How much longer did it take Ludmila to run the 100-m hurdles than it took Gail Devers to run the 100-m race?

_____ 4. How long did all the hurdlers run, total?

_____ 5. How much faster was the Canadian men's relay team than the U.S. women's relay team?

_____ 6. How much shorter was Donovan Bailey's run than Derrick Adkins' hurdle race?

_____ 7. How much longer did the slowest hurdle race take than the fastest?

_____ 8. How much faster did Marie-Jose run the 200 m than the 400 m?

_____ 9. Find the difference between the fastest of all the 400-m races and the slowest.

_____ 10. How long did all the women run, total?

Name _____

MORE TOP 10 QUESTIONS

_____ 1. Of the Top 10 Olympic Gold Medal winners of all time, 4 are U.S. athletes: Ray Ewry with 10 medals, Mark Spitz with 9, Carl Lewis with 8, and Matt Biondi with 8. Of these medals, what percentage was won by Carl Lewis?

_____ 2. Top 10 run-scoring baseball players Babe Ruth and Hank Aaron both scored 2174 runs in regular games in their careers. Ty Cobb, #1, scored 2245. Write a decimal showing the comparison of Cobb's total to Hank's and Babe's.

_____ 3. The Top 10 largest major ballparks have a total capacity of 586,252 seats. The Seattle Mariner's Kingdome holds 59,166. What percentage is this of the total capacity?

_____ 4. Of the Top 10 wage earners in the National Basketball Association in 1995–1996, Patrick Ewing is # 1 with $18,700,000. Grant Hill, #10, earned $4,000,000. Write a reduced ratio showing the comparison of Hill's income to Ewing's.

_____ 5. Secretariat is at the top of the Top 10 list of Kentucky Derby winners with a winning time, in 1973, of 1 minute 59.4 seconds. Number 10, Bold Forbes, won in 1976 in 2 minutes, 1.6 seconds. What is the difference between their times?

_____ 6. Juan Fangio is the oldest of the Top 10 oldest World Champion automobile racers. His age at the time of his win is 1.32 times older than Albert Ascari, #10. Ascari was 35. How old was Fangio when he won his title?

_____ 7. 277,004 points were scored in the regular season by 1996 by basketball's Top 10 NBA career-scorers. Kareem Abdul-Jabbar, #1 on the list, scored 38,387 of those points. What percentage of the total points are his?

_____ 8. Willie Shoemaker had the most wins of any U.S. jockey. Sandy Hawley, who is #10 on the Top 10 list, had approximately 6200 wins, which was 70% of the number of Willie's wins. Approximately how many wins did Willie have?

_____ 9. Nancy Green of Canada has won 0.07% of the women's alpine ski World Cup titles of the total held by the Top 10 women. The total is 29. How many has Nancy won?

_____ 10. Walking is first on the list of the Top 10 sports activities people choose in the U.S. 71 million people participate in this activity. Pool (billiards) is #8 on the list, with 48% as many participants as those walking. How many people said they were pool players?

Name

FRACTIONS & DECIMALS
ASSESSMENT AND ANSWER KEYS

FRACTIONS & DECIMALS
SKILLS TEST

Each answer is worth 1 point. Total possible score: 100 pts.

For 1-6, match the correct decimal letter (below right) with the written decimals (below left).

_____ 1. forty-two thousandths   A. 4.42

_____ 2. forty-two hundredths   B. 4.402

_____ 3. forty-two ten thousandths   C. 0.042

_____ 4. four and forty-two hundredths   D. 0.42

_____ 5. four and four hundred two thousandths   E. 0.0042

_____ 6. four and four hundredths   F. 4.04

7. Write the factors of 24. _____

8. Write the factors of 13. _____

9. Write the prime factors of 12. _____

10. Write the least common multiple of 4 and 5. _____

11. Write the least common denominator of $\frac{1}{7}$ and $\frac{4}{3}$. _____

12. Write the greatest common factor of 15 and 30. _____

13. Write all the common factors of 15 and 45. _____

14. Write all the common factors of 6, 18, and 24. _____

For 15-20, tell what place is in bold type by writing the correct letter.
(a) ones (b) tenths (c) hundredths (d) thousandths (e) ten thousandths

_____ 15. 6.137**2**   _____ 18. **3**1.004

_____ 16. 4.**0**11   _____ 19. 9.0**9**

_____ 17. 0.2**6**6   _____ 20. 16.20**7**

*For 21-26, write **Y** if a fraction is in lowest terms, or **N** if it is not.*

_____ 21. $\frac{7}{20}$ _____ 24. $\frac{8}{15}$

_____ 22. $\frac{11}{13}$ _____ 25. $\frac{3}{39}$

_____ 23. $\frac{9}{24}$ _____ 26. $\frac{7}{21}$

Name _____

For 27-32, place the fractions in order from smallest to largest.

½ ⅔ ⅓ ¾ ⅔ ¼

27. _____   30. _____

28. _____   31. _____

29. _____   32. _____

For 33-38, reduce each fraction to its lowest terms.

33. $^{12}/_{15}$ _____   36. $^{21}/_{49}$ _____

34. $^{16}/_{20}$ _____   37. $^{9}/_{45}$ _____

35. $^{9}/_{12}$ _____   38. $^{28}/_{42}$ _____

For 39-44, write T or F to tell whether each pair of fractions is equivalent.

____ 39. $^{3}/_{5} = {}^{15}/_{25}$ ____ 42. $^{7}/_{12} = 4^{2}/_{60}$

____ 40. $^{9}/_{12} = {}^{2}/_{3}$ ____ 43. $^{2}/_{3} = {}^{40}/_{66}$

____ 41. $^{4}/_{22} = {}^{2}/_{11}$ ____ 44. $^{11}/_{15} = {}^{22}/_{33}$

For 45-49, round the decimals to the place in bold type.

45. 0.**4**632 _____

46. 173.0**6** _____

47. 0.2**7**5 _____

48. 12.0**3**61 _____

49. 0.00**5**5 _____

For 50-54, change the decimals to fractions or the fractions to decimals. (Round decimals to the nearest hundredth.)

50. $^{7}/_{12}$ _____

51. $^{2}/_{3}$ _____

52. 0.080 _____

53. 9.33 _____

54. 73.04 _____

For 55-59, change the fractions to percents. (Round percents to nearest whole percent.)

55. ¾ _____   58. $^{9}/_{5}$ _____

56. ⅞ _____   59. ⅕ _____

57. $^{9}/_{12}$ _____

For 60-71, change the decimals to percents and the percents to decimals. (Do not round any decimals.)

60. 0.36 _____

61. 14.7% _____

62. 1.950 _____

63. 0.56% _____

64. 27.261 _____

65. 3490% _____

66. 0.0795 _____

67. 7.36% _____

68. 0.0046 _____

69. 116.43% _____

70. 33.06 _____

71. 226.7% _____

For 72-81, solve the problems below. Write the answers on the lines. (Round decimals to the nearest hundredth.)

72. $1^{2}/_{3} + 2^{6}/_{10}$ _____

73. $^{9}/_{5} + {}^{2}/_{5}$ _____

74. 1.593 + 164.001 _____

75. $6^{3}/_{4} - 6^{3}/_{5}$ _____

76. $^{5}/_{13} \times {}^{4}/_{5}$ _____

77. $^{4}/_{5} \div {}^{7}/_{8}$ _____

78. 1.8 ÷ 0.36 _____

79. 22.7 x 66.66 _____

80. $2^{1}/_{2} \div 4^{2}/_{3}$ _____

81. $7^{1}/_{10} \times 1^{9}/_{5}$ _____

Name _____

For 82-92, write the answers on the lines.

_____ 82. Which of these fractions is smallest?
   a. $\frac{1}{7}$
   b. $\frac{2}{16}$
   c. $\frac{2}{13}$
   d. $\frac{3}{11}$
   e. $\frac{4}{20}$

_____ 83. Which is the correct answer to this problem, in lowest terms?
$$\frac{3}{12} \div \frac{5}{9}$$
   a. $\frac{27}{60}$
   b. $\frac{15}{108}$
   c. $\frac{9}{20}$
   d. $\frac{5}{36}$

_____ 84. Which numeral below means sixty-six and sixty-six ten thousandths?
   a. 66.066
   b. 0.06666
   c. 66.660
   d. 66.0066

_____ 85. Which is the correct decimal for 19.076%?
   a. 1.9076
   b. 1907.6
   c. 0.19076
   d. 19.076
   e. 190.76

_____ 86. Which fraction is in lowest terms?
   a. $\frac{6}{21}$
   b. $\frac{8}{4}$
   c. $\frac{7}{49}$
   d. $\frac{9}{11}$
   e. $\frac{62}{4}$

_____ 87. What percent of 55 is 11?
   a. 20%
   b. 50%
   c. 55%
   d. 2%

_____ 88. What is the answer to 68.3 ÷ 0.01?
   a. 0.683
   b. 6830
   c. 6.83
   d. 683.0

_____ 89. What is the answer to 0.0422 x 0.001?
   a. 422.001
   b. 422,001
   c. 0.00422
   d. 0.0000422

_____ 90. 13 is what percent of 78?
   (Round to the nearest whole percent.)

_____ 91. What number is 75% of 120?

_____ 92. What number is 40% of 70?

For 93-100, solve these proportions to find x.

_____ 93. $\frac{3}{2} = \frac{x}{8}$

_____ 94. $\frac{10}{26} = \frac{x}{13}$

_____ 95. $\frac{15}{x} = \frac{5}{9}$

_____ 96. $\frac{12}{20} = \frac{36}{x}$

_____ 97. $\frac{x}{8} = \frac{20}{32}$

_____ 98. $\frac{10}{x} = \frac{30}{42}$

_____ 99. $\frac{21}{x} = \frac{7}{2}$

_____ 100. $\frac{27}{9} = \frac{42}{x}$

SCORE: Total Points _____ out of a possible 100 points

Name _____

FRACTIONS & DECIMALS
SKILLS TEST ANSWER KEY

1. C
2. D
3. E
4. A
5. B
6. F
7. 1, 2, 3, 4, 6, 8, 12, 24
8. 1, 13
9. 2, 3
10. 20
11. 21
12. 15
13. 1, 3, 5, 15
14. 1, 2, 3, 6
15. e
16. b
17. c
18. a
19. c
20. d
21. Y
22. Y
23. N
24. Y
25. N
26. N
27. $\frac{2}{9}$
28. $\frac{1}{4}$
29. $\frac{1}{3}$
30. $\frac{1}{2}$
31. $\frac{2}{3}$
32. $\frac{3}{4}$
33. $\frac{3}{5}$

34. $\frac{4}{5}$
35. $\frac{3}{4}$
36. $\frac{3}{7}$
37. $\frac{1}{5}$
38. $\frac{2}{3}$
39. T
40. F
41. T
42. F
43. F
44. F
45. 0.46
46. 173
47. 0.28
48. 12.0
49. 0.006
50. 0.58
51. 0.67
52. $\frac{8}{100}$
53. $9\frac{1}{3}$
54. $73\frac{4}{100}$ or $73\frac{1}{25}$
55. 75%
56. 88%
57. 75%
58. 180%
59. 20%
60. 36%
61. 0.147
62. 195%
63. 0.0056
64. 2726.1%
65. 34.90
66. 7.95%
67. 0.0736

68. 0.46%
69. 1.1643
70. 3306%
71. 2.267
72. $4\frac{4}{15}$
73. $2\frac{1}{5}$
74. 165.59
75. $\frac{3}{20}$
76. $\frac{4}{13}$
77. $\frac{32}{35}$
78. 5
79. 1513.18
80. $\frac{15}{28}$
81. $19\frac{22}{25}$
82. b
83. c
84. d
85. c
86. d
87. a
88. b
89. d
90. 17%
91. 90
92. 28
93. x = 12
94. x = 5
95. x = 27
96. x = 60
97. x = 5
98. x = 14
99. x = 6
100. x = 14

ANSWERS*

Some answers may vary slightly due to different rounding standards.

page 116

1. $^4/_{14}$ or $^2/_7$
2. $^6/_{14}$ or $^3/_7$
3. $^5/_{14}$
4. $^3/_{14}$
5. $^{12}/_{14}$ or $^6/_7$
6. $^{14}/_{26}$ or $^7/_{13}$
7. Labradors $^{16}/_{68}$ or $^4/_{17}$
   Alaskan malamutes $^{25}/_{68}$
   hounds $^3/_{68}$
   Irish setters $^4/_{68}$ or $^1/_{17}$
   huskies $^9/_{68}$
   non-purebred mixes $^{11}/_{68}$

page 117

1. $^{13}/_{20}$
2. $^1/_3$
3. $^{365}/_{500}$ or $^{73}/_{100}$
4. $^{295}/_{500}$ or $^{59}/_{100}$
5. $2^3/_4$
6. $^7/_{10}$
7. $^{98}/_{100}$ or $^{49}/_{50}$
8. $8^1/_2$, $9^1/_2$, $10^1/_2$
9. $^{723}/_{800}$
10. $^{10}/_{233}$
11. $^{108}/_{89}$
12. $^3/_1$

page 118

1. Canada
   Jamaica
   Switzerland
   U.S.
   Russia
2. U.S.
   Russia
   Canada
   Jamaica
   Switzerland
3. U.S. $11^1/_2$ minutes
   Jamaica 11 minutes
   Switzerland $9^5/_6$ minutes
   Canada $8^5/_6$ minutes
   Russia $10^3/_4$ minutes
Canada is the winner.

page 119

1. $2^1/_2$
2. $2^2/_3$
3. $3^1/_4$
4. $1^3/_8$
5. 3
6. $2^2/_5$
7. $3^3/_7$
8. $1^1/_2$
9. $7^1/_2$
10. $2^3/_5$
11. $^5/_4$
12. $^7/_4$
13. $^9/_4$
14. $^{11}/_5$
15. $^{14}/_5$
16. $^{21}/_5$
17. $^{11}/_{10}$
18. $^{15}/_{10}$
19. $^{31}/_{10}$
20. $^{23}/_8$

page 120

1. 12 and 6 are composite; 2 is prime
2. 24 and 6 are composite; 2 is prime
3. 13 is prime
4. 36 is composite; 2 and 3 are prime
5. 21 is composite; 3 and 7 are prime
6. 28 is composite; 2 and 7 are prime
7. 56 and 8 are composite; 7 is prime
8. 63 is composite; 3 and 7 are prime
9. 48 and 12 are composite; 2 is prime
10-20.

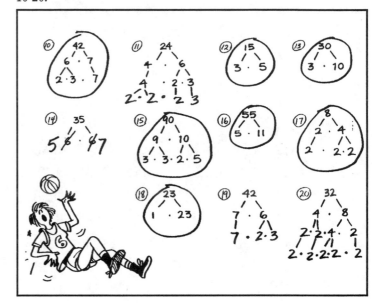

page 121

1. G	6. __ blank	11. S	16. 8
2. O	7. B	12. 3	17. 3
3. O	8. U	13. 3	18. 9
4. S	9. M	14. 4	19. 2
5. E	10. P	15. 7	20. 5

page 122

1. 8, 16, 24
2. 693
3. 18, 36
4. BJ King, S Lenglen, M Mallory, M Seles, J Fangio, T Watson, G Grafstom, W Bockl, D Jenkins, O Nepela, K Browning
5. 200
6. M Navratilova, S Graf, M Connolly, M Schumacher, J Nicklaus, B Hogan, G Player, K Schafer, G Grafstrom

page 123

Famous saying is: "It Ain't Over Til It's Over"
#s 7 and 21 are apostrophes; #s 3, 14, 18, 23 are blanks

page 124

1. $^3/_5$	5. $^{19}/_{10}$	8. $^{25}/_{110}$
2. $^{15}/_{30}$	6. $^5/_{18}$	9. $^{19}/_{11}$
3. $^{45}/_{50}$	7. a. $^{15}/_{30}$	10. $^{11}/_{44}$
4. $^3/_{10}$	b. $^{12}/_{52}$	

page 125

1. ½	20. 4/7
2. ¾	21. 5/6
3. 4/5	22. 2/3
4. ½	23. ¼
5. ⅓	24. 5/6
6. ⅓	25. 5/8
7. ⅓	26. ½
8. 4/5	27. 3/8
9. 6/7	28. ⅓
10. ½	29. ½
11. ¼	30. 2/9
12. ¾	31. no—½
13. ½	32. no—⅓
14. ⅙	33. yes
15. 2/5	34. no—1/7
16. 2/5	35. ⅓
17. 5/7	36. yes
18. 8/9	37. 2/3
19. 4/11	38. yes

pages 126-127

1. 9¾ min.
2. 3 min.
3. 10½ min.
4. 82 yds.
5. 27½ yard line; closer to Franklin's goal
6. Larry 22 yds.
   Kerry 14 yds.
   Joe 46 yds.
   Sam 31 yds.
7. yes
8. 48¼ yds.
9. 8⅙ mins.
10. 8:30 P.M.
11. 9:10 P.M.
12. 53⅔ yds.
13. 76⅓ yds.
14. 10:00 P.M.

page 128

1. individual $12\frac{11}{16}$
   personal $6\frac{15}{16}$
   group camping $8\frac{15}{16}$
   group cooking $5\frac{1}{16}$
   group food $4\frac{11}{16}$
2. Sally $6\frac{3}{8}$
   Mai $5\frac{5}{8}$
   Tamika $4\frac{7}{8}$
3. $16\frac{7}{8}$
4. $18\frac{11}{16}$
5. No; $1\frac{13}{16}$ lbs overweight

page 129

1. 9000 ft
2. 1 (all of your body)
3. 30 mph; −41°
4. 15 mph
5. 300 ft
6. 55 degrees
7. 10 hours
8. 7½ minutes; 2⅝ inches
9. 10 ft
10. 8¼ hrs

page 130

1. mints 5 lbs
   pizza 20
   nuts 12 lbs
   punch 16⅔ gallons
   cookies 10 lbs
   fudge 7½ lbs

2. hotdogs 4⅘ lbs
   hotdog buns 4 dozen
   mustard 12 ounces
   ketchup 16 ounces
   hamburger 9⅗ pounds
   hamburger buns 4 dozen
   potato chips 9 pounds
   baked beans 18 cups
   jello 2 pans
   ice cream 4½ lbs

3. hotdogs 16 lbs
   hotdog buns 13⅓ dozen
   mustard 40 ounces
   ketchup 55⅓ ounces
   hamburger 32 pounds
   hamburger buns 13⅓ dozen
   potato chips 30 pounds
   baked beans 60 cups
   jello 6⅔ pans
   ice cream 15 lbs

page 131

Brianna's catch
bass	$112 \frac{9}{128}$ ounces
bluegill	$49\frac{7}{8}$ ounces
crappie	$55\frac{11}{16}$ ounces

Simon's Catch
bowfin	$116\frac{9}{32}$ ounces
catfish	$356\frac{89}{128}$ ounces
walleye	$271\frac{1}{3}$ ounces

Nan's Catch
bass	$113\frac{77}{96}$ ounces
bowfin	$210\frac{23}{24}$ ounces
crappie	$49\frac{23}{64}$ ounces

Jason's catch
bluegill	$60\frac{7}{16}$ ounces
catfish	$389\frac{3}{8}$ ounces
walleye	$262\frac{9}{10}$ ounces

page 132

Chili
   5¼ lb hamburger
   1⅙ onion
   1¾ green peppers
   2⅝ lb tomatoes
   3⅜ T chili powder
   2¼ cans of beans

Potato Salad
   3⅙ lb potatoes
   1 lb onions
   5/6 lb celery
   4⅑ oz pickle relish
   4 eggs
   ⅙ C mustard
   5/6 T salt
   7/12 T pepper
   ¼ T paprika

Apple Crisp
   6 lb apples
   2⅚ lb brown sugar
   4⅙ C oatmeal
   1⅛ lb butter
   1¼ T cinnamon
   7/8 t. nutmeg

S'More Bars
   $2\frac{11}{20}$ C crushed chocolate bars
   5½ C crushed graham crackers
   ⅓ lb marshmallows
   3/8 C crushed peppermint candy

page 133

Cars with these numbers will crash: 3, 4, 6, 7, 12, 16, 19, 20, 21, 23, 24, and 29.

pages 134-135

0.12 — twelve hundredths

0.42 — forty-two hundredths

0.4 — four tenths

4.4 — four and four tenths

2.14 — two and fourteen hundredths

20.056 — twenty and fifty-six thousandths

33.583 — thirty-three and five hundred eighty-three thousandths

33.05 — thirty-three and five hundredths

4.87 — four and eighty-seven hundredths

0.44 — forty-four hundredths

0.08 — eight hundredths

0.8 — eight tenths

0.214 — two hundred fourteen thousandths

0.008 — eight thousandths

0.487 — four hundred eighty-seven thousandths

0.0487 — four hundred eighty-seven ten thousandths

3.305 — three and three hundred five thousandths

0.444 — four hundred forty-four thousandths

33.05 — thirty-three and five hundredths

3.35 — three and thirty-five hundredths

page 136

July 1, 1980 — Oslo
Aug 31, 1979 — Crystal Palace
Aug 26, 1979 — Crystal Palace
Sept 20, 1978 — Oslo
June 26, 1977 — Crystal Palace
May 28, 1977 — Belfast
June 30, 1975 — Stockholm
July 17, 1974 — Haringey
July 25, 1973 — Motspur Park

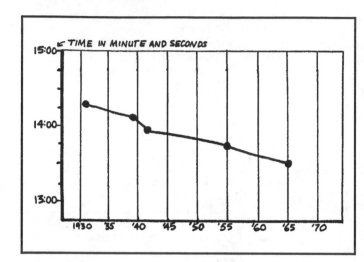

page 137

1. a. millionths
   b. ten millionths
   c. hundred millionths
2. a. thousandths
   b. hundredths
3. a. hundredths
   b. tenths
   c. ones
4. a. tens
   b. ones
5. tenths
6. ones
7. hundredths
8. tenths
9. hundreds
10. ten millions

page 138

1. 74.6 m
2. 10 sec.
3. 7.6 m
4. 8 m
5. 2.0
6. 7.4
7. 5.99
8. 9
9. 0.1
10. 41.1
11. 9.7
12. 400.1
13. 0.17
14. 2.65
15. 18.0
16. 4.99
17. 0.0
18. 45.9
19. 433
20. 87.12

page 139

1. $587.54
2. $237.54
3. $462.98
4. $52.66
5. $120.05
6. $5.59; $4.41
7. $3.50; $1.50
8. $7.35; $12.65

page 140

Melissa

Dive	Sum of Scores	Final Score
back somersault	24.3	43.74
forward 1½ somersault	26	39
inward flying somersault	22.9	43.51
Total Score:		**126.25**

Tom

Dive	Sum of Scores	Final Score
inward dive	23.6	40.12
forward double somersault	25.9	54.39
reverse 1 ½ somersault	22.9	45.8
Total Score		**140.31**

John

Dive	Final Score
back double somersault	45.2
inward flying somersault	46.93
forward triple somersault	54.75
Total Score	**146.88**

Tina

Dive	Final Score
reverse flying somersault	42.12
forward double somersault	44.31
inward double somersault	59.28
Total Score	**145.71**

Highest final score: John

page 141

1. a. Time 0.44; Rate 29.09
   b. Time 0.43; Rate 29.77
2. a. Time 0.42; Distance 1.24; Rate 2.95
   b. Time 0.45; Distance 1.24; Rate 2.76
3. a. Time 1.11; Rate 12.07
   b. Time 1.00; Rate 13
4. a. Swim 0.16; cycle 4.24; run 2.65
   b. Swim 0.16; cycle 4.52; run 2.26

page 142

1.
Player	DG	PSD
S. Valenko	0.240	0.333
T. Inqvest	0.375	0.429
J. Diskov	0.4	0.281
T. Beaufort	0.2	0.233
N. Tyler	0.166	0.192
M. Guilford	0.25	0.111

2.
Player	R/G	P/G	A/G
S. Valenko	1.7	3.3	1.1
T. Inqvest	1.55	3.33	1
J. Diskov	1.1	3.9	1.2
T. Beaufort	1	2.77	.88

N. Tyler	1.2	3.0	1.3
M. Guilford	1.4	2.88	1.11

3. Saves 14.9
   Goals 3.8

page 143

QUOTE: "Float like a butterfly;
Sting like a bee"

page 144

1. a. 44.8%
   b. 7.8%
   c. 2.9%
   d. 0.9%
   e. 6.0%
   f. 5.5%
   g. 4.3%
   h. 6.5%
   i. 4.1%
   j. 1.6%
   k. 2.8%
   l. 12.8%

2. a. 0.061
   b. 0.155
   c. 0.143
   d. 0.780
   e. 0.098
   f. 0.093
   g. 0.197
   h. 0.038
   i. 0.282
   j. 0.487
   k. 0.255
   l. 0.534

page 145

1.
category	fraction/100	decimal	percent
a. 50s-60s	8/100	0.08	8%
b. 70s	16/100	0.16	16%
c. 80s	28/100	0.28	28%
d. 90s	12/100	0.12	12%
e. current	36/100	0.36	36%

2.
category	fraction/100	decimal	percent
a. pop/rock	28/100	0.28	28%
b. country	22/100	0.22	22%
c. R&B/Rap	18/100	0.18	18%
d. Christian	14/100	0.14	14%
e. oldies	12/100	0.12	12%
f. classical	6/100	0.06	6%

page 146

1. 38.4%
2. a. 25%
   b. 37.5%
3. a. 16.7%
   b. 55.6%
   c. 27.8%
4. 30%
5. 21.9%
6. a. 13.3%
   b. 53.3%

c. 33.3%
7. a. 37.1%
   b. 15.5%
   c. 20.6%
   d. 26.8%

page 147

1. a. 50%
   b. 33⅓%
   c. 16⅔%
2. a. 19%
   b. 42.9%
   c. 38.1%
3. a. Tony 40.5%
   b. Jamie 28.6%
   c. Sheila 42.9%
   d. Jamie 71.4%

page 148

1. 70
2. 23
3. 8
4. 17
5. 17
6. 61
7. 73
8. 12
9. 20
10. 56

page 149

1. a. 7/12
   b. 7/5
2. 4/9
3. 3/4
4. 1/8
5. a. 1/2
   b. 5/2
   c. 8/5
   d. 1/2

page 150

1. a. 1055 meters per min
   b. 17.583 or 17 7/12 meters per second
2. 2 meters per second
3. 16 meters per second
4. a. 390 meters per minute
   b. 6.5 meters per second
5. a. 16.67 or 16⅔ meters per second
   b. horse
6. 10.70 meters per second
7. 86 meters per second
8. 185.87 miles per hour
9. 461.54 feet per second

page 151

1. $7/x = 1/50$; 350 m
2. a. $50/24 = 750/x$; 360 seconds
   b. $40/48 = 320/x$; 384 sec
   c. a, by 24 seconds
3. a. 32 seconds
   b. $5/x = 6/96$; 80 seconds

4. a. 322 seconds
   b. 320 seconds
   c. left, by 2 seconds
5. 7.5 cm
6. $16/48 = x/42$; 14th position

pages 152-153

1. a. $x/1000 = 11/3$; x = 366.$\overline{6}$ ft.
   b. $x/3 = 2500/1000$; x = 7.5 cm

2. a. $x/2 = 350/15$; x = 46.67 lbs.
   b. $x/15 = 48/2$; x = 360 ft.

3. $x/1 = 200/75$;
   x = 2.6 carabiners (3 are necessary)

4. $x/1 = 85/15$; x = 5.67 camming devices

5. a. $x/75 = 9/2$; x = 337.5 ft.
   b. $x/2 = 1200/75$; x = 32 cm.

6. $x/14 = 1/4$; x = 3.5 light sticks (4 are necessary)

7. a. $x/1 = 500,000/1000$; x = 50 gallons
   b. $3/1,000,000 = x/1000$; x = 3000 ml

8. $x/1 = 160/50$; x = 30⅕ knots (31 knots)

9. $5/7 = x/420$; x = 300 minutes

10. $8/30 = 30.4/x$; x = 114 lbs.

page 154

Correct answers with sky diver:
4, 5, 7, 8, 9, 12, 13, 14, 15, 16, 17, 22, 23

Incorrect answers with scuba diver:
1, 2, 3, 6, 10, 11, 18, 19, 20, 21, 24

page 155

1. 4.87 sec
2. 24.17 sec
3. 1.64 sec
4. 126.30 sec or 2 min, 6.30 sec
5. 4.26 sec
6. 38.11 sec
7. 40.24 sec
8. 26.13 sec
9. 9.33 sec
10. 188.66 sec or 3 min, 8.66 sec

page 156

1. 23%
2. 1.03
3. 10%
4. 40/187
5. 2.2 seconds
6. 46
7. 14%
8. approx. 8800
9. 2 titles
10. 34,080,000 people

PROBLEM SOLVING

Skills Exercises

2-4-6-8!

WHAT DO WE

APPRECIATE?

MATH!

SKILLS CHECKLIST FOR PROBLEM SOLVING

✔	SKILL	PAGE(S)
	Identify and define a problem	168, 169
	Identify information needed for problem solution	168–171
	Eliminate excess information	168, 169, 171
	Solve problems using information from illustrations	172
	Select appropriate operation(s) for solving problems	173, 174, 184, 191–195, 201, 202
	Solve problems using information from charts and tables	173–175, 179
	Solve multi-step problems	173–178, 184, 191–206
	Solve problems using information from graphs	176, 177
	Use estimation to solve problems	177, 182
	Solve problems using information from maps	178
	Solve problems using statistical data	179
	Choose and use formulas to solve problems	180
	Use mental math to solve problems	181, 182
	Choose correct equations to solve problems	183, 184
	Translate problems into equations	184
	Use trial and error to solve problems	185
	Create diagrams, charts, or graphs to solve problems	186–189
	Use logic to solve problems	187, 188, 201, 202
	Solve problems involving ratio	190, 196–199
	Solve problems involving proportion	190, 199
	Solve problems involving percent	190–194
	Solve consumer problems	191–195
	Solve problems involving rate, time, and distance	197, 198
	Solve problems involving time and time zones	200
	Solve open-ended problems	201, 202
	Choose appropriate problem-solving strategies	201–204
	Use alternative problem-solving strategies	201–204
	Check accuracy of solutions	205
	Determine reasonableness of solutions	206

RIGHT ON TRACK

To solve a math problem, you need to be able to identify what information in the problem is needed for finding a solution. For each problem below, circle the letters of the pieces of information that are needed in order to find the solution. Then solve the problem. Use a separate piece of paper for your work.

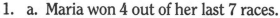

1. a. Maria won 4 out of her last 7 races.
    b. Her best time is 12 minutes 14 seconds.
    c. She runs the 100 meter race.

Problem: At this rate, how many races will she win out of the next 35?

Answer: _____

2. a. Cy's pole has broken 12 times this year.
    b. It costs $22 to fix a pole every time it is broken.
    c. Cy has used his pole for 39 track meets in the last 2 years.

Problem: How much did Cy pay this year for repairs?

Answer: _____

3. a. Hannah, a hurdler, slept 8 hours 30 minutes on Monday night.
    b. She slept 7 hours on both Tuesday night and Friday night.
    c. She slept 6 hours 20 minutes on Wednesday night.
    d. She got up at 6:30 A.M. on Thursday.

Problem: How much sleep did she get in the 3 nights before Thursday's meet?

Answer: _____

4. a. The track meet started at 4:00 P.M. on Monday.
    b. The high jump bar was knocked off 16 times.
    c. Justin has placed first 13 times in this event.
    d. There were a total of 52 jumps.

Problem: What is the ratio of unsuccessful jumps to total jumps (in lowest terms)?

Answer: _____

Name _____

168

RIGHT ON TRACK, CONTINUED

5. a. Abby washes her uniform after every meet.
    b. There are 3 meets a week.
    c. It shrinks .8% every time she washes it.
Problem: In what week of the season will the uniform have shrunk 12%?

Answer: _____

6. a. The decathlon lasts 2 days, with 5 events each day.
    b. Dylan eats 4000 calories each day for 7 days before the event.
    c. Dylan eats nothing for the 2 days of the event.
Problem: What is the average number of calories consumed per day for the 9 days?

Answer: _____

7. a. There were 900 spectators at the track meet on Friday.
    b. The crowd on Saturday was 3.5 times the size of Friday's.
    c. The crowd on Friday was 1.5 times the size of Sunday's crowd.
Problem: How many fans were there on Sunday?

Answer: _____

8. a. The male track and field athletes drank 153 gallons of sports drink at the meet.
    b. The track and field athletes drank 255 gallons of sports drink.
    c. The women track and field athletes drank 102 gallons.
Problem: What percent of the sports drink was drunk by the women?

Answer: _____

9. a. Paul's shot put weighs 16 pounds.
    b. Paul weighs 190 pounds.
    c. His record distance is 1.3 meters longer than Ray's.
    d. His record is .7 meters shorter than Gregorio's.
    e. Gregorio's record is 17.1 meters.
Problem: What is Paul's record distance for the shot put?

Answer: _____

10. a. The track and field area is 900 x 500 feet, including track and stands.
    b. The grass is mowed twice a week.
    c. 5200 square feet of the sports area is not grass.
Problem: How many square feet of grass are mowed each week?

Answer: _____

Name _____

SOMETHING'S MISSING

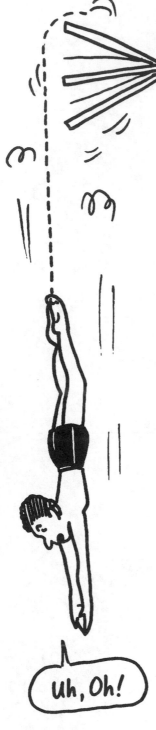

Some information is missing in these problems. For each one, tell what other information you would need in order to solve the problem.

1. This daring diver holds the record for gold medals in his state. How many more medals does he have than his nearest competitor?

   Missing: _____

2. The diving board is 12 feet above the water's surface. When David springs up, he rises 3 feet. What is the total number of feet he travels up and down from the time he leaves the board until his fingertips touch the bottom of the pool?

   Missing: _____

3. Deanna can compete with 8 different dives. She practices each of these several times a day. How many practice dives does she do in 7 days?

   Missing: _____

4. The Benson High Swimming and Diving Team used 48 towels at Tuesday's practice. What percent of the pile of towels was left unused?

   Missing: _____

5. The world record high dive is 176 feet 10 inches. What is the difference between Maria's highest dive and the world record?

   Missing: _____

6. 5 out of 7 judges each awarded Jake an 8.5 score on his high board dive. His total was 60.5 points. What score did the seventh judge give him?

   Missing: _____

7. The diving pool at Amanda's school is 48 feet wide and 84 feet long. What is the capacity of the pool?

   Missing: _____

8. Greg Louganis holds 17 U.S. national diving titles. How many of these did he win before the 1984 Olympics?

   Missing: _____

9. Randy's scores on all his springboard dives this year total 722.5 points. How does this total compare to the average for the team?

   Missing: _____

Name _____

HOW MUCH IS TOO MUCH?

Sometimes there is too much information in math problems. Then you have to decide what is really necessary. For each of these problems, underline the information that is NOT needed for a solution. Then find the answer and write it on the line.

1. Lana, a long distance runner, ran 16 miles in 3½ hours. She left home at 11 A.M. and returned at 2:30 P.M. At the end of the run her pulse was 145 beats per minute. What is the rate of her speed in miles per hour?

    Answer: _____

2. Nicole left home at 9:18 A.M. to jog with 2 friends. She ran 2.6 miles to Sam's house, and then she and Sam ran 4.1 miles to meet Rog. Rog ran with them 1.7 more miles. How many miles did Sam run?

    Answer: _____

3. After a cross-country race, Juan's team ate 12 pizzas. 6 were vegetarian, 4 were plain cheese, and 2 had pepperoni. There were 18 runners on the team. On the average, what fraction of a pizza did each runner eat?

    Answer: _____

4. Annika's best time for a 10 k race is 55 minutes. Yesterday she left home at 3:16 P.M. and returned at 4:20 P.M. She ran approximately .16 k per minute. How much time did her run take?

    Answer: _____

5. 500 runners took part in a 15 k run. 212 were male. 1.4% of the runners did not finish. 4 males did not finish. The winner was 36 years old. The average age of the runners was 28. How many women finished the race?

    Answer: _____

6. James wears out 4 pairs of running shoes each year. They cost him about $70 a pair. He spent $60 this year for entrance fees in races. Approximately how much does he spend on his shoes in 3 years?

    Answer: _____

7. Jessica traveled 830 miles by car to 12 cross-country meets this year. At these races she ran a total of 111 miles. She spent $490 on traveling expenses. How many fewer miles did she run than she traveled in the car?

    Answer: _____

8. Each member of the 36-member cross-country team has 3 different 2-piece uniforms. These uniforms cost $55 each. When they wash all their uniforms at the Laundromat on a trip, how many pieces of clothing get washed?

    Answer: _____

Name _____

SHAPE-UPS

Use the illustration to find the solutions to the following problems.

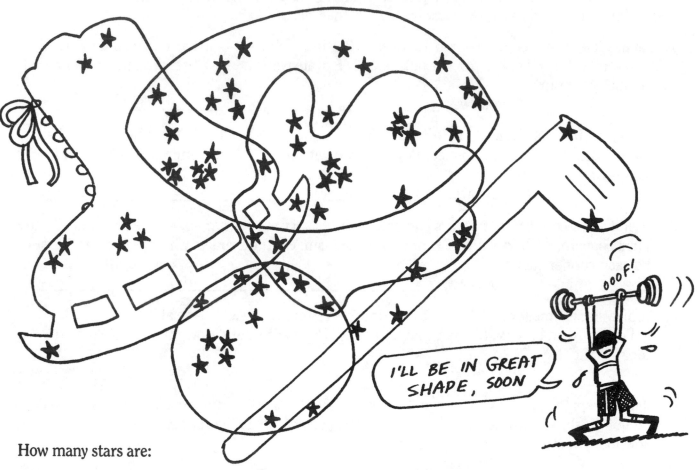

How many stars are:

1. in the intersection of the football and the baseball?

2. not in the skate?

3. in the football but not in the mitt?

4. in the golf club but outside any other shape?

5. in the intersection of the baseball and golf club?

6. in the intersection of the skate, football, and mitt?

7. in the football but outside the skate?

8. total in the mitt and in the golf club?

9. in the intersection of the baseball and skate?

10. in the mitt and in no other shape?

11. not in the glove or the football?

12. not in any shape?

13. in the skate but not in the mitt or football?

14. in the baseball but in no other shape?

15. inside only one shape?

16. total in the mitt plus total in the skate?

17. in the intersection of the football, golf club, and mitt?

18. in the intersection of the mitt, baseball, and golf club?

Name _____

FARE WARS

These players are making ticket choices for their island vacations. For each question below, tell what mathematical **operation** or **operations** the player would use to solve his or her problem. Then solve the problem. Use a separate piece of paper for your work.

Destination	Paradise Air	Tropic Jet	SunFun Jet
JAMAICA	Child $255 Adult $325	All Seats $295	All Seats $300
FIJI	Child $470 Adult $640	Child $400 Adult $690	Child $295 Adult $770
BERMUDA	All Seats $410	1st Class $800 Tourist $400	Child $399 Adult $420
HAWAII	All Seats $525	$600 3rd person flies free	Child $400 Adult $535
TAHITI	All Seats $700	All Seats $690	Child $600 Adult $750

HOLD THE PLANE! I CAN'T FIND THE COACH!

I NEED A SEAT BY THE RESTROOM, M'AM.

CAN I PAY ON THE INSTALLMENT PLAN?

1. What will Tim pay for 4 adults to Hawaii on Tropic Jet?

   Operation(s): _____ Answer: _____

2. Tad wants to take 2 adults and 1 child to Jamaica. Which airline is the best deal? What will Tad pay?

   Operation(s): _____ Answer: _____

3. How much will Ted save by flying to Tahiti on Tropic Jet instead of Paradise Air? He is traveling with his older brother and his two kids.

   Operation(s): _____ Answer: _____

4. Tom wants to take 4 friends to Bermuda first class. Can he do this for $2000?

   Operation(s) _____ Answer: _____

5. What is the cheapest tropical vacation Todd can arrange for himself, his wife, and 3 kids? On what airline?

   Operation(s): _____ Answer: _____

6. Is it cheaper to fly 4 adults and 3 children to Fiji on SunFun Jet, to Bermuda on Tropic Jet, or to Hawaii on Paradise Air?

   Operation(s): _____ Answer: _____

Name _____

ATHLETES ON THE LINE

The athletes at a California summer sports camp make a lot of phone calls. Use the information from the chart on the next page (p. 175) to answer the questions about costs of their calls. Use separate paper for your work.

1. Gymnast Joe called home to Moscow, Idaho, at 9 P.M. on Thursday. The call was 14 minutes long. How much did it cost? _____

2. Biker Becky made a 20-minute call home to Pearl City, Hawaii, that cost $24.70. When did she call? _____

3. Kayaker Suzie talked 14 minutes to her boyfriend in Paris, South Carolina, on Saturday at 9 A.M. How much did it cost? _____

4. Climber Claudia, from Romeo, Colorado, called home on Friday at 11 P.M. and talked 7 minutes. After that she called Moody, Alabama, for 5 minutes. How much did her calls cost? _____

5. Pitcher Paula talked to her sister in Sassafras, Kentucky, for 1 hour on July 4th. How much did her call cost? Was this more or less than she spent calling her friend in Sugar Hill, Georgia, the next day, Friday, at 1 P.M. for 30 minutes?
_____

6. Sprinter Shawn talked to his coach in Nutley, New Jersey, on Wednesday at 7 P.M. The call cost $12.24. How long did he talk? _____

7. Did Dan the diver spend more money talking 6 minutes to his parents in Onset, Massachusetts, at noon on Wednesday or 25 minutes to his girlfriend in Talent, Oregon, on Thursday at 9:30 P.M.? _____

8. Equestrian Eddie made three calls to friends between 10 and 11:30 P.M. on Saturday: 5 minutes to Hoxie, Kansas, 19 minutes to King Salmon, Alaska, and 12 minutes to Suncook, Nevada. How much did he spend on the calls? _____

9. Golfer Gina had only $12.30 to spend on phone calls. How long could she talk to her friend in Claypool, Arizona, after 11 P.M. on Tuesday? _____

10. How long was wrestler Ramon's $10.50 call home to Story, WY on Tuesday at 11:00 A.M.?
_____

Name _____

Use this chart to solve the problems on page 174.

CITY CALLED	WEEK DAYS, Monday–Friday						SAT, SUN, & HOLIDAYS	
	8 A.M.–5 P.M.		5P.M.–11 P.M.		11 P.M.–8 A.M.		All Hours	
	First 3 min.	Add. min.	First 3 min.	Add. min.	First 3 min.	Add. min.	First 3 min.	Add. min.
Moody, Alabama	3.60	.96	2.80	.78	1.95	.58	2.00	.62
King Salmon, Alaska	2.90	.75	2.40	.60	1.50	.43	1.80	.58
Claypool, Arizona	1.98	.50	1.66	.38	1.10	.28	1.26	.30
Romeo, Colorado	2.10	.54	1.75	.42	1.30	.28	1.62	.35
Sugar Hill, Georgia	3.15	.78	2.72	.66	1.75	.36	1.88	.45
Pearl City, Hawaii	4.30	1.20	3.96	.98	2.50	.68	2.65	.75
Moscow, Idaho	2.00	.60	1.62	.50	1.20	.35	1.46	.40
Hoxie, Kansas	2.60	.70	1.90	.58	1.50	.35	1.76	.44
Sassafras, Kentucky	3.20	1.00	2.90	.90	1.80	.64	2.00	.74
Onset, Massachusetts	3.96	1.04	3.18	.88	2.02	.66	2.32	.70
Paradise, Montana	1.95	.54	1.66	.48	1.00	.38	1.18	.44
Suncook, Nevada	2.05	.65	1.65	.55	1.25	.40	1.35	.50
Nutley, New Jersey	3.34	1.00	2.88	.78	1.86	.65	1.95	.75
Talent, Oregon	1.60	.48	1.05	.38	.90	.30	.98	.36
Pascoag, Rhode Island	3.35	1.14	2.88	.86	1.78	.66	2.00	.75
Paris, South Carolina	3.44	1.05	2.96	.95	1.85	.70	2.10	.80
Camelot, Texas	3.00	.86	2.25	.70	1.65	.50	1.75	.56
Story, Wyoming	2.22	.46	1.86	.38	1.30	.25	1.40	.30

Name

GO FOR THE GOLD

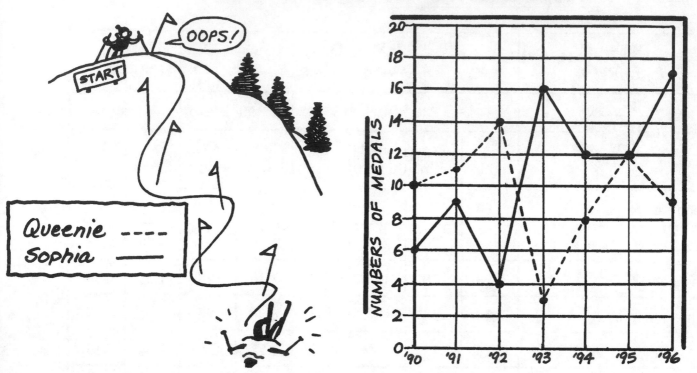

Queenie Quick-Turn and Sophia Schusher have been fierce slalom rivals for years. They are the top two women on the world circuit. The graph shows their gold medal totals for the past 7 years. Use the graph to answer the questions below.

1. As of 1992, who had the most medals (total)? _____

2. How many more did Sophia win in her best year than in her worst? _____

3. Who had the largest drop from 1 year to the next? _____

4. Who had the greatest gain from 1 year to the next?_____

5. Who had the greatest gain in a 2-year period? _____

6. What year did they tie in number of medals? _____

7. In what 3-year period did Queenie win more than Sophia?_____

8. Who had the best record from 93 to 95?_____

9. This equation shows Queenie's wins in comparison to Sophia's for what year? _____

$$Q = 3S + 2$$

10. Who won the most gold medals in the 7-year period?_____

11. In 1993, Sophia won twice as many medals as Queenie did in what year? _____

12. Who had the best record from 90-95?_____

Name _____

RECORD ATTENDANCE

Use the bar graph to answer these questions about attendance at sporting events.
Estimate the answers.

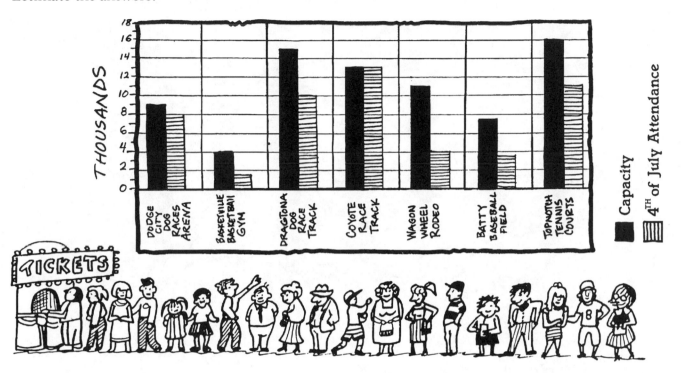

1. Which 2 centers had about the same
    attendance on July 4th?

    _____

    _____

2. What is the difference between the capacity
    of the Dodge City Dog Race Arena and the
    attendance on July 4th?

    _____

3. Which arena has a difference of about 2500
    between its capacity and the July 4th
    attendance?

    _____

4. What is the difference between the capacity
    of the largest and the smallest arenas?

    _____

5. How many more people attended the Dragtona
    Dog Race on July 4th than attended the Batty
    baseball game?

    _____

6. How many fewer people watched the
    Wagonwheel Rodeo cowboys than the
    Topnotch tennis players?

    _____

7. Which 2 centers had a difference of about 5000
    between capacity and July 4th attendance?

    _____

8. How many fewer people watched the basketball
    game than the Coyote races on July 4th?

    _____

Name _____

ON THE ROAD AGAIN

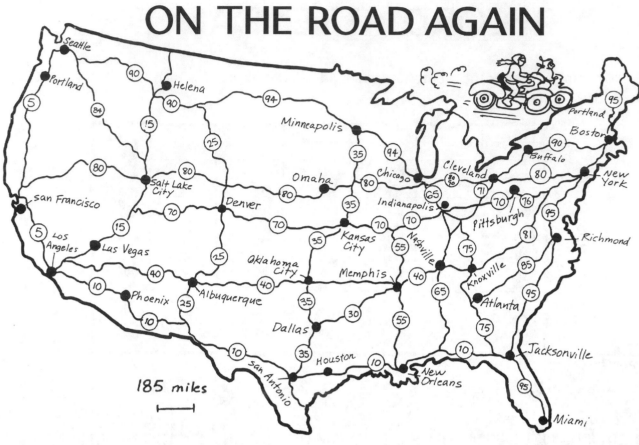

185 miles

Nora and Nancy, the Dare Devil Racing Duo, are traveling to races around the country. Use the map to help you answer questions about their travels.

1. If they ride 1480 miles west on I-80 from Chicago, where do they end up?

_____

2. Next stop: from Portland south on I-5 to San Francisco. About how far will they travel?

_____

3. For their toughest race, they head east from Salt Lake City, Nevada, on I-80, then south on I-35 to Oklahoma City. Approximately how long is their trip in miles?

_____

4. From Memphis, Tennessee, they head for New York City. Tell the shortest route and the approximate mileage.

_____

5. If they ride about 500-600 miles from Albuquerque, what cities could they reach?

_____

6. What is the approximate mileage of this route: from Indianapolis south on I-65 to Nashville, I-40 west to Memphis, I-30 west to Dallas, and I-35 south to San Antonio?

_____

7. They ride about 1500 miles north from Miami on I-95. Where do they end up?

_____

8. Their last race takes them from Helena to Oklahoma City by routes I-15, I-90, I-94, and I-35. Is this the shortest route? If not, what is the shortest route?

_____

Name

SOCCER STATISTICS

Use the statistics on the charts below to solve the problems about the performances of Suzannah, the year's highest scoring striker, and Gregory, the school's best goalie.

SUZANNAH STRIKER

GAME	ATTEMPTS	GOALS
1	8	2
2	4	0
3	9	2
4	11	3
5	12	3
6	5	1
7	7	2
8	13	4
9	5	1
10	8	1

SUZANNAH

1. Total goals she scored in 10 games _____

2. Her total attempts in the year _____

3. The ratio of goals to attempts _____

4. The percent of success in game 8 _____

5. Best game for ratio of goals to attempts _____

6. The games that had the greatest difference between attempts and goals scored_____

7. Number of unsuccessful attempts_____

8. Worst stretch of 3 games for ratio of scores to attempts _____

GREGORY GOALIE

GAME	ATTEMPTS ON GOAL	GOALS SCORED
1	8	0
2	12	1
3	9	2
4	18	3
5	16	0
6	7	1
7	10	0
8	15	2
9	11	1
10	20	4

GREGORY

9. Total goals scored against him _____

10. Total goals he stopped _____

11. Ratio of goals scored to goals attempted against him _____

12. Total goals he stopped in games 5-10 _____

13. Percent of goals stopped during 10 games _____

14. Difference between goals attempted and goals scored in game 10_____

15. Best 3 games for ratio of stops to attempts_____

16. Worst game for ratio of stops to attempts _____

Name _____

THE RIGHT FORMULA

Use the formulas below to answer these questions. Round your answers to the nearest tenth. You may need to work the problems on an extra sheet of paper.

Area of triangle .... $A = \frac{1}{2}bh$
Area of square .... $A = s^2$
Area of rectangle .... $A = l \times w$
Area of trapezoid .... $A = \frac{1}{2}h(b_1 + b_2)$
Area of circle .... $A = \pi r^2$

Perimeter of triangle ...... $P = a + b + c$
Perimeter of square .... $P = 4s$
Perimeter of rectangle .... $P = s(l + w)$
Circumference of circle .. $C = 2\pi r$

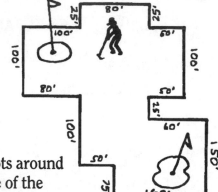

1. A figure skater goes around her figure 8 three times during a test. How much distance does she cover? _____

2. A horse trots around the outside of the golf course. How far does she trot?
_____

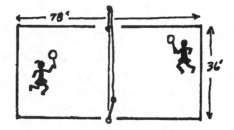

3. How much area is on either side of the net on the tennis court? _____

4. Jan's coach paces around the tennis court 5 times before the match begins. How far does the coach walk? _____

5. How much area is there for the boxers to dance around in?
_____

6. A little kid runs around the trampoline twice. How far does he run?

7. What area is available for the trampolinist to land on?
_____

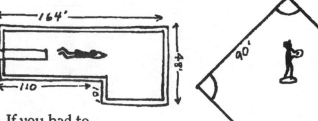

8. If you had to paint the bottom of the pool, how much area would you cover? _____

9. How far does a batter run to complete a home run?
_____

10. It's Nyoko's job to clean the sail on her mom's boat. After she scrubs the front and back of the sail, how much surface area has she cleaned?
_____

Name _____

MENTAL PUSH-UPS

Try to solve each of these problems in your head. Write your answer on the line.

1. Jay does 90 sit-ups in 2 minutes. At this rate, how many can he do in 10 minutes? _____

2. Lu does 18 push-ups, 166 sit-ups, 37 jumping jacks, and 11 chin-ups. How many repetitions of exercises has she completed? _____

3. Chad grunts 3 times as often as Jeff when he's doing pull-ups. Jeff grunts 11 times a minute. How many times does Chad grunt in 5 minutes? _____

4. Jennifer walks the treadmill slowly for 8 minutes and fast for another 68 minutes. What fraction of the total time is she going slowly (in lowest terms)? _____

5. Tomas begins his workout at 1:35 P.M. and finishes at 3:01 P.M. How long does he work out? _____

6. Jo's pulse climbs 115 beats per minute to 190 bpm while he is jumping rope. What was his heart rate when he started?_____

7. Jess exercised 40 minutes every day this week except for 55 minutes on Tuesday and Friday. What is her total exercise time this week? _____

8. Bryan's dad gave him 5 cents for every sit-up and 50 cents for each push-up he could do. He did 130 sit-ups and 35 push-ups. How much money did he receive? _____

9. Drinking water costs 85 cents at the gym. How many bottles can Moe buy for $10?_____

10. Melanie has 8 different exercise outfits. She wears a different one each day and doesn't wear it again until she's worn all the others. How many times will she wear outfit # 1 in the month of December if she wears it on December 1st and exercises each day? _____

11. The exercise mat is 13 meters long and 9 meters wide. Lulu jogs around it once. How far around is it?_____

12. Jan does 80 back stretches today. Mandy does ⅝ as many. How many is that? _____

13. Jenna's workout this Monday is on June 25. What day is her August 10 workout? _____

14. Joe talks to a friend 3 minutes after every 7 minutes he exercises at the gym. After 1 hour at the gym, how many minutes has Joe exercised? _____

Name

SWIMMER'S SNACK BREAK

Tacos----- $ .80
Burritos-----.99
Hot Dogs-----1.50
Hamburgers--1.75
Pizza Slice--1.25
Sandwiches--1.90
Rice Bowl--1.00
Fries------.95
Salad----1.10
Chips------.50
Shakes-----1.50
Drinks------.90
Ice Cream-----.95
Candy------.45

The championship Surfside Swim Team is taking some time out from their strenuous practice for a snack break. Estimate each swimmer's total bill. Write your estimate on the ticket.

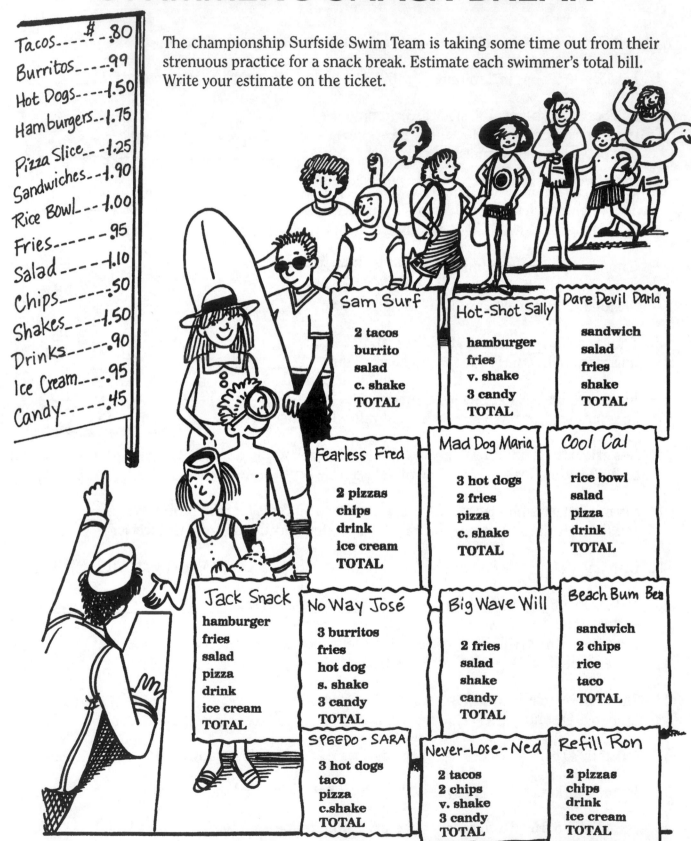

Sam Surf

2 tacos
burrito
salad
c. shake
TOTAL

Hot-Shot Sally

hamburger
fries
v. shake
3 candy
TOTAL

Dare Devil Darla

sandwich
salad
fries
shake
TOTAL

Fearless Fred

2 pizzas
chips
drink
ice cream
TOTAL

Mad Dog Maria

3 hot dogs
2 fries
pizza
c. shake
TOTAL

Cool Cal

rice bowl
salad
pizza
drink
TOTAL

Jack Snack

hamburger
fries
salad
pizza
drink
ice cream
TOTAL

No Way José

3 burritos
fries
hot dog
s. shake
3 candy
TOTAL

Big Wave Will

2 fries
salad
shake
candy
TOTAL

Beach Bum Bea

sandwich
2 chips
rice
taco
TOTAL

SPEEDO - SARA

3 hot dogs
taco
pizza
c. shake
TOTAL

Never-Lose-Ned

2 tacos
2 chips
v. shake
3 candy
TOTAL

Refill Ron

2 pizzas
chips
drink
ice cream
TOTAL

Name

A CAREFUL BALANCE

Often you can solve a word problem by turning it into an equation. For each of these, write the letter of the equation that correctly fits the problem. Then solve the problem.

1. Tatiana falls from the balance beam 3 times during her first 8 routines. At this rate, how many times will she do her routine to end up with 27 falls?

    a) $3/8 = 27/x$
    b) $27/x = 8/3$
    c) $3/27 = x/8$

    Correct Equation:_____

    Solution: _____

2. 5 days a week Tatiana spends 8 hours at the gym with a $2\frac{1}{4}$-hour break in the late afternoon. On the fourth day, she also takes a $1\frac{1}{2}$-hour morning break. How much time does she spend in actual training at the gym?

    a) $5(8 - 2\frac{1}{4}) + 1\frac{1}{2} = n$
    b) $n = 5(8 - 2\frac{1}{4} - 1\frac{1}{2})$
    c) $n = 5(8 - 2\frac{1}{4}) - 1\frac{1}{2}$
    d) $8 - 2\frac{1}{4} + 1\frac{1}{2} = 5n$

    Correct Equation:_____

    Solution: _____

3. 26 gymnasts started for the team at the beginning of the year. 2 dropped each week for 8 weeks. Then 3 joined. The final total was equal to 5 less than the number of members on last year's team. How many were on last year's team?

    a) $26 - 2 + 8 - 5 = x$
    b) $26 - (8 \times 2) + 3 = x - 5$
    c) $x = 26 + 5 - 2(8 + 3)$

    Correct Equation:_____

    Solution: _____

4. Kate's floor routine lasts 0.6 minute less than Meg's and 0.3 longer than Brie's. Brie's routine is 2.4 minutes long. How long does Meg's last?

    a) $2.4 - 0.6 + 0.3 = M$
    b) $M = 2.4 + 0.3 + 0.6$
    c) $2.4 - 0.3 - 0.6 = M$

    Correct Equation:_____

    Solution: _____

5. Sandra won 9 gold medals in 1993, 14 in 1994, and 8 in 1995. Her total gold medals in these 3 years was twice what she won in 1996. How many in 1996?

    a) $2n = 9 + 14 + 8$
    b) $3(9 - 14 + 8) = n$
    c) $n = 2(9 - 14 + 8)$

    Correct Equation:_____

    Solution: _____

6. Todd had 8 injuries last year. He had 2 less than 3 times that many this year. How many injuries this year?

    a) $n = 3(8 - 2)$
    b) $n = (3 \times 8) - 2$
    c) $n = 8 - (3 \times 2)$

    Correct Equation:_____

    Solution: _____

Name

FAN-TASTICS

Translate each problem into an equation. Write your equation. Then use the equation to find the solution.

RAH-RAH-SISS-BOOM-BAH!

GO! GO! GO!

WOOF WOOF

1. The Grizzly football fans are a loyal crowd. In the 1994 season their attendance rose 880 over the '93 season. In '95 it was 1000 more than in '94, setting a season record of 17,964. What was the attendance in '93?

2. When Grandpa Cheer took over leadership of the Grizzly Booster Club, there were 44 members. Now there are 8 less than 3 times that many. How many members are there now?

3. The principal's twins found 26 wallets under the bleachers. This was 6 less than 4 times the number of wallets the coach's triplets found. How many did the coach's kids find?

4. The Grizzly cheerleaders cheered 12 less than 42 dozen cheers. How many cheers?

5. The Sitalot family came to the game with $12. They bought 4 bags of popcorn at 75¢ each and 3 drinks at $1 each in the first half. At halftime, Sammy Sitalot found 6 quarters under the bleachers. The family went home with $3.45. How much did they spend in the second half?

6. Little Frannie Francis bought a bag of popcorn with 1087 pieces of popcorn in it. She spilled 12 pieces for every 1 she put in her mouth. At the end of the game, there were 34 pieces left. How many pieces actually went into her mouth?

Name

ON A ROLL

The trial and error method is one strategy for problem solving. First, you choose a solution you think might work and try it out. If it doesn't fit the problem, keep trying others until you find one that works.

Eric is pretty good on his skates, but he's doing such wild stuff that he takes plenty of falls. Find the number that tells how many falls Eric took each day.

DAY 1
An even, 2-digit number whose 2 digits have a difference of 1 and the first digit is larger than the second. The sum of the digits and the product are < 10 and > 0.

DAY 2
The smallest even number other than 2 that is a factor of 78.

DAY 3
A prime number < 10 with a square that is > 40 but < 80.

DAY 4
A 2-digit multiple of 3 whose digits total 6, but neither digit is 1, 2, or 0.

DAY 5
The smallest prime number with more than 1 digit, the sum of whose digits is > 5.

DAY 6
A 2-digit square whose digits add up to an even number.

DAY 7
A number < 50 that is divisible by 1, 2, 3, 5, and 10.

DAY 8
The smallest number divisible by 9.

DAY 9
A number that when added to 52 gives a square number, when subtracted from 48 gives another square, and when divided by 3 gives another square.

DAY 10
A number > 95 and < 115 that is the product of 2 prime numbers (other than 1).

Name

CROSS-COUNTRY CHALLENGE

One strategy for problem solving is to make a chart with the information you're given. For some problems, this is the easiest way to find a solution. For each of these problems below, make a chart to help you find the answer. Show your chart on a separate piece of paper.

1. On the first day Margot skied the Camelback Cross-Country Course, she did it in 26 minutes. Each day after that, she cut 10 seconds off her time. Skier Holly did the same course in 23 minutes on Day 1, cutting 5 seconds off her time each day after that. On what day will the two skiers have the same time on this course?

   Answer: _____

2. Michael wants to buy 2 items of food for each of the friends skiing with him. The snack shop has 5 kinds of snacks: granola bars, energy bars, chocolate bars, peanuts, and bananas. How many different combinations of 2 items could he possibly choose?

   Answer: _____

3. Four skiers, Ted, Jed, Ned, and Fred, want to practice today. Practice sessions are from 8 to 10:40 A.M. only. Skiers must start the course 10 minutes apart and no more than 3 skiers may be on the course at once. Each skier is allowed to stay on the course for only 30 minutes. Can all 4 skiers practice today and finish before 9:40 A.M.?

   Answer: _____

4. Katarina skied 2 miles on Day 1. Each day after that, she skied 1.5 miles more than the day before. On what day did she ski over 30 miles?

   Answer: _____

Name _____

WHO'S WHO AT THE STADIUM?

You will need to use logical thinking to find a solution for these problems. The clues will help you.
For each problem, draw a diagram to show your thinking.

1. Only one of the cheerleaders at Ashland High has brought a pet to the game. The pets that
    aren't here are a tarantula, a llama, an iguana, and a pig. The cheerleaders' names are Tori,
    Tom, Tad, Tish, and Tara. Their ages are 14, 15, 16, 17, and 18. Which cheerleader owns the
    poodle, and how old is she (or he)?

    Tad is 4 years older than Tara.
    Tish hates dogs and Tom hates pigs.
    Tom's mom won't allow a large pet.
    Tara owns the iguana.
    Tad is afraid of arachnids.
    Tori is older than Tom.
    Tara does not own the pig.
    Tori is allergic to dogs.
    Tish is 2 years younger than Tori.
    Tad is 1 year older than the tarantula owner.
    The pig owner is 3 years older than the llama owner.

    Answer: _____

2. The players here are Tyler, Craig, Ray, Sean, and Elijah. Their positions are fullback, quarter-
    back, center, guard, and tackle. What is the name and number of the quarterback?

    Elijah is not a tackle.
    Craig is on one end of the line.   The fullback is not Tyler.
    Ray is not # 4 or # 8.   The quarterback is between the guard and tackle.
    The guard is # 8.   Craig is next to Ray.
    Tyler is not the tackle.   # 2 is not Ray.
    The quarterback is not Ray.   Elijah is not next to Sean.
    The center is # 2.

    Answer: _____

CONFUSION AT THE FINISH LINE

Draw a diagram to help you solve each of these four logic problems. Each person in each race is mentioned.

1. Daryl and Jake are behind Raoul.
   Kai is faster than Guy.
   There are 2 runners ahead of Hank.
   There are 2 runners between Raoul and Jake.
   Guy is faster than Jake but slower than Hank.
   Hank is behind Kai.
   Jake is ahead of Daryl.

   Who wins the race?_____

2. Fran and Meghan are ahead of Patrice.
   Fran is behind Anya and ahead of Tonia.
   Carla is the second runner ahead of Fran.
   3 runners are between Tonia and Carla.
   Meghan is ahead of Fran but behind Anya.

   Who wins the race?_____

3. Josh is ahead of Wynn, but behind Gabe.
   There are 3 people between Gabe and Bryan.
   Andy is behind Josh.

   Who wins the race?_____

4. Tori is behind Tracy
   Trina is ahead of Tracy.
   Trish is ahead of Tori.
   Tori is the 4th runner behind Tami.

   Who wins the race? _____

Name

BOUNCE BACK

Draw a diagram or a picture to help you solve each of these problems.

1. As Jamey bounces on the trampoline, 11 coins totaling $1.37 fall out of his pocket.

   What are these coins? _____

2. He keeps bouncing and more coins bounce out of the other pocket. The total this time is $2.10 from 14 coins.

   What are the coins?_____

3. A group of kids are standing evenly spaced around a circular trampoline, watching the tricks of the trampolinist. Kid #11 is directly across from Kid #27.

   How many spectators are there around the trampoline? _____

4. The instructor is trying to divide a group of trampolinists into teams for a competition. If he puts them into groups of 2, 4, or 6, one is left over. If the groups have 7, none are left over.

   How many trampolinists are there? _____

5. Ryan is trying to walk across the length of a trampoline while Jude is bouncing. The trampoline is 27 feet long. Each step Ryan takes moves him forward 2.3 feet, but each time he moves, one of Jude's bounces sends him back .5 foot.

   How many steps will it take him to get across?_____

Name

CHANCE FOR A BULL'S-EYE

You may not be as sharp as Alonzo with an arrow, but you can probably help him solve some of these problems about percent and ratio. Round each problem to the nearest whole number.

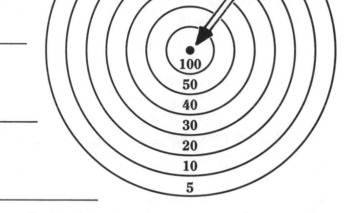

1. If Alonzo got 4 bull's-eyes out of 22 shots, what is his percentage of perfect shots? _____

2. He hit the wall 3 times out of 33 shots. What percent of all shots is this? _____

3. 40% of Alonzo's 55 shots today have been hitting the 50 ring. How many shots is this? _____

4. Alonzo's archer friend, Abigail, practices 7 out of every 10 days. How many days has she practiced in the last 10 weeks? _____

5. Today, Abigail has brought 12 sandwiches to share with friends at practice. Unfortunately, her pet mouse got into her backpack and ate parts of 5 of them. What percent of the sandwiches are still in good shape? _____

6. Alonzo's first practice round score is 165. If he shot 6 arrows, then he scored what percent of the total possible points for that round? _____

7. Each arrow costs $3.40, and Alonzo breaks 10% of all the arrows he buys. If he buys 150, how much money does he lose on broken arrows? _____

8. Abigail's high school has 2500 students. The girls' archery team has .6% of the school's students as members. How many members does the team have? _____

9. If Alonzo hits the 100 ring once, the 50 ring twice, the 40 three times, the 30 twice, and the 10 twice, what percent of the total points are provided by the arrows that have hit the 10 and 30 rings? _____

10. If the archery team gets a bull's-eye on 20% of their total shots today, and the number of bull's-eyes is 27, how many shots did they take all together? _____

Name _____

SPORTS STUFF ON SALE

The Giorgiano family went shopping before Tim, Tom, Tami, Terry, and Troy went off to sports camp. They found a great sale at the Super Duper Sports Center. Find the price they paid at each section of the store.

1. soccer shoes   89.50
    football cleats   63.96
    basketball shoes   89.99

    total   _____

    discount   _____

    sale price   _____

2. tennis shorts   32.00
    tennis shoes   66.85
    duffel bag   24.95
    (can) tennis balls   2.90

    total   _____

    discount   _____

    sale price   _____

3. aquasox   35.50
    swimsuit   30.00
    snorkel   24.85
    wet suit   177.00
    fins   55.00

    total   _____

    discount   _____

    sale price   _____

4. jogging shoes   79.95
    warm-up suit   126.00
    sweatbands   10.00
    stop watch   17.99

    total   _____

    discount   _____

    sale price   _____

5. helmet   34.45
    bike shorts   19.00
    gloves   18.00
    reflectors   2.50

    total   _____

    discount   _____

    sale price   _____

6. What is the total they saved? _____

Name _____

The BASIC/Not Boring Middle Grades Math Book   Copyright ©2000 by Incentive Publications, Inc., Nashville, TN.

TICKET TIE-UPS

Use the information on the chart to answer each question about discounted prices for these fans who are buying tickets to sports events.

TICKETS

Baseball Game	29.00 Adult
	18.00 Child
Tennis Match	16.00 All Tickets
Gymnastics Events	10.00 Semifinals
	30.00 Finals
Diving Finals	22.00 Adult
	10.00 Child
Fencing Finals	36.00 All Tickets
Volleyball Game	40.00 All Tickets
Golf Tournament	36.00 All Tickets
Swim Events	15.00 Adult
	12.00 Child
Track Events	19.00 1-Day Pass
	35.00 2-Day Pass

1. The Perez family bought tickets for 2 adults and 3 children to the diving finals and the gymnastic finals. They have a coupon for a 15% discount. How much will they pay? _____

2. The Johannes sisters, both children, have a coupon for a 10% discount on the 2-day track events and 20% off the baseball game and the swim events. How much will they pay if they go to all three? _____

3. Mrs. Switchalot gets a 35% discount for senior citizens. She wants to turn in her 2 tickets from the golf tournament and see the volleyball game and the fencing finals with a friend. If she pays for her friend's tickets as well as her own, how much more will she pay? _____

4. The whole Cue family reunion of 16 adults and 22 kids wants to see the diving finals. They qualify for a 40% group discount. How much will they pay? _____

Name _____

TICKET TIE-UPS, CONTINUED

5. Mrs. Shivers qualifies for a 25% discount as a member of the Friends of Spiders and other Arthropods Club. How much will it cost her to buy 4 child and 2 adult tickets to both gymnastics events if she uses her 25% discount coupon? _____

6. Ranch Dude Dan thinks the fencing competition is a bunch of cowboys putting up fences, and this he wants to see! How much will it cost for him and 7 ranch hands to go? _____

7. Which is a better price for the Achoo family of 2 kids and 2 adults: the fencing finals at 15% off, the swim events at 10% off, or 2-day track passes at 30% off? _____

8. Will Mr. Splash save more money if he gets 30% off both gymnastic events or 25% off the volleyball and golf tournaments? _____

9. The Lions Baseball League gets a 40% group discount. How much will they save when they buy tickets for 38 children and 20 adults to see the baseball game? _____

10. The tennis match and the volleyball game each have 5 seats left. If Ms. Courtside purchases them all at a 15% discount, how much money will the ticket center take in from her? _____

11. Mr. Cheapskate qualifies for the 15% miser's discount. Can he and his wife see both gymnastics events and the tennis match for under $100? _____

12. An old golf pro wants 22 tickets to the golf tournament. If he has a coupon for a 10% discount, can he get these tickets for under $700? _____

Name _____

THE VICTORY MEAL

The Panthers Basketball team is having a celebration meal after winning the big game against their rivals, the Coyotes. They're not thinking about it now, but the cost is adding up! Look at the bill for each player. Figure out how much each will spend by totaling the bill and adding a 6% tax and 15% tip. (Figure the tip on the food total only, not the total after tax is added.) What is the total bill for the team?

1. SARA

Nachos	4.00
Ham Sandwich	4.70
Choc. Shake	1.85

Subtotal _____

Tax _____

Tip _____

TOTAL _____

2. TARA

Egg Rolls	3.00
Rice Plate	3.50
Chow Mein	2.50
Iced Tea	1.00

Subtotal _____

Tax _____

Tip _____

TOTAL _____

3. KARA

Turkey Plate	6.00
Salad	3.25
Sundae	2.50

Subtotal _____

Tax _____

Tip _____

TOTAL _____

4. LARA

Pizza	7.00
Salad	3.25
Breadsticks	2.50
Cola	1.00

Subtotal _____

Tax _____

Tip _____

TOTAL _____

5. DARA

Cheese Sticks	1.65
Lasagna	6.50
Salad	3.25
Pie	1.50

Subtotal _____

Tax _____

Tip _____

TOTAL _____

6. COACH

Spaghetti	5.50
Garlic Bread	2.00
Salad	3.25
Iced Coffee	2.75

Subtotal _____

Tax _____

Tip _____

TOTAL _____

Name _____

7. TOTAL BILL = _____

DEEPWATER DEBT

Scuba Diver Scott bought all new equipment. He was not able to pay for it all at once, so he's making some monthly payments. The store is not charging interest. Fill in the blanks with the missing information about his payments.

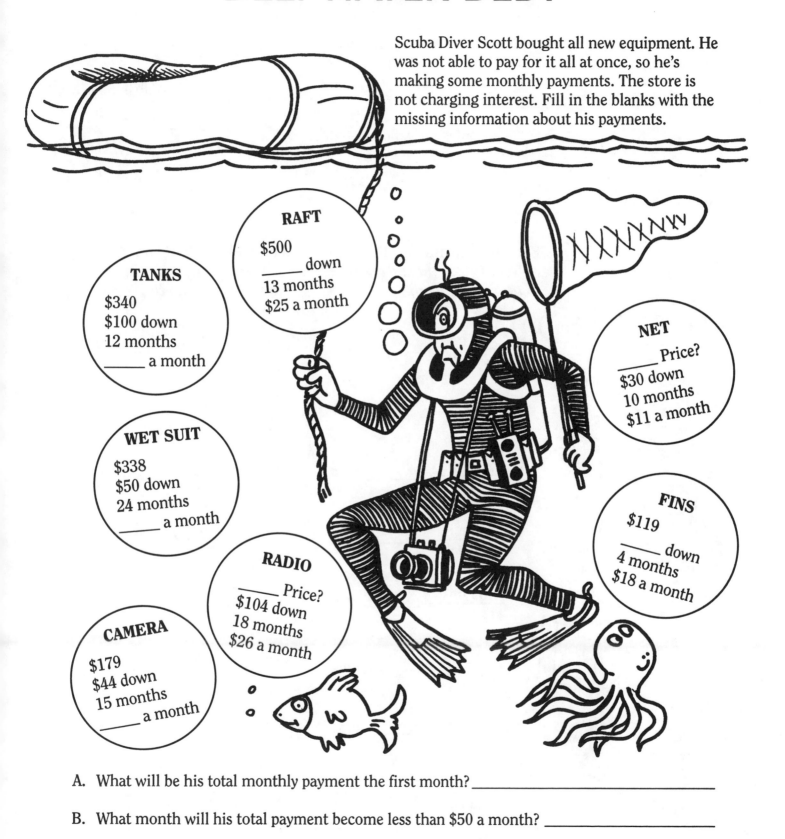

RAFT

$500
_____ down
13 months
$25 a month

TANKS

$340
$100 down
12 months
_____ a month

NET

_____ Price?
$30 down
10 months
$11 a month

WET SUIT

$338
$50 down
24 months
_____ a month

FINS

$119
_____ down
4 months
$18 a month

RADIO

_____ Price?
$104 down
18 months
$26 a month

CAMERA

$179
$44 down
15 months
_____ a month

A. What will be his total monthly payment the first month? _____

B. What month will his total payment become less than $50 a month? _____

Name

OUT OF GAS

The team has great batting averages, but Coach struck out at calculating his gas mileage for this trip. You can find out ahead of time what kind of mileage the van will get on their trips, or how much gas they'll need, by using these ratios:

$$\frac{\text{miles}}{\text{gas used}} = \text{_____ miles per gallon (mpg)}$$

$$\frac{\text{miles}}{\text{miles per gallon (mpg)}} = \text{_____ gas used (in gallons)}$$

For questions 1-8, find the gas mileage (mpg). *(Round answers to the nearest tenth.)*

For questions 9-16, find the amount of gas used. *(Round answers to the nearest tenth.)*

JUST KEEP ON TRUCKIN'!..

COACH

GAS

NEXT GAS 8 mi

1. $\frac{400 \text{ mi}}{20 \text{ gal}} = \text{_____ mpg}$

2. $\frac{420 \text{ mi}}{25 \text{ gal}} = \text{_____ mpg}$

3. $\frac{252 \text{ mi}}{16.4 \text{ gal}} = \text{_____ mpg}$

4. $\frac{310 \text{ mi}}{21.6 \text{ gal}} = \text{_____ mpg}$

5. $\frac{199 \text{ mi}}{12.5 \text{ gal}} = \text{_____ mpg}$

6. $\frac{100.2 \text{ mi}}{12.6 \text{ gal}} = \text{_____ mpg}$

7. $\frac{515.8 \text{ mi}}{28.2 \text{ gal}} = \text{_____ mpg}$

8. $\frac{287.9 \text{ mi}}{17.3 \text{ gal}} = \text{_____ mpg}$

9. $\frac{179 \text{ mi}}{10 \text{ mpg}} = \text{_____ gal}$

10. $\frac{226 \text{ mi}}{18.5 \text{ mpg}} = \text{_____ gal}$

11. $\frac{216 \text{ mi}}{22 \text{ mpg}} = \text{_____ gal}$

12. $\frac{344 \text{ mi}}{20.2 \text{ mpg}} = \text{_____ gal}$

13. $\frac{395 \text{ mi}}{23.1 \text{ mpg}} = \text{_____ gal}$

14. $\frac{133 \text{ mi}}{6 \text{ mpg}} = \text{_____ gal}$

15. $\frac{198 \text{ mi}}{12 \text{ mpg}} = \text{_____ gal}$

16. $\frac{395 \text{ mi}}{25 \text{ mpg}} = \text{_____ gal}$

Name

WHITE WATER CALCULATIONS

To find the rate at which Katarina Kayaker paddles on her practice sessions on different runs, use this ratio:

$$\text{rate in miles per hour (mph)} = \frac{\text{distance}}{\text{time}}$$

If you know the rate, but not the time, use this ratio:

$$\text{time} = \frac{\text{distance}}{\text{rate (mph)}}$$

Fill in the missing information on the chart. Round answers to the nearest tenth.

NAME of RUN	Distance	Time	Rate (mph)
1. Wallawalla River Run	4.8 mi	.4 hrs	_____ mph
2. Ripping Rapids	7.21 mi	.7 hrs	_____ mph
3. Pacific Ocean Edge	8.64 mi	1.1 hrs	_____ mph
4. Danger Drop Gorge	19.04 mi	1.6 hrs	_____ mph
5. Crazy Canyon Rapids	4.09 mi	.66 hrs	_____ mph
6. Watch-out Whirlpool	14.59 mi	.9 hrs	_____ mph
7. Lazy Current	12.25 mi	2.5 hrs	_____ mph
8. Twenty Falls River	29 mi	2.9 hrs	_____ mph
9. Broken Back Bend	7.44 mi	.8 hrs	_____ mph
10. Last Chance Gorge	14.08 mi	1.6 hrs	_____ mph
11. Eternity Run	24.84 mi	_____ hrs	6.9 mph
12. Snake River Scourge	6.16 mi	_____ hrs	8.8 mph
13. Never Never Rapids	8.33 mi	_____ hrs	11.1 mph
14. Big Wave Gorge	10.92 mi	_____ hrs	9.1 mph
15. Switchback River	19.92 mi	_____ hrs	8.3 mph

THEY CALL THIS THE PRACTICE RUN ?!?

LAST CHANCE GORGE

On what run does she have her fastest speed? _____

What run is the slowest? _____

Name _____

ON COURSE

At each of these courses, some information is missing. Find either the rate, time, or distance for each sport that has taken place there.

Remember that: <u>distance (d)</u> = <u>rate (r)</u> x <u>time (t)</u>

So: $r = d/t$ and $t = d/r$

MOUNTAIN CLIMBER

1. mountain climber

   13.5 mi

   _____ hr

   .5 mph

3. ski jumper

   3 mi

   _____ hr

   60 mph

2. skier

   _____ mi

   3.33 hrs

   7 mph

4. speed skater

   300 meters

   _____ min

   75 meters per min

SKI JUMP

SPEED SKATE RINK

BOBSLED TRACK

MOUNTAIN BIKE RACE COURSE

6. bobsled racer

   4.25 mi

   .05 hr

   _____ mph

5. powerboat pilot

   _____ mi

   .15 hr

   120 mph

POWERBOAT RACES

8. race car driver

   114 mi

   .6 hr

   _____ mph

7. mountain biker

   35 mi

   1.4 hr

   _____ mph

RACE CAR TRACK

Name

INJURY PROBLEMS

Boxer Bruno has gotten injured 4 out of every 5 times he's had a match. If he's fought in 320 matches, how many times has he been injured?

You can answer this question by using this proportion: $\frac{4}{5} = \frac{n}{320}$

Solve the proportion by cross multiplication:
5 times n = 4 times 320 (5 x n = 4 x 320 or 5n = 4 x 320).

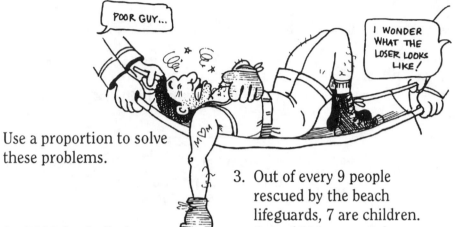

Use a proportion to solve these problems.

1. Of 20 football players surveyed, 12 were injured last season. There are 80 players in the school football program. At this rate, how many injuries were there?

_____

2. The cost of hospital visits for soccer team injuries averages $900 for the first 2 months of the season. At this rate, how much will injuries cost over the 5-month season?

_____

3. Out of every 9 people rescued by the beach lifeguards, 7 are children. Out of 504 rescues, how many are for children?

_____

4. Tennis player Tom lost 45 minutes over 3 games for a bloody nose. At this rate, how much time will be lost in 7 games?

_____

5. Out of every 7 members on the ski team, 2 quit before the end of the season because of injuries. If 28 quit because of injuries, how many started the season?

_____

6. The ratio of jumps to falls for ice skater Rhonda is 4 falls to every 15 jumps. At this rate, how many times will she NOT fall in 360 jumps?

_____

7. 350 out of 500 bike injuries in the state last year were head injuries. Of each 10 bike injuries, how many are to the head?

_____

8. The hurdlers on the Cougar team bang up their shins 35 times in 4 hours of practice. At this rate, how many shin injuries will there be in 300 hours of practice?

_____

Name _____

IT'S ABOUT TIME

A volleyball team from Minneapolis is on the road for several weeks. They're on a tight schedule, so they have to pay attention to their time. Solve their time problems for them. Remember to consider time zone changes in your calculations.

1. Leave Minneapolis (CT) for Portland, Maine, (ET) at noon on Sunday. Arrive at 1 P.M. on Monday. How long did they travel?

_____

2. Head out of Portland (ET) for Buffalo (ET) Monday at 7:30 P.M. for a 13-hour trip. Arrival time in Buffalo?

_____ Time _____ Day

3. Drive 14 hours from Buffalo (ET) to Chicago (CT). Arrive at 5:15 A.M. on Friday. When did they leave Buffalo?

_____ Time _____ Day

4. Travel from Chicago (CT), leaving after a party at midnight on Sunday. Arrive in Minneapolis (CT) for home game 8 hours later. Arrival time?

_____ Time _____ Day

5. Leave Minneapolis (CT) for Salt Lake City (MT) at 6 A.M. Wednesday. Travel 38 hours plus a 5-hour delay for bad weather. Arrival time?

_____ Time _____ Day

6. Fly from Salt Lake City (MT) to Calgary, Canada (MT). Plane leaves at 8:10 A.M. for a 1 hour 54 minute flight. Arrival time?

_____

7. Fly from Calgary (MT) to Anchorage, Alaska (AT), on a 2 hour 20 minute flight leaving at 11:49 A.M. Arrival time?

_____

8. Fly from Anchorage (AT) to meet bus in Seattle (PT). Flight departure, scheduled for 9:33 A.M. was delayed 1 hour 45 minutes. Flight is 2 hours 10 minutes long. Arrival time in Seattle?

_____

9. Drive from Seattle (PT) to Denver (MT). Arrive 6:05 P.M. Monday in Denver after a 22 hour 30 minute trip. When did they leave Seattle?

_____ Time _____ Day

10. Head home to Minneapolis (CT) from Denver (MT), leaving at 10:30 A.M. on Monday. Two 10-hour stops to sleep and eleven 30-minute stops for gas and food. The actual driving time is 26 hours. Arrival time home?

_____ Time _____ Day

Name _____

DROP-IN SOLUTIONS

Some problems are open-ended problems. They have more than one possible answer. Solve these open-ended problems about sports.

1. Find two different numbers that could show how many jumps the skydiving team took today. The number is a 2-digit odd number under 40. Both digits are odd. The sum of the digits is 10; their product is odd. Tell at least two different numbers of jumps the team could have made.

_____

2. While golfer Greg was searching for his ball, he found 24 coins totaling $2.40. Tell two different combinations of coins he might have found.

_____

_____

3. At the end of a good game, three bowlers each had scores above 250 and the fourth had a score of 225. The total of all 4 scores was 1110, and no bowler scored a perfect 300. Name two possible combinations of the bowlers' scores.

_____

_____

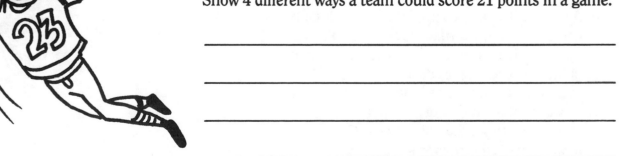

4. There are 5 ways a football team can score points:
   6 pts......(TD) Touchdown
   3 pts......(FG) Field Goal
   2 pts......(R) Run after a touchdown
   1 pts......(K) Kick after a touchdown
   2 pts......(S) Safety
Show 4 different ways a team could score 21 points in a game.

_____

_____

_____

_____

Name _____

SPEED DOESN'T COUNT

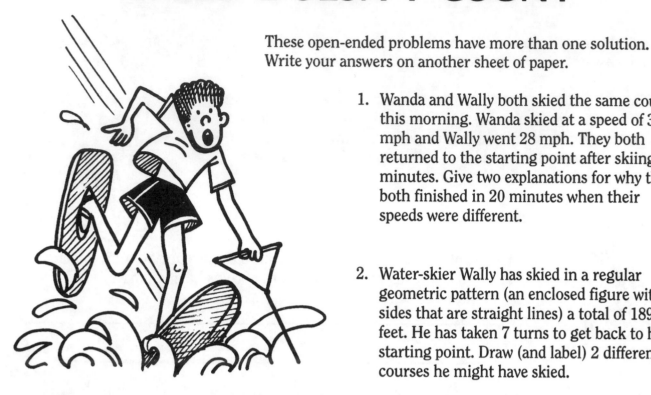

These open-ended problems have more than one solution. Write your answers on another sheet of paper.

1. Wanda and Wally both skied the same course this morning. Wanda skied at a speed of 35 mph and Wally went 28 mph. They both returned to the starting point after skiing 20 minutes. Give two explanations for why they both finished in 20 minutes when their speeds were different.

2. Water-skier Wally has skied in a regular geometric pattern (an enclosed figure with sides that are straight lines) a total of 1890 feet. He has taken 7 turns to get back to his starting point. Draw (and label) 2 different courses he might have skied.

3. Last week, skier Wally fell once more than half as much as Dan, who fell 3 times as often as Jen. Jen fell a number of times that has 2 even digits and is < 30. How many times did Wally fall? Give at least 2 different answers.

4. The gasoline tank on Dana's boat holds 26 gallons. Dana filled it up by carrying gas to her boat in a 3-gallon can and a 2-gallon can. Tell 3 different ways she could have filled her tank using these 2 cans to carry gas.

5. Ari, like all skiers, does a lot of bouncing across waves. Yesterday, he bounced a record number! The number of bounces is a 3-digit palindrome whose digits add up to 27. (A palindrome is a number that reads the same forwards and backwards.) All digits are < 7. How many times did Ari bounce? Give at least two possible answers.

Name

202

HORSING AROUND

For each problem, choose the problem-solving strategy that you think would be the best one to help you with the solution.

1. A jockey is 62 inches tall. Is this about 5 feet tall?

    a) Use mental math
    b) Draw a diagram
    c) Translate problem into a ratio

2. Each bale of hay in the barn is 2 cubic feet. The barn has 575 cubic feet of space. How many bales will fit in the barn?

    a) Use trial and error
    b) Make a number line
    c) Estimate

3. You know the times that 8 races begin and the lengths of each race. How will you set up a plan for 24 horses to race at different times?

    a) Translate into an equation
    b) Make a chart
    c) Use a formula

4. Horse C is ahead of Horse B who is 3 horses behind Horse F. Horse A is 2 horses ahead of Horse D, who is 2 horses ahead of Horse E. Which horse is closest to the finish line?

    a) Draw a diagram
    b) Use statistical data
    c) Use trial and error

5. Fresh Paint won 4 out of the last 13 races. At this rate, how many will he win in the next 65 races?

    a) Make a number line
    b) Estimate
    c) Translate into a proportion

6. You know the number of first place wins for 2 horses, Shooting Star and Record Breaker, for each of the past 10 years. You want to answer some questions about the comparison of their wins during these years.

    a) Write an equation
    b) Make a number line
    c) Make a graph

7. Heartbreaker runs for .15 hours and covers a distance of 4.95 miles. At what rate in miles per hour is he running?

    a) Translate into a ratio
    b) Trial and error
    c) Use mental math

8. 2500 spectators are seated in 6 stands. If 5 hold the same amount and the 6th holds 12 times that amount, how many spectators do the first 5 hold?

    a) Translate into a proportion
    b) Write an equation
    c) Estimate

Name

TO RIDE A WAVE

There are many strategies for solving problems. Sometimes one problem can be solved using more than one strategy. Choose a strategy that you think is best for each problem, and find the solution.

Trial and Error . . .
Write an Equation . . .
Make a Diagram . . .
Make a Chart . . .
Make a Graph . . .
Use Mental Math . . .
Estimate . . .
Use a Formula . . .
Make a Number Line . . .
Translate into a
Ratio or Proportion . . .
Guess and Check . . .

1. Hot Shot Surfer Stu catches 4 great waves every half hour. At this rate, how long will it be before he has ridden 44 waves?

   Answer: _____

2. Beach Bum Bonnie is 75 feet from the shore at 9 A.M. Every hour she moves forward 18 feet and is pulled backward 7 feet. What time will she reach the shore?

   Answer: _____

3. Two surfers, Al and Alison, have the same 2 digits in their ages, but the digits are reversed. $1/11^{th}$ of the sum of their ages is the square root of the differences between their ages plus 1. What are their ages?

   Answer: _____

Name _____

HEAVY MATH FOR STRONG MINDS

The answer is given for each of these weighty problems. But is it correct? Check each answer for accuracy. Use any method you choose. For each problem write YES or NO to tell whether it is accurate. If it is incorrect, find the right answer.

HUH?

OX

1. Ox is 6 times the weight of Tiny, yet Tiny can lift Ox even when he's holding 80 pounds. Tiny is holding up 410 pounds right now (Ox plus 80 lbs). How much does Tiny weigh?
55 lbs
Accurate? _____

2. The number of bones in a weight lifter's foot is 26. How many bones are there in the feet of 26 weight lifters?
676 bones
Accurate? _____

3. Ox, Puduka's Weight Lifting Champion, added 28 pounds to each side of his bar. Then, he took off two 10-pound weights from each side and added seven 3-pound weights to each side. He began with 73 pounds on each side. How much TOTAL weight is there on the bar now?
102 lbs
Accurate? _____

4. Ox puts spherical weights at the ends of his bar. They have a radius of 5.5 inches. What is the volume of each weight? (The formula for the volume of a sphere is $\frac{4}{3}\pi r^3$.)
696.6 in.³
Accurate? _____

5. Ox eats 3.7 lbs of pasta every day for 10 days before a competition. How much pasta would he eat if he had 3 competitions this month?
117 pounds
Accurate? _____

6. The weight lifting team of 5 members ate 80 tacos in 12 minutes. On the average, how many tacos did each member eat per minute?
1.3 tacos
Accurate? _____

7. Ox lifted 203 pounds this morning. Zorro lifted 174 pounds. Write a ratio, in lowest terms, that compares Ox's lift to Zorro's.
⁶/₇
Accurate? _____

8. At the end of every contest, Ox takes a walk around the mat 10 times. The mat is 30 x 40 feet. How far does he walk?
1200 feet
Accurate? _____

Name _____

YOUR FISH WAS HOW BIG?

Sometimes fishermen or fisherwomen (and other sports persons) stretch the truth about their accomplishments. For each of these sports tales, decide whether or not the answer is **reasonable.** If it is not, explain why.

YOU SHOULD HAVE SEEN THE ONE THAT GOT AWAY!

1. Fisherman Frank's fish weighed 2.2 pounds per foot. The scales showed a weight of 7.3 pounds. Frank claims his fish was 14.6 feet long. Is his claim reasonable? _____

2. Fisherman Frank is 40 years old. His son Frankie is 16. How many years ago was Frank 6 times as old as his son? Frankie calculates the answer to be 18 years. Is this reasonable? _____

3. Nicole's tennis balls have a radius of 1.25 inches. Her container for balls is a can 2.75 inches in diameter and 13 inches tall. She says her can holds 5 tennis balls. Is this reasonable? _____

4. Trixie the trampolinist bounces at a rate of 2 bounces every 6 seconds. At this rate, how long will it take her to bounce 3600 times? Trixie's answer is 20 minutes. Is this reasonable? _____

5. Brady bicyclist takes a ride one day at 25.4 mph for 8 hours. Wayne Walker takes a walk for the same amount of time at 3.5 mph. How many miles does each cover? Brady says he rides 203.2 miles and Wayne claims he walks 28 miles. Is this reasonable? _____

6. A volleyball tournament has 16 teams. A team is eliminated when they lose one game. Winners go on to play winners of other games. If 400 tickets are sold to each game, how many tickets will be sold for the tournament? Referee Rachael says 1000 tickets will be sold. Is this reasonable? _____

7. Pole-vaulter Paula leaps 2.1 times as far as her little sister Polly. Polly's highest leap is 5.8 feet. Paula claims her highest is 28 feet. Is this reasonable? _____

8. Cross-country skier Cassie skied at a pace of 3.8 mph for 4 hours and 6.3 mph for 22 hours one afternoon. She claims she skied a distance of 314.5 miles. Is this reasonable? _____

Name _____

206

PROBLEM SOLVING
ASSESSMENT AND ANSWER KEYS

PROBLEM-SOLVING
SKILLS TEST

Each answer is worth 2 points. Total possible score: 100 pts.

For questions 1–12, write the letter of the correct answer.
Use the picture below to answer questions 1-3.

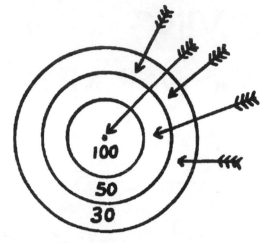

_____ 1. The total score received from these 5 arrows is:
   a. over 250   c. under 200
   b. exactly 210   d. exactly 240

_____ 2. The ratio that shows the number of arrows scoring 30 to the number scoring over 30 is:
   a. ⅗   c. ⅔
   b. 3/2   d. 5/3

_____ 3. If the next three arrows shot are 30, 30, and 100, what will be the average score for all the arrows shot?
   a. 50   c. 45
   b. 40   d. 80

_____ 4. Jana's pulse rate tripled during her morning run. Her resting pulse was 63. To find her pulse rate during her run, you should:
   a. add
   b. multiply
   c. multiply, then add
   d. divide

_____ 5. Sports drinks cost 75 cents a bottle. Each player on the volleyball team drinks 3 a game. There are 17 players. To find how much the team spends on drinks over 4 games, you would:
   a. multiply 4 times
   b. add, then multiply
   c. multiply twice
   d. multiply 3 times

_____ 6. A bowler knocked down an average of 6 pins in each frame. She bowled 30 frames every day for 10 days. A good problem-solving strategy for finding out how many pins she knocked down in 10 days would be:
   a. make a number line
   b. use mental math
   c. translate into a ratio
   d. draw a diagram

_____ 7. 4 pole vaulters line up in order of their height. Bob is taller than Bill and Bud. Brad is shorter than Bob and Bill. Brad is taller than Bud. To find out who is tallest, a good problem-solving strategy would be:
   a. make a graph
   b. estimate
   c. write an equation
   d. draw a diagram

_____ 8. 288 hot dogs were sold during the first 3 innings of the baseball game. 506 more were sold during innings 3–7. During the 7th inning stretch, they sold 390. Another 113 were sold during innings 8 and 9. A good estimate of the total sold would be:
   a. 1000   c. 1300
   b. 1100   d. 1200

Name _____

_____ 9. Hockey Team A has scored twice as many goals as Team B, who has scored 6 goals. Team C has scored 3 less than A and B together. Which equation represents the number of goals Team C has scored?
   a. $n = 2(6 + 3) - 3$
   b. $n = 6 + (6 \times 2) - 3$
   c. $n = 6 - (3 \times 2) + 6$
   d. $n = 2(6-3) + 6$

_____ 10. Zoie sold her wet suit to a friend for $146 and her snorkel and mask for $95 less. Then she bought a used suit for $90 and a used mask and snorkel for $26. Which equation shows how much money she still has?
   a. $n = 146 - 95 + 90 - 26$
   b. $n = 90 + 26 - 146 - 95$
   c. $n = 146 + 95 - 90 - 26$
   d. $n = 146 + (146 - 95) - 90 - 26$

_____ 11. Dr. Foil gave 16 physical exams to the fencing team members. Dr. Goal gave 3 less than twice as many to the soccer team. Which equation represents the number Dr. Goal gave?
   a. $n = (2 \times 16) - 3$
   b. $n = (2 \times 16) / 3$
   c. $n = 16 + (3 \times 2) - 3$
   d. $n = 16 - 3/2$

_____ 12. Chen Li had 3 more than twice as many injuries as Amy. Together the 2 had 18. Which equation shows this situation?
   a. $x + 2x - 3 = 18$
   b. $x + 3/2 = 18$
   c. $x + (2x + 3) = 18$
   d. $2x + 3 - x = 18$

For questions 13–50, write the correct answer on the line.

_____ 13. Estimate the answer to this problem: Hockey practice lasted 4 hours each day last week except for Friday and Saturday. On these days the team practiced 6 hours 45 minutes. There is no practice on Sunday. What was the average length of a practice?

_____ 14. 1658 football fans attended Friday's game. 152 left before half time. 823 sat in reserved seats. 82 fans left during halftime. 221 left during the 3rd and 4th quarters. What information is NOT needed to find out how many fans were left at the end of the game?

_____ 15. Tickets to the swim meet cost $8.50 for adults, $3.00 for children, $6.00 for senior citizens, and $ 5.00 for students. The total receipts for the game were $9670.00. What **missing** information do you need in order to find out how many students were at the game?

_____ 16. Carla does 161 pushups a week. She does 14 on Monday and 27 on Tuesday. What **missing** information do you need to find out the percent of the total she has finished by Thursday?

_____ 17. James scored 16 runs in 4 baseball games. He scored 4 in Game 1 and 3 less than twice as many in Game 2. He had 5 hits in Game 3 and scored 4 in Game 4. Which information is NOT needed to find out how many runs he scored in Game 2?

_____ 18. Natasha knocked down 2 out of 9 hurdles. At this rate, she figures she will knock down 24 out of the next 108. Is this accurate?

_____ 19. Springs on Yuri's trampoline cost $2.59 each, and he estimates that he can replace all 98 of them for under $250.00. Is he correct?

Name _____

The BASIC/Not Boring Middle Grades Math Book

_____ 20. A golfer hit a ball at 10:59 A.M. Eastern Standard Time across a state line into the Central Standard Time Zone. The ball was in the air for over 1 minute. He claims that it landed in the next time zone at 12:01 P.M. Central Standard Time. Is he correct?

_____ 21. Find two different solutions for the following problem: The number of dives James took today is a 2-digit prime number. The sum of the digits are = or < 10, and the difference is equal to or greater than 4. What number is it?

_____ 22. Find two different solutions for the following problem: Ty and Cy both slept more than 6 hours a night the 3 nights before the ski race. Ty slept a total of 8 hours more than Cy. Neither slept a total of more than 33 hours. How many hours did Ty sleep each night? (He slept the exact same number each night.)

Use the table to solve problems 23–26.

CONFERENCE 2-YEAR WIN-LOSS RECORD			
	Wins	_Losses_	_Ties_
Panthers	4	16	0
Grizzlies	20	0	0
Rams	15	3	2
Cougars	1	19	0
Kings	8	12	0
Cyclones	10	8	2

23. What team had the second best win–loss record? _____

24. How many teams had a worse record than the Kings? _____

25. What was the total number of games played by the Cougars in the 2-year period? _____

26. How many games did the Cyclones **not** win over the 2-year period? _____

27. Brie exercises her horse by running him around a ring which has a radius of 11 feet. If the horse completes this circle 127 times, how far does he run? _____

28. Two friends need 50 square feet of blanket to wrap them up and keep them warm at a football game. They have a blanket that is 5 feet long and 4½ feet wide. Is it big enough? _____

Use the graph to solve problems 29-31.

SKI TEAM TRYOUTS

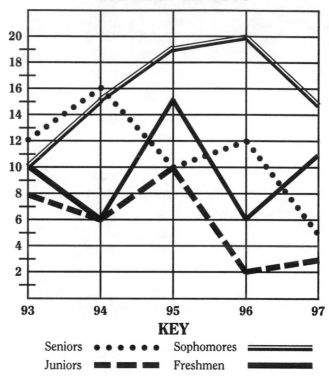

KEY

Seniors	• • • • •	Sophomores	══════
Juniors	▬ ▬ ▬ ▬	Freshmen	▬▬▬▬

29. Which class has the greatest increase in tryouts over a 2-year period? _____

30. Which classes had the same number of tryouts in 1995? _____

31. Which class has consistently had the lowest number of tryouts over the 5-year period? _____

32. Surfer Samantha has caught a ride on 3 out of the last 32 waves. At this rate, how many rides will she get out of the next 192 waves? _____

33. The Coast Tennis Training Camp accepts 4 out of 7 kids who apply. If 56 are accepted, how many applied? _____

Name _____

34. In a motorcycle race, Jed drives 242 miles in 2.75 hours. What is his speed? _____

35. Paula's powerboat goes 283.5 miles on 5 gallons. What kind of mileage is she getting? _____

36. Sue's soccer game ran long because of an overtime and a shoot-out. The game started at 1:45 P.M. and ended at 4:03 P.M. How long did the game last? _____

37. Thomas is catching up on his sleep after a tournament in Europe. He wakes at 6:30 A.M. on Thursday. He went to sleep at 11:11 P.M. on Tuesday. How long ago was that? _____

38. Marta has 7 hours and 13 minutes left to practice and rest before she takes her skating test. It is now 8:55 A.M. What time is her test? _____

39. 3 skateboarders are ages 12, 14, and 17. One has a brand-new board, one has an old beat-up board, and one uses a borrowed board. Jody is not 17. The owner of the old board is younger than Jen. Jo is older than Jody. The 12-year-old has the new board. The old board owner is not 17. Which skater has the used board? _____

40. 4 basketball teams compare the heights of their players. The Tigers are taller than the Panthers. The Vikings are shorter than the Chargers and the Tigers. The Panthers are shorter than the Vikings. The Tigers are taller than the Chargers. Which team has the tallest players? _____

41. Jan bought 3 videotapes of the surfing contest. They cost $16 each, plus 8% tax. How much did she pay? _____

42. Ski calendars that are regularly priced at $18 are on sale for 25% off. How much would Tori pay for 7 calendars? _____

43. Team A ate 12% less pasta than Team B. Team B ate 22 pounds. How much did Team A eat? _____

44. 40% of all the first-time sky divers who take lessons at the Take-a-Leap Sky Diving School get cold feet and don't jump. They had 510 first-time students last year. At this rate, how many jumped? _____

45. Attendance at the second district track meet was 1,925. The first meet's attendance was 76% of that. How many attended the first meet? _____

46. 730 fans came to see the Blue Ridge County Equestrian competition. 20% of them traveled about 100 miles to get there. 60% of them only traveled about 5 miles. The rest traveled about 30 miles. About how many miles did all the fans travel? _____

47. The wrestling team uses 12 bars of soap each time they shower. They have had 6 practices and 2 meets a week this season. They shower after each of these. How many bars of soap has the team used in a 13-week season? _____

48. Heptathlon Camp for junior athletes began on Wednesday, August 21, at noon. It ended 143 hours later. When was that? (Day, date, time?) _____

49. Anika paid $860 for gold-coated skates. They last for about 125 days of skating. She skates 6 days a week. How much will skates cost her a year? _____

50. The cross-country ski team burns up 228,000 calories in 3 races. There are 20 team members. Assuming each person burns the same amount in each race, how many calories does each member burn in each race? _____

SCORE: Total Points _____ out of a possible 100 points

Name _____

PROBLEM SOLVING
SKILLS TEST ANSWER KEY

Give 2 points to each correct answer. Total possible score is 100 points.

1. d
2. b
3. a
4. b
5. d
6. b
7. d
8. c
9. b
10. d
11. a
12. c
13. about 5 hours
14. 823 sat in reserved seats
15. the number of adults, children, and senior citizens who attended
16. the number of pushups Carla did on Wednesday and Thursday
17. 5 hits in Game 3 and the score of 4 runs in Game 4
18. yes
19. no
20. no
21. Give 1 point each for any two of these answers: 17, 19, 37, 61, 71, 73, 91
22. Give 1 point each for any two answers which are greater than 6 hours and equal to or less than 8.33 hours.
23. Rams

24. 2
25. 20
26. 10
27. 8773.16 feet
28. no
29. sophomore class
30. junior and senior classes
31. junior class
32. 18 rides
33. 98 applied
34. 88 miles per hour (mph)
35. 56.7 miles per gallon (mpg)
36. 2 hours 18 minutes
37. 31 hours 19 minutes
38. 4:08 P.M.
39. Jen
40. Tigers
41. $51.84
42. $94.50
43. 19.36 pounds
44. 306 jumped (204 did not)
45. 1463 attended
46. 21,170 miles
47. 1248 bars of soap
48. Tuesday, August 27, at 11:00 A.M.
49. $2580.00 spent in a year
50. 3800 calories per person per race

The BASIC/Not Boring Middle Grades Math Book   Copyright ©2000 by Incentive Publications, Inc., Nashville, TN.

ANSWERS

pages 168–169

1. a .... Answer: 20 races
2. a, b .... Answer: $264
3. a, b, c .... Answer: 21 hrs, 50 min
4. b, d .... Answer: $16/52$ (or $4/13$ in lowest terms)
5. a, b, c .... Answer: Week 5
6. b, c .... Answer: 3111 calories
7. a, c .... Answer: 600 fans
8. b, c .... Answer: 40%
9. d, e .... Answer: 16.4 meters
10. a, b, c ...... Answer: 889, 600 ft²

page 170

1. the number of his medals
   the number of competitor's medals
2. the depth of the pool
3. the number of times she practices each dive
4. the total number of towels
5. Maria's highest dive
6. the score of the 6th judge
7. the depth of the pool
8. dates of the titles
   or the number earned at the '84 Olympics and after
9. the team average

page 171

1. • left home at 11 A.M.
   • returned at 2:30 P.M.
   • pulse was 145 bpm
   Answer: 4.57 mph

2. • left home at 9:18 A.M.
   • ran 2.6 miles to Sam's
   Answer: 5.8 miles

3. • 6 vegetarian
   • 4 plain
   • 2 pepperoni
   Answer: $12/18$ or $2/3$

4. • best time for 10 k 55 minutes
   • ran .16 k per minute
   Answer: 1 hr 4 min

5. • winner was 36 years old
   • average age was 28
   Answer: 285

6. • spent $60
   Answer: $840

page 172

1. 0	7. 22	13. 10
2. 39	8. 26	14. 7
3. 20	9. 2	15. 30
4. 4	10. 0	16. 40
5. 1	11. 22	17. 0
6. 2	12. 0	18. 0

page 173

1. multiply
   Answer: $1800
2. multiply, add
   Answer: Tropic Jet, $885
3. multiply, add, subtract
   Answer: $40
4. multiply
   Answer: no
5. multiply, add
   Answer: Jamaica on Paradise Air
6. multiply, add
   Answer: Bermuda on Tropic Jet

page 174

1. $7.12
2. Mon-Fri, 8 A.M.-5 P.M.
3. $10.90
4. $5.53
5. $44.18, more
6. 15 minutes
7. girlfriend
8. $ 19.57
9. 43 minutes
10. 21 minutes

page 176

1. Queenie
2. 13
3. Queenie
4. Sophia
5. Queenie
6. 95
7. 90-91-92
8. Sophia
9. 1992
10. Sophia
11. 1994
12. Sophia

7. • went to 12 meets
   • spent $490
   Answer: 719 miles

8. • uniforms cost $55
   Answer: 216 pieces

page 177

1. Wagon Wheel Rodeo
   Batty Baseball Field
2. 1000
3. Basketville Basketball Gym
4. 12,000
5. about 6500
6. 7000
7. Dragtona Dog Race Track
8. about 12,000

page 178

1. Salt Lake City
2. about 700 miles
3. about 1500 miles
4. I-40 W to Knoxville and I-81 N to New York, about 1100 miles
5. San Antonio, Phoenix, or Oklahoma City
6. about 1200 miles
7. Boston
8. no, I-90 E to I-25, I-25 S to I-40 and I-40 E to Oklahoma City

page 179

1. 19
2. 82
3. $19/82$
4. 30.8%
5. Game 8
6. Games 5 and 8
7. 63
8. Games 1, 2, 3
9. 14
10. 112
11. $14/112$ or $1/8$
12. 71
13. 89%
14. 16
15. Games 1, 5, 7
16. Game 3

page 180

1. 188.4 ft
2. 1230 ft
3. 1404 ft²
4. 1140 ft
5. 256 ft²
6. 87.9 ft
7. 153.9 ft²
8. 6672 ft²
9. 360 ft
10. 216 ft²

page 181

1. 450
2. 232
3. 165
4. $^2/_{19}$
5. 1 hr, 26 min (or 86 min)
6. 75 beats per min
7. 310 min
8. $ 24.00
9. 11
10. 4 times
11. 44 meters
12. 32 back stretches
13. Friday
14. 42 minutes

page 182

Answers will be approximate. Give credit for anything close to amount below.

Sam Surf	$ 5.00
Hot-Shot Sally	$ 5.50
Dare Devil Darla	$ 5.50
Fearless Fred	$ 5.00
Mad Dog Maria	$ 9.00
Cool Cal	$ 4.00
Jack Snack	$ 7.00
No Way Jose	$ 8.50
Big Wave Will	$ 5.00
Beach Bum Bea	$ 5.00
Speedo Sara	$ 8.00
Never-Lose Ned	$ 5.50
Refill Ron	$ 5.00

page 183

1. Equation: a Solution: 72 times
2. Equation: c Solution: 27¼ hrs
3. Equation: b Solution: 18 members
4. Equation: b Solution: 3.3 min.
5. Equation: a Solution: 15 medals
6. Equation: b Solution: 22

page 184

Equations students write may differ slightly from these answers, but must include the same elements.

1. $n = 17,964 - 880 - 1000$
   Answer: 16,084

2. $n = 3(44) - 8$
   Answer: 124

3. $26 = 4n - 6$
   Answer: 8

4. $n = 42(12) - 12$
   Answer: 492

5. $n = 12.00 - 4(.75) - 3(1.00) + 6(.25) - 3.45$
   Answer: $ 4.05

6. $n = \dfrac{1087 - 34}{13}$
   Answer: 81

page 185

Day 1	32
Day 2	6
Day 3	7
Day 4	33
Day 5	15
Day 6	64
Day 7	30
Day 8	9
Day 9	12
Day 10	111

page 186

1. Day 37
2. 15
3. Yes
4. Day 20

page 187

1. Tom–poodle–16
   Order: Tara–iguana–14, Tish–llama–15, Tom–poodle–16, Tori–tarantula–17, Tad–pig–18
2. #3 QB Tyler
   Order: #8 Guard Elijah, #3 QB Tyler, #4 Tackle Sean, #17 Full-back Ray, #2 Center Craig

page 188

Answers in bold print.
1. **Kai**, Raoul, Hank, Guy, Jake, Daryl
2. **Anya**, Carla, Meghan, Fran, Patrice, Tonia
3. Gabe, Josh, **Wynn**, Andy, Bryan
4. Tami, Trina, Tracy, Trish, **Tori**

page 189

1. 3 quarters, 6 dimes, 2 pennies
2. 5 quarters, 8 dimes, 1 nickel or 7 quarters and 7 nickels
3. 32 kids
4. 49 trampolinists
5. 15 steps

page 190

1. 18%
2. 9%
3. 22 shots
4. 49 days
5. 58%
6. 27.5%
7. $ 51.00
8. 15 members
9. 20%
10. 135 shots

page 191

1. $ 243.45, $ 48.69, $ 194.76
2. $ 126.70, $ 63.35, $ 63.35
3. $ 322.35, $96.71, $ 225.64
4. $ 233.94, $23.39, $ 210.55
5. $ 73.95, $ 11.09, $ 62.86
6. $ 243.23

pages 192–193

1. $ 190.40
2. $ 111.00
3. $ 52.00
4. $ 343.20
5. $ 180.00
6. $ 288.00
7. swim events
8. volleyball and golf
9. $ 505.60
10. $ 238.00
11. yes
12. no

page 194

1.	Sara	$ 12.76
2.	Tara	$ 12.10
3.	Kara	$ 14.22
4.	Lara	$ 16.64
5.	Dara	$ 15.61
6.	Coach	$ 16.34
7.	Total	$ 87.67

page 195

Raft	$ 175 down
Tanks	$ 20 a month
Wet Suit	$ 12 a month
Radio	$ 572 price
Camera	$ 9 a month
Net	$ 140 price
Fins	$ 47 down

A. $ 121.00 a month
B. month 14

page 196

1. 20 mpg
2. 16.8 mpg
3. 15.4 mpg
4. 14.4 mpg
5. 15.9 mpg
6. 8 mpg
7. 18.3 mpg
8. 16.6 mpg
9. 17.9 gal
10. 12.2 gal
11. 9.8 gal
12. 17 gal
13. 17.1 gal
14. 22.2 gal
15. 16.5 gal
16. 15.8 gal

page 197

1. 12 mph
2. 10.3 mph
3. 7.9 mph
4. 11.9 mph
5. 6.2 mph
6. 16.2 mph
7. 4.9 mph
8. 10 mph
9. 9.3 mph
10. 8.8 mph
11. 3.6 hrs
12. .7 hrs
13. .75 hrs
14. 1.2 hrs
15. 2.4 hrs

Fastest: Watch-out Whirlpool
Slowest: Lazy Current

page 198

1. 27 hours
2. 23.31 miles
3. .05 hours
4. 4 minutes
5. 18 miles
6. 85 mph
7. 25 mph
8. 190 mph

page 199

1. 48
2. $ 2250
3. 392
4. 105 minutes (or 1 hr, 45 min)
5. 98
6. 264
7. 7
8. 2625

page 200

1. 24 hours
2. 8:30 A.M. on Tuesday
3. 4:15 P.M. on Thursday
4. 8:00 A.M. on Monday
5. 12:00 A.M. on Friday
6. 10:04 A.M.
7. 12:09 P.M.
8. 2:28 P.M.
9. 7:35 P.M. on Sunday
10. 3:00 P.M. on Wednesday

page 201

Answers will vary. Students are to give 2 answers for each problem. Give credit to students for any workable solution.

page 202

Answers will vary. Students are to give 2 answers for each problem. Give credit to students for any workable solution.

page 203

1. a
2. c
3. b
4. a
5. c
6. c
7. a
8. b

page 204

Students should show that they have chosen and used a specific problem-solving strategy for each of these.
1. 5.5 hours
2. about 3-4 P.M.
3. ages 12 and 21
(other possible solutions)

page 205

1. yes
2. no, There are 1352 bones in **2 feet** each of 26 persons
3. no, 204 pounds
4. yes
5. no, 111 pounds
6. yes
7. no, ⅙
8. no, 1400 feet

page 206

Students will be explaining why they do not find answers reasonable. Accept any sensible explanation for their decisions.
1. no
2. no
3. yes
4. no
5. yes
6. no
7. no
8. no

GRAPHING, STATISTICS, & PROBABILITY

Skills Exercises

ROLLER BLADE JUMP SCORES				
TRIXIE	7	4	0	2
PIXIE	6	5	7	6
KATE	10	9	9	7
MAY	6	7	2	8
JUMP:	1	2	3	4

SKILLS CHECKLIST FOR GRAPHING, STATISTICS, & PROBABILITY

✔	SKILL	PAGE(S)
	Construct a frequency table from statistical data	218–219
	Read & interpret tables of statistics	218–225, 236, 239–241
	Read & interpret frequency graphs (histograms)	220
	Construct a frequency graph from statistical data	221, 222
	Analyze data to find range and mean	224
	Analyze data to find median and mode	225
	Read & interpret a line graph	226, 229, 232, 242
	Read & interpret a bar graph	227, 230, 234, 235, 237, 238
	Construct a line graph from statistical data	228
	Read, interpret, & construct a circle graph	229
	Construct a bar graph from statistical data	230
	Read & interpret a scattergram	231
	Read & interpret a multiple line graph	232
	Construct a multiple line graph from statistical data	233
	Read & interpret a double bar graph	234
	Construct a double bar graph	235
	Make interpretations & draw conclusions from data	236, 237
	Solve problems from statistics shown on a graph	238, 242
	Solve problems from statistical tables	239–241
	Describe possible outcomes of events	243–250, 253–255, 257, 258
	Identify events; find probability of an event	244–250, 253–258
	Describe all the possible outcomes of two events	246–249
	Use tree diagrams to show possible outcomes of two actions	248, 249
	Use the counting principle to find possible outcomes	250
	Describe the permutations of sets	251
	Identify possible combinations of sets within a larger set	252
	Find the probability of independent events	253, 254
	Find the probability of dependent events	255
	Find the odds in favor or against the occurrence of an event	256
	Use probability concepts and calculations to solve problems	257
	Use random samplings to make probability predictions	258

GOING TO EXTREMES

Welcome to the Extreme Sports Event of the year!

Athletes are arriving to register for the competition. The box below shows data for the first 50 people in line to show which sport each one is here to enjoy. The data is in the form of letters, which are codes for different sports.

Finish the Frequency Table to show how many athletes in this group are registering for each of the sports.

EXTREME DATA

SPCL	SPCL	HGGD
AILS	AILS	BNGY
BNGY	HGGD	WSRF
WSRF	SPCL	BNGY
BCYS	WKBD	SKYS
HGGD	SKBD	AILS
SKBD	SKYS	JTSK
BFJP	WSRF	BNGY
JTSK	SPCL	AILS
WKBD	SKYS	SKYS
WKBD	JTSK	AILS
BFJP	HGGD	BNGY
SKBD	BNGY	JTSK
BNGY	WKBD	AILS
SKBD	WSRF	JTSK
JTSK	SKBD	BCYS
WKBD	JTSK	STLG

FREQUENCY TABLE
Sports Participation

SPORT	CODE	TALLY	FREQUENCY
jet skiers	JTSK		
windsurfers	WSRF		
aggressive in-line skaters	AILS		
barefoot waterski jumpers	BFJP		
bicycle stunt riders	BCYS		
skateboarders	SKBD		
street lugers	STLG		
hang gliders	HGGD		
skysurfers	SKYS		
wakeboarders	WKBD		
sport climbers	SPCL		
bungee jumpers	BNGJ		

Name

GOING TO EXTREMES, CONT.

The athletes at this year's competition come from all over the United States. The data shows the home state for each of the competitors. Use the data to complete the Frequency Table to show how many athletes live in each state represented.

FREQUENCY TABLE
Home States of Competitors

State	Tally	Number	State	Tally	Number
AK			MN		
AL			MO		
AR			MT		
AZ			NC		
CA			NJ		
CO			NM		
FL			NY		
GA			OR		
HI			SC		
ID			TX		
LA			WA		
ME			UT		
MI			VT		

EXTREME DATA

OR	WA	TX	AZ
ME	TX	UT	OR
CA	HI	CO	CO
MT	OR	HI	MT
ID	CA	ME	CO
CO	HI	CO	LA
CA	WA	CA	WA
HI	MT	CO	AK
GA	AL	AR	AL
WA	AK	HI	ID
CO	CA	ME	CO
HI	AK	HI	WA
ID	OR	NM	ME
MT	ID	HI	CA
CA	HI	MT	UT
SC	VT	NC	MI
MI	NY	SC	VT
HI	MT	UT	FL
CO	OR	HI	HI
WA	HI	CA	AK
AK	OR	AK	CO
CA	TX	WA	HI
CO	MT	CA	FL
FL	OR	HI	FL
NJ	CO	HI	CA
WA	CO	CA	NM
FL	HI	UT	MN
VT	ID	WA	CA
CA	AK	AK	AK
HI	HI	HI	CA
MO	CA	ID	CO
OR	CO	CA	MT

Name

WINTER EXTREMES

Competitors have been braving extreme weather conditions (blizzards, winds, and cold temperatures) to win medals in extreme winter sports. There is an extreme difference in the ages of the athletes this year.

Use the data on the histogram (frequency graph) to find out about their ages.

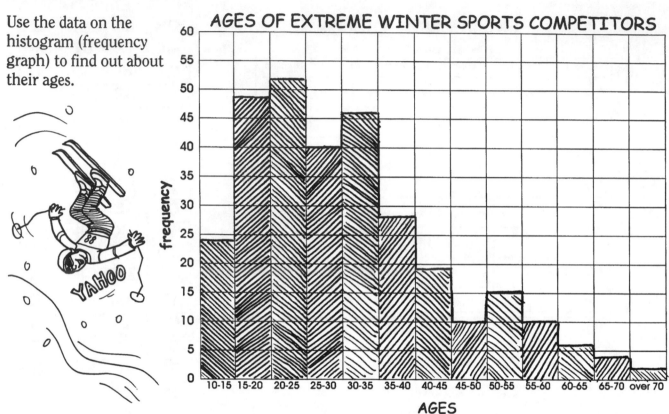

AGES OF EXTREME WINTER SPORTS COMPETITORS

1. Which age group has 19?_____

2. Which age group has 6?_____

3. Which age group has 28?_____

4. Which age group has 46 ?_____

5. Which age group has the most?_____

6. About 25 are in the _____ age group.

7. About 35 are _____ or older.

8. About how many are 60 or older?_____

9. About how many are aged 10-20?_____

10. Which has about 20 less than the 30-35-year old group?_____

11. Which groups have less than the 45-50 year old group?_____

12. Which two groups have the same number?

_____

13. Which 10-year age span has about 30 competitors?_____

14. Which group has about the same as the 10-15 age group?_____

15. Which has about seven times as many competitors as the 60-65 year old group?

_____

16. Does the 35-40-year old age group have more than any younger groups?_____

Name _____

WINTER EXTREMES, CONT.

Some of the athletes have traveled long distances in the cold, winter weather to get to the Extreme Winter Competition. The Tally Sheet shows the travel frequencies.

Use this data to finish the frequency chart. For each mileage category on the graph, color a vertical bar to show the number of athletes traveling those distances.
Use a different color for each bar.

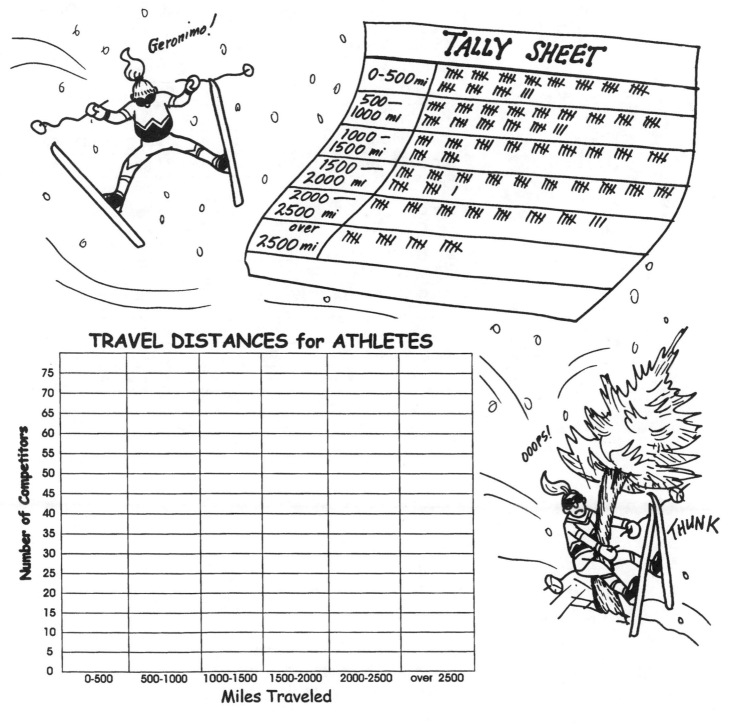

Name

RECORD-SETTING ADVENTURES

It seems that people with a competitive spirit will go to any lengths to set (or break) a record! Here are some adventures where challengers set records for throwing, moving, jumping, driving, or spitting something the farthest.

FAR-OUT ADVENTURES

Description of the Farthest.....	Record-Setting Distance
Egg Toss (without breaking the egg)	223 feet, 2 inches
Boot Throw	209 feet, 9 inches
Flying Disc Throw	656 feet, 2 inches
Cow Pie Throw	266 feet
Spear Throw	848 feet, 6 ½ inches
Grape Throw (caught in the mouth)	327 feet, 6 inches
Crawl	870 miles
Dance	23 miles, 385 yards
Cricket Spitting (Yes! People actually spit dead crickets in competition!)	32 feet, ½ inch
Ramp Jump in a Car	232 feet
Jump on a Motorcycle	251 feet
Underwater Dive (while holding breath)	925 feet
Underwater Dive (using equipment)	35,797 feet
Dive from a Diving Board	176 feet

1. Which went farther: the cow pie or the spear? _____

2. Which went farther: the egg or the grape? _____

3. Which went farther: the flying disc or the spear? _____

4. How much farther did the egg travel than the boot? _____

5. How much farther was the spear thrown than the boot? _____

6. How much farther did the motorcycle jump than the car? _____

7. How much farther did the crawler travel than the dancer? _____

8. Which went about 450 feet farther than the cow pie? _____

9. Which went about 75 feet farther than the diving board diver? _____

10. How much farther did the underwater diver with the
    equipment descend than the diver holding his breath did? _____

Name _____

AN EXTREMELY WET EVENT

Is it possible to complete a white-water rafting race without getting wet? These teams certainly took plenty of spills during the 5-day Wild Water Competition. The table shows the statistics for the number of tips and spills for each team. Use the tables to answer the questions below.

WHITE WATER RAFTING COMPETITION
UPSIDE-DOWN SPILLS

Team	# of Spills				
	Mon	Tue	Wed	Thur	Fri
Splashin' Six	20	19	5	0	3
White-Water Wizards	11	13	15	17	18
River Racers	7	1	1	0	2
Speed Demons	18	18	12	12	4
The Wet Ones	9	6	7	0	5
River Rats	5	9	2	6	1
The Untouchables	5	8	14	11	10
Floating Phantoms	5	15	19	19	7
The Rapids Racers	0	6	0	7	0
The Unsinkables	3	3	3	3	3
The Water Diggers	12	4	6	0	3
Kings of the Rapids	0	0	5	1	6

Find the total spills for:

1. The Splashin' Six _____

2. The White-Water Wizards _____

3. The River Racers _____

4. The Speed Demons _____

5. The Wet Ones_____

6. The River Rats _____

7. The Untouchables _____

8. The Floating Phantoms _____

9. The Rapids Racers _____

10. The Unsinkables_____

11. The Water Diggers _____

12. The Kings_____

13. Monday_____

14. Wednesday _____

15. Friday_____

16. Who had the most days with no spills? _____

17. Who had the fewest (total) spills?_____

18. Who had the most spills?_____

19. Which team had the same number each day? _____

20. Which day was the worst for spills?_____

21. Which day was the best for spills?(fewest spills)_____

22. Which team had more spills every day than the day before? _____

Name _____

FLIPS, TRICKS, & FLAT TIRES

In the BMX (bicycle motorcross) categories, nothing is quite as exciting as the freestyle and ramp riding competitions. Courageous bikers do wild tricks in the air: like spins, flips, rotations, wheelies, and hops. All that action can be hard on tires. Just look at how many went flat during this year's events!

Biker's Name	A.J. Ryder	J.R. Crash	Tom Elite	Gabe McTrick	Angie deWheel	B.J. Wynn	Z.Z. Tops	Flip Skyler
Number of Flat Tires	13	6	14	21	18	3	6	7

1. What is the range of the set of data? (Range is the difference between the least and greatest numbers.)

   _____

2. What is the mean of the set of data? (Mean is the sum of the data divided by the number of items.)

   _____

3. These are the numbers of quarts of water drunk by the different bikers: 7, 2, 4, 3, 5, 3, 6, 2.

   What is the range? _____

   What is the mean? _____

4. These are the weights of the bikers: 95 lb, 120 lb, 90 lb, 125 lb, 140 lb, 110 lb, 90 lb, 102 lb

   What is the range? _____

   What is the mean? _____

5. These are the numbers of falls the different bikers endured: 14, 5, 16, 14, 7, 1, 0, 9

   What is the range? _____

   What is the mean? _____

6. These are the numbers of injuries to the 8 different bikers: 16, 16, 22, 20, 15, 15, 32, 16

   What is the range? _____

   What is the mean? _____

Name

THE STRANGEST GAMES OF ALL

You might call this the Weird and Wacky Olympics! Competitors have gathered to join in contests and races of the strangest sort. The table gives data about the numbers of competitors in each event for five years of competitions.

Follow the directions to find the median (the middle number in a set of data) and the mode (the number that appears most frequently in a set of data) for the data given.

Numbers of Competitors, 1996-2000
The "Strange Games" Events

Sporting Event	1996	1997	1998	1999	2000
Sausage Eating	27	14	9	12	4
Alligator Wrestling	11	27	21	20	29
Bed Racing	18	30	18	20	32
Bathtub Racing	16	27	40	13	14
Ladder Climbing	15	33	6	20	10
Hair Cutting	21	16	21	20	9
Hand Sprinting	5	7	7	6	23
Pancake Tossing	11	15	21	2	9
Leapfrog Jumping	6	7	7	11	16
Egg Eating	10	9	15	15	9
Coconut Tree Climbing	11	4	21	20	11
Median					
Mode					

Finish the table by writing the median and mode for each year (each column).

1. Look at these scores from the egg-eating competition:

   14   26   12   22   15   18   9   20   6

   What is the median? _____

2. Look at these distances for the pancake toss:

   54 ft   36 ft   52 ft   29 ft   50 ft   44 ft   56 ft   47 ft   39 ft   26 ft   36 ft   36 ft

   What is the mode? _____

3. Look at these heights of coconut trees:

   7½ m   12 m   8½ m   10 m   14½ m   13m   17m

   What is the median? _____

4. Look at these weights of bathtubs used in the races:

   102 lb   98 lb   77 lb   101 lb   104 lb   77 lb   150 lb   116 lb   99 lb   115 lb   97 lb

   Circle the median. Draw a box around the mode.

Name _____

THE HUMAN SPIDER

Who, besides a spider, could possibly climb a building that is several hundred feet tall? Some pretty adventurous climbers try such ventures often!

Scaling buildings is another extreme idea for fun. Read the graph to find and learn about the heights of ten different buildings Spider Samson climbed last year.

1. Spider climbed the 348-meter T & C Tower in Taiwan in the month of _____ .

2. In July, he climbed the Shanghai World Finance Center, a height of _____ .

3. In _____ , he traveled to Thailand to climb the 319-meter Baiyoke II Tower.

4. South Africa's Carlton Center, which is _____ high, was an easy climb for Spider in March.

5. In the month of _____ , Spider reached the 381-meter top of the Empire State Building in New York City.

6. The Petronas Tower in Malaysia, climbed in June, is about _____ high.

7. Spider climbed the 347-meter John Hancock Center in Chicago in _____ .

8. In _____ and _____ , Spider climbed two Australian Towers: the 214-meter Chifley Tower and the 242-meter Rialto Tower.

9. In January and November, Spider climbed a church tower in his home town. It is _____ high.

Spider's Heights

Meters — 500, 400, 300, 200, 100

Jan Feb Mar Apr May Jun Jly Aug Sep Oct Nov

Name _____

SURFING AT EXTREME HEIGHTS

Can you imagine riding a surfboard through the sky? What an idea! Skysurfers ride the wind, doing awesome tricks while they freefall from a plane. They can ride and fall for several thousand feet before opening a parachute. It may sound scary, but at least there are no sharks to worry about!

Nine different surfers jumped from a plane at 9500 feet. They each surfed while falling a distance through the air. The graph shows the number of vertical feet each one used for surfing before opening the parachute.

1. Sal's drop was about _____ feet.

2. Sly's drop was about _____ feet.

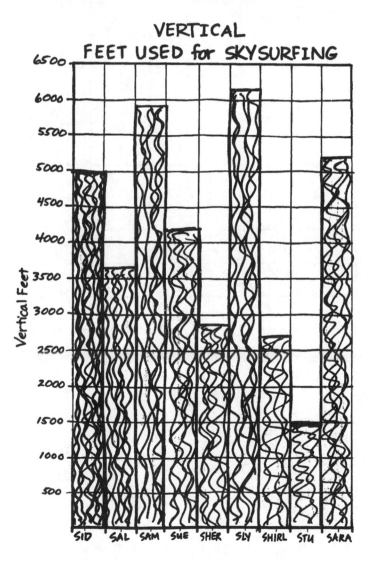

VERTICAL FEET USED for SKYSURFING

Vertical Feet: 6500, 6000, 5500, 5000, 4500, 4000, 3500, 3000, 2500, 2000, 1500, 1000, 500

SID SAL SAM SUE SHER SLY SHIRL STU SARA

3. Who used more distance than Sara?
   _____

4. How many surfers used less distance than Sue?
   _____

5. Who surfed for 4250 feet?
   _____

6. Who used about 2700 feet to surf?
   _____

7. How many vertical feet did Sid use?
   _____

8. Who used about 5950 feet to surf?
   _____

9. How many less feet did Stu use than Sid? _____

10. Who used about 200 feet less than Sher? _____

11. Who surfed for a 5200-foot drop?
    _____

12. Whose drop was about 4500 feet greater than Stu's?
    _____

Name _____

SINKING TO EXTREME DEPTHS

Exploring shipwrecks is a favorite adventure for many scuba divers. Some of them will go to great depths to snoop around in ghostly, sunken ships.

The Data Table shows the depths of 12 different dives. Show the depths by completing the line graph. Finish labeling the intervals for feet measurements. Plot each data item. Then, draw the line to show the depths of the dives over a 12-day period.

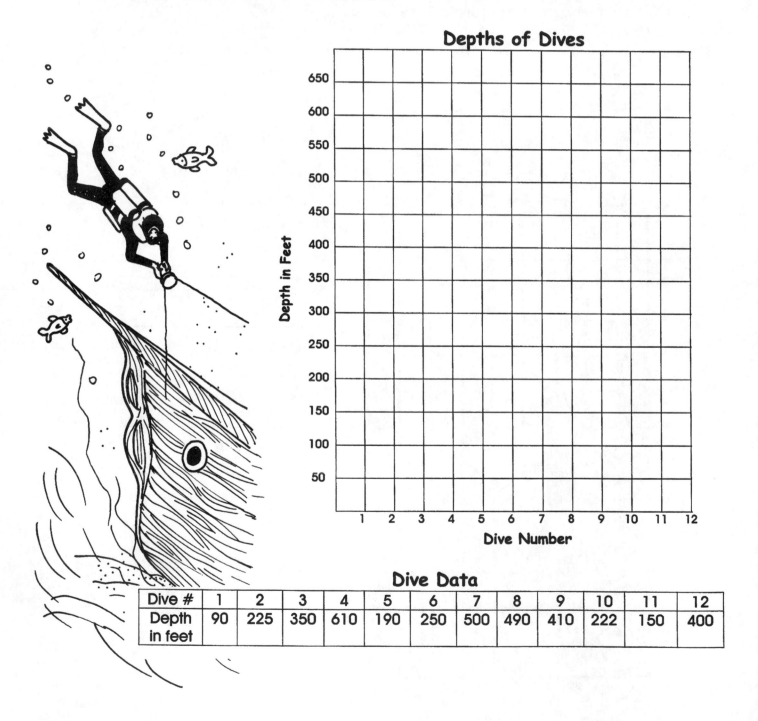

Depths of Dives

Dive Number

Dive Data

Dive #	1	2	3	4	5	6	7	8	9	10	11	12
Depth in feet	90	225	350	610	190	250	500	490	410	222	150	400

Name _____

SCUBA ECONOMICS

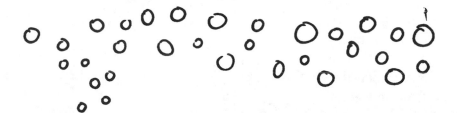

Before you start your scuba diving lessons, you probably should stop by the bank. Like many sports, scuba diving is expensive. Get a look at some of the prices Samantha paid for her equipment. Use the data beside the surfer to complete the circle graph. The graph will show how the $2600 she spent was used.

Look at the price for each piece of clothing or equipment. Decide which piece of the graph represents that amount. Write the name and price of the item in the correct circle wedge. Color each wedge a different color.

HOOD $50.

SNORKEL $50.

REGULATOR $300.

MASK $200.

TANKS $600.

GLOVES $50.

GAUGES $400.

KNIFE $100.

WET SUIT $800.

BOOTS $50.

FINS $100.

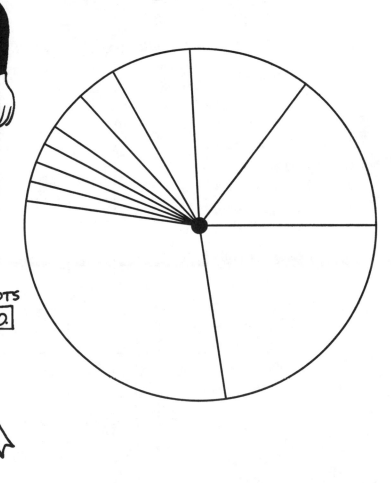

Name _____

BUMPS, BRUISES, OLLIES, & McTWISTS

Ollies, McTwists, fakies, iguana flips, tail grabs, back scratchers, nose roles, slob airs . . . these are some of the tricks snowboarders are doing as they sail up ramps and over jumps. Needless to say, they get a lot of injuries as they flip, turn, and crash!

The table shows data about the different injuries a team suffered during a recent season of competition. Use the data to finish the graph. Color a bar on the graph to show the correct number for each type of injury.

INJURIES

Kind of Injury	Number
Broken Legs	1
Broken Arms	2
Broken Feet	3
Broken Wrists or Fingers	6
Broken Noses	3
Broken Teeth	17
Sprained Ankles	5
Sprained Wrists or Fingers	28
Pulled Ligaments	23
Back Injuries	12
Head Injuries	5
Shoulder Injuries	25
Serious Cuts	32
Bloody Noses	26
Frostbite Cases	13
Serious Sunburn	22

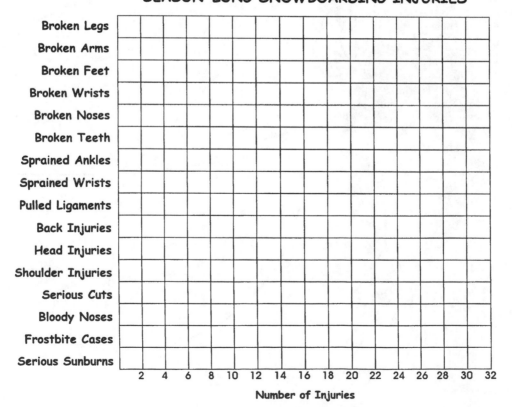

SEASON-LONG SNOWBOARDING INJURIES

Number of Injuries

Name

A SPORT WITH TEETH

Can this possibly be fun . . . wrestling a scaly reptile with snapping jaws and sharp teeth? Some people must think it is, because they wrestle alligators for sport.

This scattergram gives some information about how often alligators bit the contestants at the Great Gatorama Grappling Contest. Since a scattergram shows the relationship between two quantities, you'll see that the number of bites is related to the size of each gator. Use the information from the graph to answer the questions.

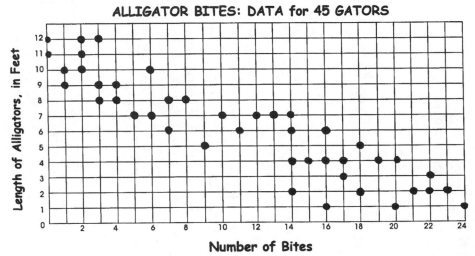

ALLIGATOR BITES: DATA for 45 GATORS

Length of Alligators, in Feet

Number of Bites

1. How many gators were 4 feet long? _____

2. How many gators were less than 4 feet long? _____

3. How many gators were 7 feet long? _____

4. How many gators were more than 8 feet long? _____

5. How long was the gator that bit 9 times? _____

6. How long was the gator that bit 24 times? _____

7. How long was the gator that bit 12 times? _____

8. Did a 3-foot gator bite less than 10 times? _____

9. Did a 6-foot gator bite 6 times? _____

10. Did a 10-foot gator bite more than 5 times? _____

11. What were the most times a 9-foot gator took a bite? _____

12. What lengths were the gators that did not bite at all? _____

13. What was the total number of bites from the 9-foot gators? _____

14. What was the least number of times a 2-foot gator took a bite? _____

15. Circle the statements which are true (according to the data):

   a. In general, the smaller gators bit more.

   b. In general, the larger alligators bit more.

   c. The length of the gator had no relationship to the number of bites.

   d. There were more gators 1–8 feet long than 9–12 feet long.

   e. There were more 4-foot long gators than any other size.

   f. In general, the larger alligators bit less.

   g. The 11 and 12-foot long alligators did not bite at all.

Name _____

NO WATER SKIS ALLOWED

No skis are needed at this waterskiing competition. The competitors ski and jump on their bare feet. The graph shows the jump scores for ten different jumps for each of four barefoot skiers. How well did they do?

1. Which skier had the most consistent scores?

   _____

2. Which skier had the greatest drop in score between 2 jumps in a row?

   _____

3. Which skier had the greatest rise in score between 2 jumps in a row?

   _____

4. Which skier probably won this competition? _____

5. Which skier scored below 12 most often?

   _____

6. Which skier made the best recovery from a drop in scores? _____

7. Do Nicole's 10 scores average above 14?

   _____

8. Did the majority of Brandy's scores fall above or below 12.0? _____

9. Between which 2 dives did Jennifer make the most improvement?

   _____

10. Between which 2 dives did Amanda make the most improvement?

    _____

11. Who had the third best score on the 9th dive?

    _____

12. Which skier received the score of 14.8 twice and 14.0 three times?

    _____

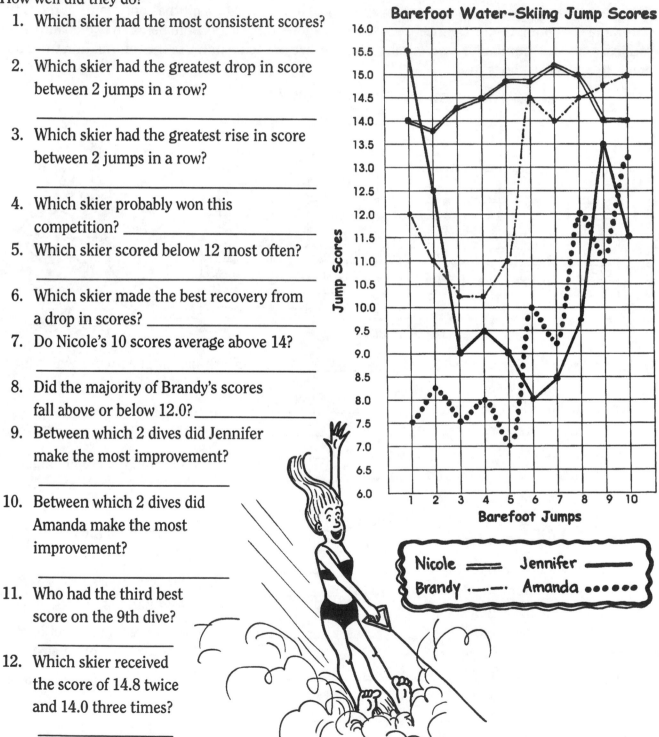

Barefoot Water-Skiing Jump Scores

Jump Scores vs. Barefoot Jumps

Nicole ═══ Jennifer ────
Brandy ─·─·─ Amanda ••••••

Name

EXTREME RISKS

Along with the thrill of most extreme sports comes a high risk factor. In all the sports, athletes use good equipment and follow rules to keep safe, but accidents are always a possibility. And when the sport takes place high up in the air above the ground, the accidents or injuries can be even more scary!

Three teams of friends from different sports kept track of the injuries each year over a 10-year period. The table shows the results of their count. Use this data to finish the line graph. Plot the amounts for each team for each year. Use the correct color of dots for each sport. Connect the dots with the line of the same color.

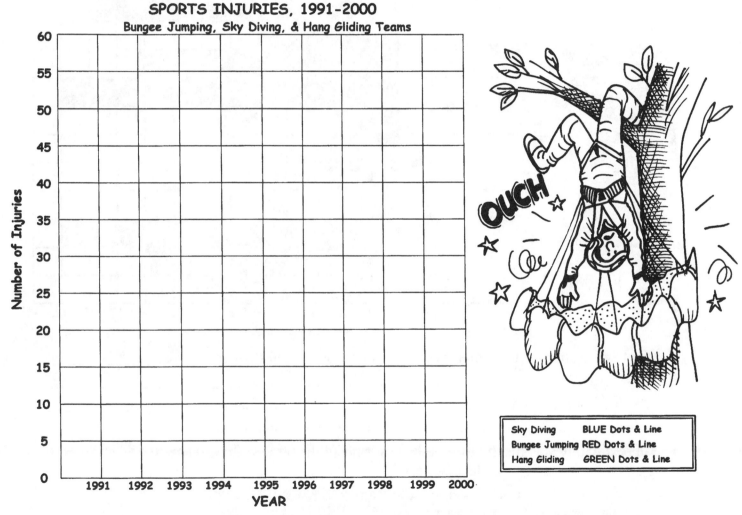

SPORTS INJURIES, 1991-2000
Bungee Jumping, Sky Diving, & Hang Gliding Teams

Sky Diving   BLUE Dots & Line
Bungee Jumping RED Dots & Line
Hang Gliding   GREEN Dots & Line

Sport	Color for line	1991	1992	1993	1994	1995	1996	1997	1998	1999	2000
Sky Diving	blue	33	44	44	56	47	54	58	28	25	20
Bungee Jumping	red	8	4	18	12	30	38	45	50	43	37
Hang Gliding	green	20	26	19	38	55	59	60	56	60	60

Name

NO SLEEPING ALLOWED

Don't try to take a nap in any of these beds. They're being used for one of the world's most unusual sports . . . bed racing! Today's race is one mile long. The graph shows the record time for a 1-mile race for each team entering today. Also shown is each team's amount of experience at bed racing.

Use the data on the graph to answer the questions.

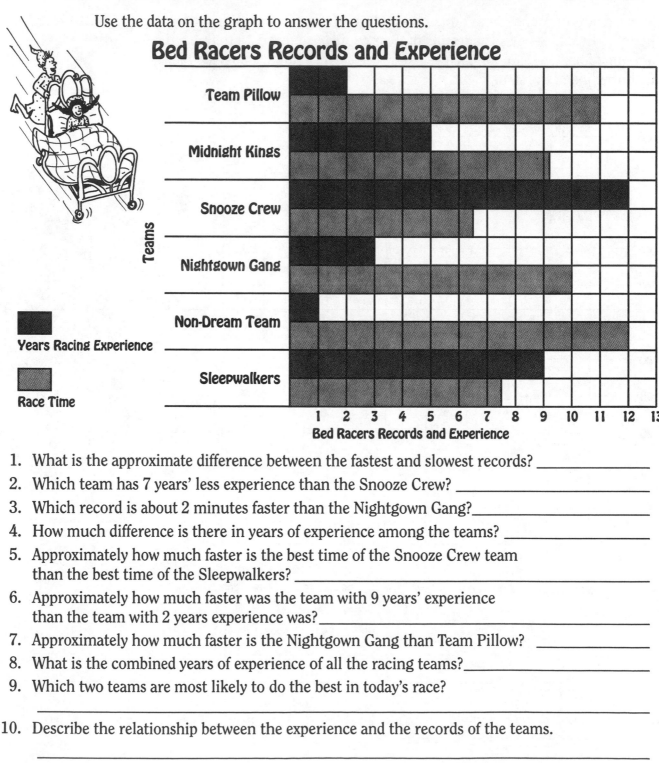

Bed Racers Records and Experience

Teams: Team Pillow, Midnight Kings, Snooze Crew, Nightgown Gang, Non-Dream Team, Sleepwalkers

■ Years Racing Experience
▨ Race Time

Bed Racers Records and Experience

1. What is the approximate difference between the fastest and slowest records? _____

2. Which team has 7 years' less experience than the Snooze Crew? _____

3. Which record is about 2 minutes faster than the Nightgown Gang? _____

4. How much difference is there in years of experience among the teams? _____

5. Approximately how much faster is the best time of the Snooze Crew team than the best time of the Sleepwalkers? _____

6. Approximately how much faster was the team with 9 years' experience than the team with 2 years experience was? _____

7. Approximately how much faster is the Nightgown Gang than Team Pillow? _____

8. What is the combined years of experience of all the racing teams? _____

9. Which two teams are most likely to do the best in today's race?

_____

10. Describe the relationship between the experience and the records of the teams.

_____

Name

ICY CLIMBING

You can find adventuresome people climbing frozen surfaces all over the world. The ice-climbing competition is a "hot" event at the Extreme Winter Games, too.

An ice climber can win medals for climbing speed or for difficulty. The table below shows some data for five ice-climbing friends. Use the data on the table to finish the graph. For each climber, color a green bar (on the left) to show the number of medals won for climbing speed, and a yellow bar (on the right) to show the number of medals won for climbing difficulty.

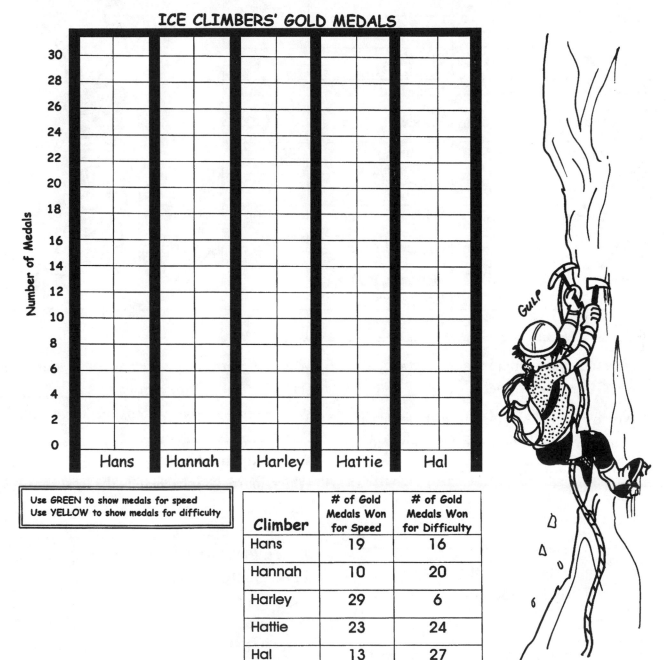

ICE CLIMBERS' GOLD MEDALS

Number of Medals

Hans   Hannah   Harley   Hattie   Hal

Use **GREEN** to show medals for speed
Use **YELLOW** to show medals for difficulty

Climber	# of Gold Medals Won for Speed	# of Gold Medals Won for Difficulty
Hans	19	16
Hannah	10	20
Harley	29	6
Hattie	23	24
Hal	13	27

Name

EXTREME JOURNEYS

A journey can be taken in many ways . . . on foot, by sled, on stilts, on hands and knees, in a wheelchair, on skates . . . or even just walking on hands. Here are statistics about some records set for the most unusual journeys. These distances are almost unbelievable! Use the data to answer the questions.

RECORDS for EXTREME JOURNEYS
(According to 1999 Guinness Book of World Records, Rounded to the nearest mile)

Journey	Distance in Miles	Journey	Distance in Miles
Taxi	21,691	Polar Sled	3,750
Motorcycle	457,000	Bicycle	226,800
Snowmobile	10,252	Backwards Walk	8,000
Lawn Mower	3,366	Backwards Run	3,100
Wheelchair	24,903	Hitchhike	501,750
Unicycle	2,361	Stilt Walk	3,008
Walk on Hands	870	Walk on Water	3,502
Leapfrog	996	Parachute Fall	6
Skates	19,000	Unicycle, riding backwards	53
Crawling	870	Dancing	23

870 mi

1. How much farther did the motorcycle travel than the bicycle? _____

2. Which record is the longest distance for a journey that did not involve a motorized vehicle? _____

3. How much further did the backwards walker travel than the backwards runner? _____

4. How much shorter was the dancer's journey than the crawler's? _____

5. Which record surprises you most? _____

   Why? _____

6. Which appears to be more difficult: a journey on skates, or walking on your hands? _____

7. Which journey probably took the longest time? _____

   Why do you think so? _____

8. Which journey probably took the least time? _____

   Why do you think so? _____

9. What is the difference between the record times for the frontwards and backwards unicycle rides? _____

10. From what the data tells you, does it appear to be easier to travel while crawling or dancing? _____

Name _____

RIDING THE WAKE

Stay awake when you're riding the wake! An exciting new sport, called wakeboarding takes advantage of the thrill of riding the crest of water created behind a motor boat. Wakeboarders use the power of the wake to do all kinds of fancy tricks.

Walter is practicing his wakeboarding tricks. He wants to do 30 of each in good form this week. How is he doing so far? Use the information on the graph to answer the questions.

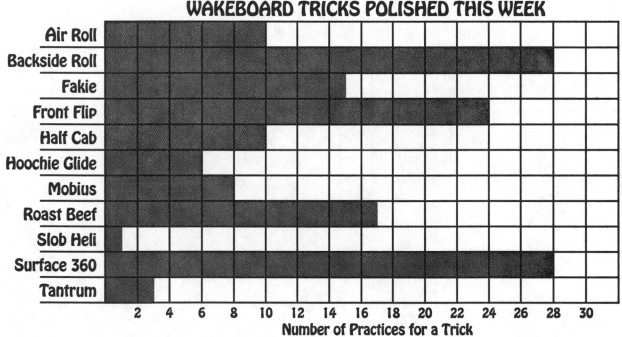

WAKEBOARD TRICKS POLISHED THIS WEEK

Number of Practices for a Trick

Yahoo!

1. How many good front flips does Walter have left to do this week to reach his goal? _____
2. How many more good roast beefs does Walter need? _____
3. How many more half cabs has he done than hoochie glides? _____
4. How many more backside rolls has he done than air rolls? _____
5. How many more good tantrums is he working for this week? _____
6. How many more front flips has he done than roast beefs? _____
7. Does Walter seem to be doing well at polishing his surface 360s? _____
8. How many more times does he need a good practice of a mobius to meet his goal? _____
9. Which appears to be harder for Walter, the fakie or the half cab? _____
10. Which trick seems to be giving Walter the most trouble in his work to complete 30 good samples of each? _____
11. It is Tuesday night. If he continues accomplishing his goals at the same rate as he has since Sunday, will Walter have all his 30 good roast beefs by Saturday night? _____
12. Will he have 30 good half cabs by Saturday night, continuing at this pace? _____

Name _____

EXTREME THRILLS

Bungee Jumping is perhaps the wildest thrill of all the sports! Brave people of all ages leap off high places, attached only by a stretchy, bouncy cord that lets them fall, then bounces them back and forth for a while. More and more adventuresome folks are trying group bungee jumping . . . leaping while grouped together with many other jumpers.

The graph shows data which compares ages of some bungee jumpers to the number of jumps they've taken in the past year. Use the data to solve the problems.

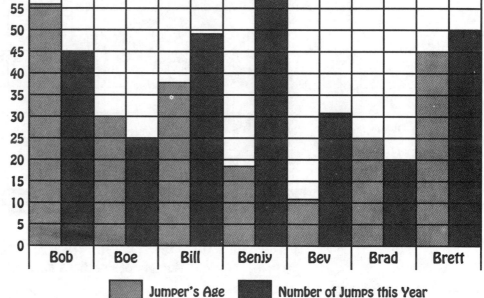

BUNGEE JUMPERS: JUMPS & AGES

1. What is the difference in age between the oldest and youngest jumpers?

    _____

2. What is the difference between the greatest and least number of jumps? _____

3. For which jumpers is this statement true? **A (age of jumper) > N (number of jumps)**

    _____

    _____

4. Is this statement true? **The youngest 2 jumpers together did more jumps than the oldest 2 jumpers.** _____

5. The 56-year old did how many more jumps than the 25-year old? _____

6. The 11-year old did how many more jumps than the 25-year old? _____

7. In the following statement, who is x and who is y *(x and y stand for the number of jumps)*?
    x − y = 19
    x = _____ **y =** _____

8. In the following statement, who is x and who is y *(x and y stand for the number of jumps)*?
    3y = x
    x = _____ **y =** _____

9. In the following statement, who is a and who is b *(a and b stand for the ages)*?
    b = 2 a + 6
    a = _____ **b =** _____

10. What is the average age of the jumpers *(round to nearest whole number)*? _____

Name _____

EXTREMELY HIGH WALKING

It is a very long way down from the place where this extreme activity takes place. Tightrope walkers spend years practicing their art high above the ground. Some walkers go to great heights without any sort of safety net at all.

The table shows the records for a group of tightrope-walking friends. Notice that the record height and the record length (distance) is included for each of twelve tightrope walkers.

Use the data to solve the problems below.

Records for Tightrope Walks
Mile High County Tightrope Club

Tightrope Walker	Record Height of Wire (in feet)	Record Length of Walk (in feet)
Francine	430	48
Flossie	610	45
Frankie	225	30
Frenchie	80	55
Phillipe	610	35
Flo	390	72
Phyllis	850	29
Flip	1000	120
Fran	305	85
Phoebe	700	29
Frank	903	68
Fred	275	72

1. How much higher has Frank performed than Frankie?_____

2. How much longer a distance did Flo walk than Flossie? _____

3. Who walked about twice the distance as Phillipe? _____

4. Who walked about one-fourth the distance as Flip?_____

5. Whose record height was twice as high as Fran's?_____

6. Who performed at a height 513 feet higher than Flo? _____

7. Who has performed almost twice as high as Francine? _____

8. What is the difference between Phillipe's record for height and Flossie's? _____

9. How much higher has Fred performed than Frenchie?_____

10. Who performed at a height 150 feet higher than Phoebe?_____

11. How many club members have performed at greater heights than Francine? _____

12. How much difference is there between the longest and the shortest of the records for length of walk? _____

13. How much difference is there between the greatest and the least records for height of wire?_____

14. If a new performer successfully walks 81 feet across a wire, how many records of other club members will this exceed? _____

Name _____

LONG HOURS & STEEP DROPS

The highest rollercoaster in the United States is Superman, The Escape, at Six Flags Magic Mountain in California. There is a 415 foot distance between its base and its highest peak.

Marco and several friends have caught "rollercoaster fever." They love the thrill of those steep drops—over and over. They compete with each other for rollercoaster-riding records, riding different coasters for as long as they can at one time. (They stop to sleep occasionally.) The table shows the lengths of times different riders spent on different coasters. Use the data to solve the problems on the next page.

ROLLERCOASTER RIDES

Name of Coaster	Location of Rollercoaster	Length of Ride (Hours)
Silver Bullet	Oklahoma City, OK	18
The Cannonball	Gulf Shores, AL	73
Shockwave	Gurnee, IL	29
Twisted Sisters	Louisville, KY	52
Red Devil	Maggie Valley, NC	23
Big Bad Wolf	Williamsburg, VA	44
Desert Storm	Phoenix, AZ	66
Desperado	Primm, NV	50
Batman, The Ride	Atlanta, GA	20
Black Widow	Agawam, MA	110
Top Gun	Santa Clara, CA	83
Steel Phantom	West Mifflin, PA	55
Mean Streak	Sandusky, OH	70
Swamp Fox	Myrtle Beach, SC	31
Tidal Wave	Ocean City, MD	52
Colossal Fire Dragon	Farmington, UT	93
Great American Scream Machine	Jackson, NJ	88
The Outlaw	Des Moines, IA	39
Texas Twister	Houston, TX	52
Mind Eraser	Denver, CO	7

Name

LONG HOURS & STEEP DROPS, CONT.

1. Marco rode in Arizona and Alabama. What was his total time on these rides? _____

2. Mei Chen rode one coaster for 110 hours. In what state did she ride? _____

3. How much longer was Marco's ride on Top Gun than on Big Bad Wolf? _____

4. Joe rode in Utah and Georgia last week. How long did he ride? _____

5. How much longer was the longest ride than the shortest ride? _____

6. How many hours were ridden all together by Marco and his friends? _____

7. Marco's favorite ride was for 83 hours. What state was this in? _____

8. Which ride was twice as long as the ride on the Steel Phantom? _____

9. Which ride was about ⅓ as long as the ride on the Colossal Fire Dragon? _____

10. How much shorter was the Outlaw ride than the Steel Phantom ride? _____

11. Pete rode these three coasters in one week: Mind Eraser, Swamp Fox, and Shockwave.

    How long did he ride that week? _____

12. Angelo rode Silver Bullet and Desperado.

    Maria rode the Mean Streak. Whose riding time was longer? _____

    How much longer? _____

13. Which coaster was ridden half as long as the ride on Great American Scream Machine?

    _____

14. Brianna rode in Kentucky, Pennsylvania, and Maryland.
    Pete rode in South Carolina, Illinois, and Texas. Who rode longer? _____

15. Which three coasters were ridden the same amount of time? _____

    What was the total of the hours ridden on these three? _____

16. Which coaster was ridden 16 hours longer than the Red Devil? _____

Name _____

LONG-JUMPING MOTORCYCLES

In 1997, Fiona Beale, of Derby, England, jumped 190 feet, 2 inches over 12 trucks. She was riding a Kawasaki KX500 when she became the new record-holder for the longest distance jumped by a woman on a motorcycle.

Motorcycle jumping is a thrill for the rider, and a thrill for spectators, too. Four thrill-seeking competitors (B. J., J. J., R. J., and P. J.) showed their expertise by challenging each other to a week-long jumping contest. The graph shows the number of cars each challenger jumped every day for five days. Use the graph to solve the problems.

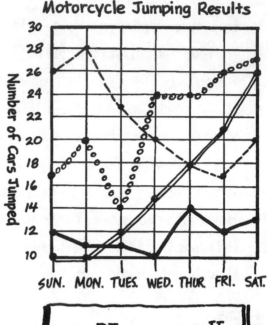

Motorcycle Jumping Results

Number of Cars Jumped

SUN. MON. TUES. WED. THUR. FRI. SAT.

=== BJ   ooooo JJ
— PJ   ---- RJ

1. What is the total of all R. J.'s jumps? _____

2. Whose average of all 7 jumps was less than 12? _____

3. What is the average of all the jumps on Monday? _____

4. Is R. J.'s average jump for the week more than 15 cars? _____

5. Which jumpers have the same total number of jumps? _____ _____ _____

6. What is the difference between J. J.'s best and worst jumps? _____

7. Whose best jump is almost twice her own worst jump? _____

8. Whose worst jump cleared more cars than P. J.'s best jump? _____

9. On Wednesday, who jumped 50% of the cars as R. J.? _____

10. On Thursday, who jumped 75% of the cars that J. J. jumped? _____

11. Who had the greatest difference between her best and worst jumps? _____

12. Who jumped twice the cars on Monday that J. J. jumped on Tuesday? _____

13. The expression **x − 14** can be used to represent the number of cars P. J. jumped on Saturday. Whose jump is represented by **x**? _____

14. At the last competition, P. J. jumped 100 cars. How many more is that than this week's total? _____

Name _____

TO RIDE A WILD BULL

Sometimes they stay on. Sometimes they fall off! Riders of wild bulls have plenty of experience with falls, throws, and flying trips through the air.

Staying on the bull may be a matter of skill. Today, since all the riders are brand new, it's a matter of chance.

The probability of an event that is impossible is 0. The probability of an event that is certain is 1.

When you don't know the outcome, the probability is somewhere between 0 and 1, usually expressed as a fraction; staying on the bull is somewhere between 0 and 1.

For each bull rider in today's contest, there are four possible results or outcomes that may occur. Assume there is an equal probability of all four shown on the chart.
1. The probability of F1 (falling off before the 1st bell) = P (F1) = $\frac{1}{4}$
2. P (F2) = _____
3. P (not falling at all) = P (S1 + S2) = _____
4. P (falling) = P (F1 + F2) = _____

POSSIBLE OUTCOMES FOR BULL RIDERS	
F1	Fall off before 1st bell
S1	Stay on just until 1st bell
F2	Fall off between 1st & 2nd bells
S2	Stay on until 2nd bell

Write a number to show the probability for each of these. It will be 0, 1, or a fraction between 0 and 1.

5. The sun will rise tomorrow. _____

6. A coin toss will yield heads. _____

7. 2 odd numbers will have an even sum. _____

8. The sun will set in the east. _____

9. You'll spend the summer on the moon. _____

10. If you toss one die, you will get a 6. _____

11. 2 even numbers will have an even sum. _____

12. You will have homework today. _____

13. The next president of the United States will be from your state. _____

14. Winter will follow fall. _____

What are the number of possible outcomes for these events?

15. Flip of a coin _____

16. Toss of one die _____

17. Choosing a month beginning with J _____

18. Choosing a day beginning with T _____

19. How many possible outcomes are there from spinning this spinner? _____

20. Which is the most likely? _____

21. Which is the least likely? _____

22. Which outcomes are equally likely? _____

Name _____

EXTREMELY AWESOME BIKE TRICKS

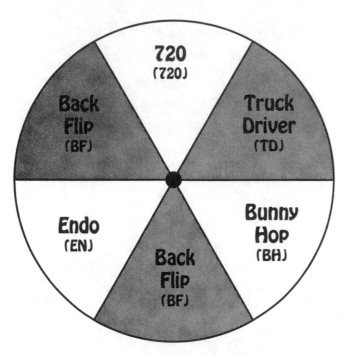

Freestyle bike tricks are exciting events to watch. The adventuresome bikers do wild tricks like Bunny Hops (hopping the bike into the air), Back Flips (jumping in the air and spinning around once, then "sticking" the landing), 720s (performing two full 360° rotations in the air), Truck Drivers (spinning the handlebar while doing a 360° rotation in the air), and Endos (balancing on the front wheel of the bike).

The bikers will start the competition with a spin of the spinner to tell them which trick to try. The set of one or more outcomes from the spinner is called an event. Tell the probability of the events described below.

Remember: P(E event) = <u>number of a particular outcome</u>
number of possible outcomes

1. P(EN) = _____

2. P(BF) = _____

3. P(TD) = _____

4. P(BF or TD) = _____

5. P(anything but BF) = _____

6. P(BH or 720) = _____

7. P(720) = _____

8. P (EN or BF) = _____

Use the numbered spinner to find the probability of these events:

9. P(odd number) = _____

10. P(prime number) = _____

11. P(10 or 15) = _____

12. P(less than 14) = _____

13. P(divisible by 3) = _____

14. P(multiple of 2) = _____

15. P(sum of digits < 3) = _____

16. P(greater than 10) = _____

17. P(sum of digits is 6) = _____

18. P(multiple of 5) = _____

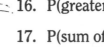

Name

EQUALLY AWESOME SKI TRICKS

Freestyle skiing is even more thrilling to perform than it is to watch (although the watching is definitely easier and safer). Three kinds of tricks fit into the freestyle category. Skiers may do all three, but they often excel in one. Aerial tricks involve fancy jumps in the air. Acro tricks are airborne ballet moves. In mogul skiing, athletes ski over bumps, often doing tricks as they bounce up into the air.

The chart shows the numbers of skiers from three countries specializing in each of the three kinds of tricks. Finish the chart. Then find the probability of each event.

	Country	AR (Aerials)	AC (Acro)	M (Moguls)	Totals for each Country
J	Japan	20	10	20	_____
C	Canada	10	50	30	_____
U	USA	20	20	20	_____
	Totals	_____	_____	_____	_____

You meet a skier. What is the probability . . . .

1. P(Skier is from C) = _____

2. P(Skier is not from U) = _____

3. P(Skier is from J) = _____

4. P(Skier is a mogul skier from C) = _____

5. P(Skier is an aerial skier from J) = _____

6. P(Skier is not an acro skier) = _____

7. P(Skier is mogul or acro skier) = _____

8. P(Skier is not a mogul skier) = _____

9. P(Skier is an aerial skier from U) = _____

10. P(Skier is an acro skier from C) = _____

11. You meet a USA skier.
    P(Skier is an M skier) = _____

12. You meet a Japanese skier.
    P(Skier is not an AC skier) = _____

13. You meet a Canadian skier.
    P(Skier does not ski M) = _____

14. You meet an acro skier.
    P(Skier is from J) = _____

15. You meet an aerial skier.
    P(Skier is from J or U) = _____

16. You meet a USA skier.
    P(Skier is AR or AC) = _____

17. You meet a mogul skier.
    P(Skier is from C) = _____

18. You meet an aerial skier.
    P(Skier is not from U) = _____

19. You meet an acro skier.
    P(Skier is from C) = _____

20. You meet a Japanese skier.
    P(Skier is an AC skier) = _____

Name _____

TAKING CHANCES ON THE RIVER

Kayaking is a wild sport, with plenty of wild white water, thrills, and spills.

These kayakers spin to choose which one of the three runs they will take down the river. The race takes two days. Each kayaker spins each day.

What are the possible outcomes for two spins? List them on the chart. Use the letter codes.

OUTCOMES for 2 Spins		

Use the chart to find the probabilities:

1. P(D one of the days) = _____

2. P(R neither day) = _____

3. P(N both days) = _____

4. P(R and D on the 2 days) = _____

5. P(same run both days) = _____

6. P(different runs both days) = _____

Kayak Runs

After the routes are chosen, each pair of racers flips a coin to see who does the run first. Alexander always calls for heads. See how he did at starting first in four different races. Use the chart to list all the possible outcomes for flipping a coin four times.

7. P(Alexander started first) = _____

8. P(two of each) = _____

9. P(three of one) = _____

10. P(4 heads or 4 tails) = _____

11. P(no heads) = _____

12. P(HTTH or THHT) = _____

OUTCOMES FOR 4 FLIPS		

Name _____

TAKING CHANCES ON THE RIVER, CONT.

OUTCOMES for ROLLING 2 DICE				

Sometimes the kayakers use dice to decide who will go first in the race. Each athlete rolls the dice, and they watch for the highest sum of the two dice.

Finish the table to show all the possible outcome when two dice are rolled. Write the outcomes this way (first roll, second roll) e.g., (4,6).

Find the probabilities:

1. P(6,6) = _____

2. P(both numbers the same) = _____

3. P(2 even numbers) = _____

4. P(2 prime numbers) = _____

5. P(2 odd numbers) = _____

6. P(sum of 6) = _____

7. P(sum of > 10) = _____

8. P(sum of 8) = _____

9. P(sum an even number) = _____

10. P(sum of 10) = _____

11. P(sum of < 5) = _____

12. P(sum of 9) = _____

13. P(difference of 4) = _____

14. P(difference of 1) = _____

15. P(difference of 5) = _____

16. P(sum of 11) = _____

Name

FOLLOWING THE WIND

You don't need an ocean for this kind of surfing. But you do need wind. Windsurfers travel to the places where they can usually count on high winds to sweep them along rivers and other bodies of water on a surfboard attached to a sail.

Of course, they hope for excellent winds every day. Sometimes the winds are less than top speed, but are okay for good surfing. Other days, the winds are just downright poor for the sport. On two consecutive days of judging the winds, what are the possible outcomes? A tree diagram can be used to show the number of outcomes. Finish the tree diagram to show all the possible outcomes on the diagram.

1. How many possible outcomes? _____

What are the probabilities of these?

2. P(G on both days) =

   _____

3. P(anything but P on both days)

   _____

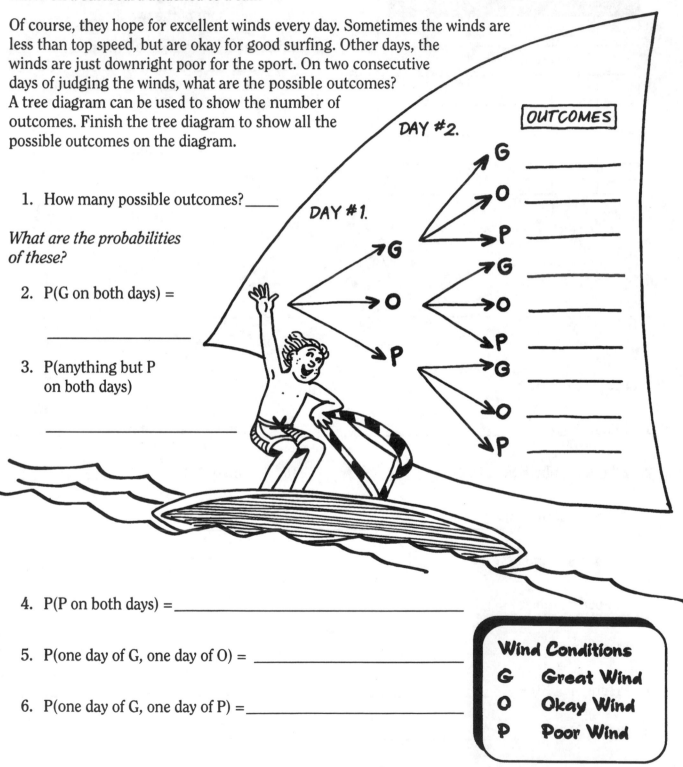

4. P(P on both days) = _____

5. P(one day of G, one day of O) = _____

6. P(one day of G, one day of P) = _____

Wind Conditions
G   Great Wind
O   Okay Wind
P   Poor Wind

Name _____

The BASIC/Not Boring Middle Grades Math Book

FOLLOWING THE WIND, CONT.

Today there is prize money waiting for the top finishers in the windsurfing races.
There are two races, and two chances to win. With five racers, each racer has a chance to come in 1st, 2nd, 3rd, 4th, or 5th.

PRIZES

1st	$200
2nd	$100
3rd	$ 80
4th	$ 50
5th	$ 0

1st both days $500

What are the possibilities for Miranda's finishes in two races?
Use the tree diagram to show all the possible outcomes for her.

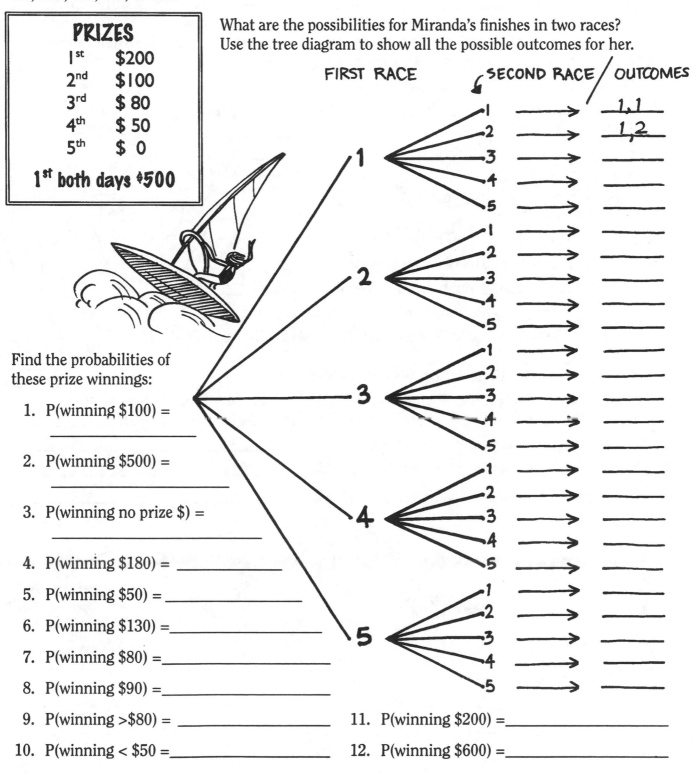

FIRST RACE   SECOND RACE / OUTCOMES

Find the probabilities of these prize winnings:

1. P(winning $100) = _____

2. P(winning $500) = _____

3. P(winning no prize $) = _____

4. P(winning $180) = _____

5. P(winning $50) = _____

6. P(winning $130) = _____

7. P(winning $80) = _____

8. P(winning $90) = _____

9. P(winning >$80) = _____

10. P(winning < $50 = _____

11. P(winning $200) = _____

12. P(winning $600) = _____

Name _____

FAST TRACKS

Making tracks through the snow is the hobby for snowmobilers . . . and the faster the tracks are, the better.

In this snowmobile race, there is more than one way to make tracks from Start to Finish. Sometimes counting is the most practical way to find the number of outcomes for a probability problem. This is one of those times. Find out the number of possible outcomes by counting the snowmobile routes.

START

FROZEN FAST TRACK

SLIPPERY SLOPE

WIND WHIP WAY

NECKBREAKER POINT

AVALANCHE ALLEY

RIDGE RIDER

SNOWSHOE HILL

ICE-CREAM SLOPE

HIP-HOP DROP

SERPENTINE TRAIL

FINISH

1. Number of routes from START to Snowshoe Hill _____
2. Number of routes from Snowshoe Hill to Neckbreaker Point _____
3. Number of routes from Neckbreaker Point to the FINISH line _____
4. Routes from START to FINISH = # from START to SH x # NP x # to FINISH
   = _____ x _____ x _____ = _____
   (If you want to, try listing all the routes on another piece of paper.)
5. What is the probability Chuck took this route in the race: Slippery Slope to Snowshoe Hill, Wind Whip Way to Neckbreaker Point, and Ice Cream Slope to the FINISH? _____
6. What is the number of possible routes from A to D? _____
7. What is the number of possible routes from 1 to 5? _____
8. What is the number of possible routes from W to Z? _____

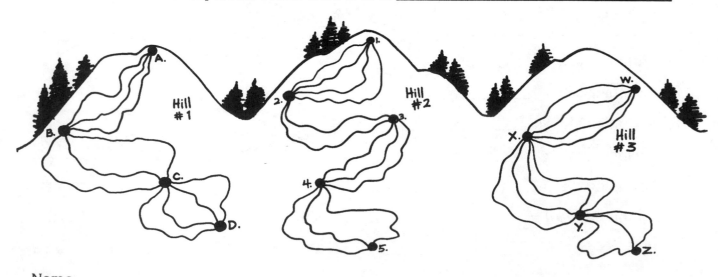

Name _____

HIGH ALTITUDE RACING

Hot air balloons of all sizes, shapes, and designs are scattered through the sky during a balloon race. The imaginations of the balloon designers seem to be unlimited. In this race, these three balloons (the mouse, the cat, the piece of cheese) are the first ones to approach the finish line.

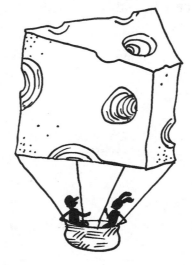

There are several different ways they could finish in 1st, 2nd, and 3rd place. The different arrangements, or orders, in which they could finish, are called **permutations**.

Finish the chart to write down all the possible arrangements.

How many permutations? _____

PERMUTATIONS for 3 BALLOONS								
CH = Cheese M = Mouse C = Cat								
1st	2nd	3rd	1st	2nd	3rd	1st	2nd	3rd
CH, C, M								
1st	2nd	3rd	1st	2nd	3rd	1st	2nd	3rd

To find the number without counting, do this:

<u>3 choices for 1st place</u> x <u>2 choices for 2nd place</u> x <u>1 choice for 3rd place</u>

3 x 2 x 1 = _____

Name the number of permutations for each of these:

1. five books on a shelf _____

2. four cars parked for the balloon race _____

3. three kids in line for tickets _____

4. eight wet suits hanging in a closet _____

5. six different skateboarding tricks _____

6. seven runners crossing the finish line _____

7. ten skiers waiting for a ski lift _____

8. four kayakers paddling down the river single file _____

Name _____

PARACHUTE COMBINATIONS

Before the jumpers head for the plane to start their day of skydiving practice, each one chooses two parachutes. On the outside, the parachute packages all look the same, but when the chutes open, the colors are different.

There are three parachutes laid out for each jumper: one red (R), one green (G), one yellow (Y). The jumper chooses two.

These are the combinations she might choose. (They are listed like this: 1st choice color, 2nd choice color.)

Notice that some of the combinations are actually the same. (Green and yellow is the same as yellow and green, since order is not important.)

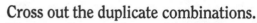

Cross out the duplicate combinations.
How many possible combinations are there when choosing 2 out of 3 parachutes? _____

_____

A. There are five prizes that can be won for a good jump: concert tickets (T), a giant pizza (P), a spaghetti dinner (D), movie tickets (M) or cash (C). The winner can choose 4 of the 5 prizes.

How many possible combinations are there of 4 prizes from 5? ____

Name them in the space below. Do not include duplicates.

B. The parachute club is forming pairs of jumpers from 6 jumpers: Ben (B), Carly (C), Daren (D), Evan (E), Fran (F), Georgia (G).

How many different pairs of jumpers can be formed from 6? ____

Name them in the space below. Do not include duplicates.

Name _____

NO LONGER JUST A SUMMER SPORT

What an idea! A snow-covered mountain may seem like the place for skiing or snowboarding. But some inventive folks thought of another use for steep snowy mountain trails . . . biking! Competitors race mountain bikes on snow in a new sport called Snow Mountain Biking.

In this competition, each biker flips a coin to see which trail she or he will ride. Then, bikers roll a die to decide the order of the riders. When James rolls a die and flips a coin, there are several different possible outcomes of these two events.

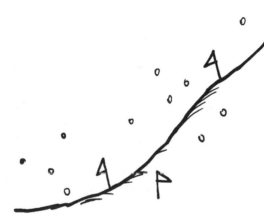

> **If two events are independent, the probability that both events occur is the product of their individual probabilities.**
>
> P(A and B) = P(A) × P(B)

OUTCOMES	
1 die roll & 1 coin toss	
H, 1	**H, 2**

Finish the table to show all the possible outcomes.

What is the probability of these?

Use the table to help you answer.

1. P(H and even number) =_____

2. P(T and even number) = _____

3. P(T and number > 2) = _____

4. P(H and 1, 2, 3, or 4) = _____

5. P(H and 4 or 5) =_____

6. P(T and number < 5) = _____

7. P(H and odd number) = _____

8. P(H and number > 1) =_____

9. P(T and multiple of 3) = _____

10. P(H and number > 4) =_____

11. P(T and number < 3) = _____

12. P(T and 1, 3, or 6) = _____

Name _____

WAITING FOR THE BIG ONE

Surfer Sal waits a long time for the best wave.

Of the next six waves, one will be 2 feet high, one will be 3 feet high, one will be 4 feet high, one will be 5 feet high, one will be 6 feet high, and one will be 7 feet high.

Sal will catch only one of them. When she does, she may ride it all the way, or she may wipe out!

What is the probability that she'll catch a 5-foot wave and ride it all the way?

$$P\ (5\ and\ R) = P\ (5)\ x\ P\ (R) = ⅙\ x\ ½ = ¹/_{12}$$

POSSIBLE OUTCOMES

Write all the possible outcomes for the events of catching the 2, 3, 4, 5, 6, or 7-foot wave and falling (F) or riding (R) the wave.

Find these probabilities:

1. Probability of catching a wave over 3 feet and falling.

   P(4, 5, or 6 and F) = P (3) x P (F) = _____ x _____ = _____

2. Probability of catching a wave under 4 feet and riding it.

   P(2 or 3 and R) = _____

Finish the table. Fill in an answer for each ?

	EVENTS	P(1ˢᵗ Event)	P (2ⁿᵈ Event)	(Both Events)
3) Toss a coin twice	H, H	P(H) = ½	P(H) = ½	P(H and H) = ?
4) Roll a die, toss a coin	4, T	P(4) = ?	P(T) = ?	P(4 and T) = ?
5) Toss a coin, Roll a die	T, even #	P(T) = ?	P(even #) =?	P(6 and even #) = ?
6) Roll a die twice	4, 4	P(4) = ?	P(4) = ?	P(4 and 4) = ?

Name _____

UNBELIEVABLE BALLOON FLIGHTS

People actually take flights with toy balloons. Of course, they use dozens of large, sturdy balloons. The record-holder for this sport used 400 helium-filled toy balloons to fly to a height of 1 mile, 1575 yards.

This bunch of balloons has 200 red, 20 blue, 10 green, and 70 orange.

Suppose two pop. The probability of the 1st being green is $\frac{10}{300}$. What is the probability that the 2nd popping balloon is blue? The results are affected by the fact that one of the original balloons is gone. The probability of this second event is $\frac{20}{299}$.

The probability that both these events will happen is shown like this:

P(G and B) = P(G green) x (B/G blue given that green popped first)

$P(G \text{ and } B) = \frac{10}{300} \times \frac{20}{299} = \frac{200}{89,700}$ or $\frac{2}{897}$

Two balloons pop in each of the events below.

Finish the table to find the probabilities.

Original Balloon Bunch	1st Event (1st Popping Balloon)	2nd Event (2nd Popping Balloon)	Probability of Both Events
1) 2 red 1 green 4 blue 3 orange 2 yellow	P (Y) = ?	P (O) = ?	P (Y and O) = ?
2) 10 red 20 yellow 10 blue	P (B) = ?	P (R) = ?	P (B and R) = ?
3) 3 red 4 green 8 blue 5 yellow	P (Y) = ?	P (Y) = ?	P (Y and Y) = ?
4) 2 red 2 green 2 blue 2 orange 2 yellow 2 purple	P (G) = ?	P (G) = ?	P (G and G) = ?
5) 96 red 4 purple	P(P) = ?	P (R) = ?	P (P and R) = ?

Name _____

255

THOSE WACKY, WILD, WING-WALKERS

Here's another daredevil sport . . . walking on the wings of flying airplanes! Yes, people actually have done this for sport! Don't try it on your next airplane trip!

These wing-walkers have a chance of winning prizes.

When they land successfully, each can draw an envelope from a group of five. Three of the envelopes have prizes, and two do not.

The **odds in favor** of getting a prize are 3 to 2.

The **odds against** getting a prize are 2 to 3.

Odds are different from probability.
But if you know the odds, you can find the probability.

Find the odds and probabilities for the prize possibilities below.

1. **7 boxes; 3 contain a prize**

   a. odds in favor of getting a prize = _____

   b. odds against getting a prize = _____

   c. probability of getting a prize = _____

2. **4 boxes; 1 contains a prize**

   a. odds in favor of a prize = _____

   b. odds against a prize = _____

   c. probability of NO prize = _____

3. **8 envelopes; 5 contain cash**

   a. odds in favor of getting cash = _____

   b. odds against getting cash = _____

   c. probability of getting cash = _____

4. **6 boxes; 2 contain prizes**

   a. odds in favor of a prize = _____

   b. odds against a prize = _____

   c. probability of NO prize = _____

5. **10 envelopes; 7 contain prizes**

   a. odds in favor of a prize = _____

   b. odds against a prize = _____

   c. probability of NO prize = _____

6. **9 boxes; 8 contain a prize**

   a. probability of getting a prize = _____

   b. odds in favor of getting a prize = _____

   c. odds against getting a prize = _____

7. **11 envelopes; 1 contains cash**

   a. odds in favor of getting cash = _____

   b. odds against getting cash = _____

   c. probability of getting cash = _____

8. **12 envelopes; 9 contain cash**

   a. probability of NOT getting cash = _____

   b. odds in favor of getting cash = _____

   c. odds against getting cash = _____

Name

SOCK PROBLEMS

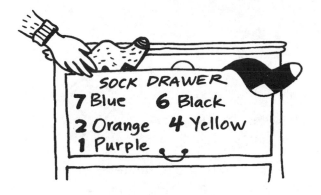

SOCK DRAWER
7 Blue   6 Black
2 Orange 4 Yellow
1 Purple

She's late for the downhill race, and Sasha can't find the right socks. She's reaching in this drawer and madly pulling out socks. The drawer is labeled with the numbers and colors of the socks.

Refer to Sasha's sock drawer to solve the probability problems below.

If Sasha pulls out one sock . . .

1. What is P (black)? .... _____
2. What is P (not yellow)? .... _____
3. What are the odds in favor of getting purple?............. _____
4. What are the odds in favor of getting blue? .... _____
5. What are the odds against getting black? .... _____

If Sasha gets a blue sock on her first grab . . .

6. What is P(blue) on her second try? .... _____
7. What is P (orange) on her second try? .... _____

If Sasha pulls out 2 socks at once . . .

8. What is P (yellow and black)? .... _____
9. What is P (orange and blue)? .... _____
10. What is P (purple and blue)? .... _____
11. What is P (2 blue socks)? .... _____
12. What is P (2 orange socks)? .... _____

13. You approach 20 skiers on the way to the race.

    8 are males, 12 are females.

    6 are wearing black gloves. 14 are wearing red gloves.

    You pass the first skier. What is the probability that this skier is . . .

    a. P (male wearing red gloves) =................................ _____
    b. P (female wearing red gloves) =............................. _____
    c. P (female wearing no gloves) =.............................. _____
    d. P (male wearing black gloves) =............................. _____

Name

EXTREME JUGGLING

Jacko can juggle lots of stuff at the same time. Balls are the ordinary things to juggle, but he also is great with plates, vegetables, kitchen supplies, and shoes.

He has a huge bag with 1200 items of three kinds: shoes, tomatoes, and teacups. To estimate the probability of choosing any one item when he reaches in the bag to grab something, some friends sampled the items. Each of six friends chose 4 items from the bag (in each case, taking the first thing they touched) then replaced them. The table shows the results of their samples.

Use the table to estimate the probability for each kind of item in the sample.

1. P (shoes) = _____

2. P (tomatoes) = _____

3. P (teacups) = _____

4. P (shoes or teacups) = _____

5. P (not shoes) = _____

6. P (not tomatoes) = _____

Out of 1200 items, predict the number that would be:

7. shoes _____

8. tomatoes _____

9. teacups _____

10. A sampling of 30 athletes at the Extreme Competition found 6 with measles.

Predict the number out of all 900 athletes that had measles.

_____

11. A bag of Ener-G Bars contains 2400 bars. A random sampling of 40 showed these results: 12 chocolate, 15 caramel, 5 banana, 8 marshmallow.

Predict the number of each bar in the bag:

a. chocolate = _____

b. caramel = _____

c. banana = _____

d. marshmallow = _____

Results of Sampling of Items for Juggling			
Friend	Shoes (S)	Tomatoes (T)	Cups (C)
Jimbo	2	0	2
Angie	1	1	2
Marco	0	1	3
Sal	1	0	3
Bobbo	2	1	1
Franco	0	1	3
Totals			

Name _____

GRAPHING, STATISTICS, & PROBABILITY
ASSESSMENT AND ANSWER KEYS

GRAPHING, STATISTICS, & PROBABILITY
SKILLS TEST

Each answer is worth 1 point. Total possible score: 100 pts.

Choose the matching term for each definition. Write the letter on the line.

a. histogram   d. statistics   h. mean
b. data   e. frequency   i. scattergram
c. median   f. mode   j. range
         g. line graph

_____ 1. the number of times an item appears in a set of data

_____ 2. information given in numerical form

_____ 3. a bar graph showing frequency data

_____ 4. the average of a number of data items

_____ 5. the collection, organization, and interpretation of sets of numerical data

_____ 6. the number that appears most often in a set of data

_____ 7. the difference between the least and greatest numbers in a set of data

_____ 8. a graph that shows the relationship between two items

_____ 9. a graph that uses lines to show changes in data over time

_____ 10. the number that falls in the middle of a set of data arranged in order

Use this frequency table for questions 11–14.

Number of Extreme Sports Events Held in Crash County, 1994-2000				
Sport	1994	1996	1998	2000
Wakeboarding	14	18	21	26
Barefoot Skiing	3	5	5	12
Jet Skiing	39	28	24	30
Windsurfing	0	1	4	6
Skysurfing	0	0	4	9
Dirt Bike Jumping	20	18	19	20

11. Which kind of sporting event was held most frequently over the years shown?

_____

12. How many sports increased in events from 1994 to 2000? _____

13. Which sport nearly doubled in number of events?

_____

14. Which quadrupled in number of events?

_____

Use this graph to answer questions 15–20.

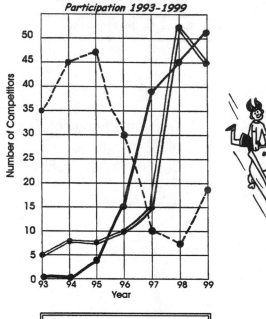

OUTRAGEOUS RACES
Participation 1993-1999

Number of Competitors / Year

Bathtub Racing ———
Lawnmower Racing ═══
Backward Unicycle Racing ─ ─ ─

15. Which races had less than 35 competitors in 1996?

_____

_____

16. Which sport made the greatest gain in competitors from 1995 to 1999?

17. Which sport had the greatest loss in participation? _____

18. Did the lawnmower races have more total participants in '95–'97 than the backward unicycle races? _____

19. In which year were the 3 sports closest in number of competitors? _____

20. Which sport made the greatest gain in participation between '98 and '99?

_____

Name _____

Use this Data Table for questions 21–29.

MOTORCYCLE JUMPS					
Numbers of Cars Jumped During Contest					
BIKER	Mon	Tue	Wed	Thur	Fri
J. J.	12	14	5	9	0
R. J.	16	15	15	15	14
P. J.	7	9	10	10	7
L. J.	12	10	8	7	15
T. J.	15	8	6	15	0

21. What is the mean of J. J.'s jumps? _____
22. What is the mode of all the data on the table? _____
23. What is the mean of R. J.'s jumps? _____
24. Who has the greatest range in jumps? _____
25. What is the median for Wednesday? _____
26. What is the mean for Friday's jumps? _____
27. What is the median of L. J.'s jumps? _____
28. What is the range of the data on the table? _____
29. What is the mean of T. J.'s jumps? _____

Use this graph for questions 30–34.

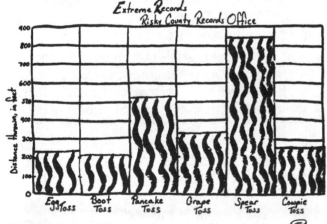

30. Which record was a distance about twice the egg toss? _____
31. Which toss was about 200 less than the pancake toss? _____
32. Which records were the closest? _____
33. Which record was about 500 less than the spear toss? _____
34. Which record was about 600 more than the cowpie toss? _____

Use this Data Table for questions 35–39.

TICKETS SOLD ON ROLLERCOASTERS			
Rollercoaster	June	July	August
Tsunami	20,110	14,980	6,050
The Tarantula	5,070	9,310	6,800
The Terminator	12,400	24,100	17,700
Toronto Twister	10,000	10,900	10, 500
Tummy Turner	3,100	8,650	9,700
Texas Torture	8,020	5,070	16,300

35. Which coaster dropped in ticket sales between June and July? _____
36. Which coaster made the biggest gain in ticket sales between June and August? _____
37. Which coaster made the biggest gain in ticket sales between June and July? _____
38. Overall, which month was the best for ticket sales on the coasters? _____
39. Which coaster sold almost 5 times as many tickets in July as The Tarantula sold in June? _____

Use this graph for questions 40–44.

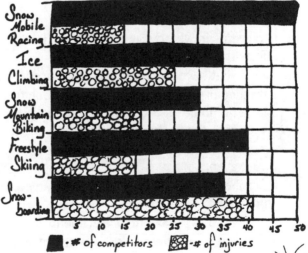

40. Which sport had more than one injury per athlete? _____
41. Which 2 sports had 15 less competitors than snowmobile racing? _____
42. Which sport had the fewest number of injuries in relation to the number of competitors? _____
43. Which sport had an injury for just less than half of its competitors? _____
44. Did any sport have about one injury for every 3 competitors? _____

Name _____

Use this circle graph for questions 45–47.

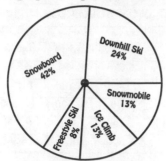

Competition Accidents

45. What % of the accidents were not ski accidents? _____

46. Which sports had a combined accident rate of 26%?
_____

47. What % of the accidents were skiing or snowboarding accidents? _____

Write the letter of the correct definition for each term.

____ 48. combination   ____ 52. random

____ 49. dependent events ____ 53. probability

____ 50. independent   ____ 54. permutation
      events   ____ 55. outcomes

____ 51. sampling   ____ 56. event

  a. two events in which the result of the first affects the outcome of the second

  b. events that have equal probability of occurring

  c. a method of getting data from a selection from a larger amount of data, in order to make predictions about the larger amounts

  d. events whose outcomes have no effect on future events

  e. a number describing the chance that an event will happen

  f. the result of a probability experiment

  g. a selection of a set of things from a larger set without regard to order

  h. an arrangement of data in a particular order

  i. a set of one or more outcomes

Write the probability for each event. Use 0 or 1 or any fractional number in between.

_____ 57. 2 odd #s will have an even sum

_____ 58. a toss of a die will yield a 6

_____ 59. a flipped coin will land on tails

_____ 60. 2 odd numbers will have an odd sum

_____ 61. a month begins with the letter M

Write the number of possible outcomes for each of the following:

____ 62. Flip of a coin   ____ 65. Toss one die
____ 63. Toss of one die   and flip a coin.
____ 64. You'll be sick one   ____ 66. Flip a coin
      day next week.   twice.

Use this spinner to answer questions 67–70.

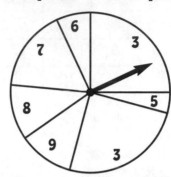

67. How many possible outcomes? _____

68. Which is most likely? _____

69. Which is least likely? _____

70. Which are equally likely? _____

71. Joe, a sky diver, is in a contest that he has a chance of winning or losing. At the end of the contest, ALL competitors will be given an envelope that has one of these amounts in it: $10, $20, $50, $100. There is an equal chance he could get any of the amounts of money.

What are all the possible outcomes of the race and his winnings? Write the outcomes in the box. Use a letter and amount (such as W50 or L20, where W stands for win and L stands for lose).

```
┌─────────────────────────────────────┐
│                                     │
│                                     │
└─────────────────────────────────────┘
```

72. Toss a coin. P(H) = _____

73. Toss 2 coins. P(TT) = _____

74. Toss 2 coins. P(one H and one T) = _____

75. Toss 1 die. P(odd #) = _____

76. Toss 1 die P(# < 5) = _____

77. Toss 1 die, flip 1 coin P(H, #<6)= _____

78. Toss 1 die, flip 1 coin P(H, 4) = _____

79. Toss 1 die, flip 1 coin P(H, #<4) _____

80. Toss 1 die, flip 1 coin P(T, odd #) = _____

81. Toss 2 dice. P(6,5) = _____

82. Toss 2 dice. P(both # same) = _____

83. Toss 2 dice. P(sum of 6) = _____

Name

Charlene will race in two handsprinting races against 4 other sprinters. She could come in 1st through 5th in either race.

84. What is the number of possible outcomes for her two races? _____

85. What is the probability of 1st and 3rd place finishes? _____

86. What is the probability of no 1st place finishes? _____

87. What is the probability that she'll finish in the same place both days? _____

88. Before biking, Bob goes to his sock drawer. It contains 5 red, 7 white, 3 purple socks. He grabs one out without looking. It is red. What is the probability that the second one is purple? _____

89. Yesterday, his drawer had 5 red and 4 white socks. What is the probability he would draw a red on the first grab and a white on the second grab? _____

90. Tom reaches into a bag of 100 snorkels, and chooses one. The pulls out 5, then returns them and takes out 5 a few more times. After a sampling of 25 snorkels, he finds that 5 of the 25 were broken. Predict the number of snorkels that will probably be broken in the whole bag of 100.

_____

91. After a long dive, Tom and his friends take a random sample of 30 Ener-G bars from a bag of 3000. The sample yielded 5 cinnamon, 15 peach, 4 apple, and 6 fudge. Predict the number of each kind of bar in the bag of 3000:

_____ 91. cinnamon

_____ 92. apple

_____ 93. peach

_____ 94. fudge

95. Three envelopes. Two contain cash. Choose one envelope.

a. Odds in favor of getting cash _____

b. Odds against getting cash _____

c. Probability of getting cash _____

96. Seven envelopes. Five contain cash.
a. Probability of NOT getting cash _____
b. Odds in favor of getting cash _____
c. Odds against getting cash _____

These 3 skiers will end the race in 1st–3rd places. What are the possible arrangements of order (permutations) in which they might finish?

97. The number of arrangements _____

98. List the possible arrangements

_____

_____

99. How many permutations (possible different arrangements) are there of 5 ski outfits hanging in a closet? _____

100. Two of the skiers arrive at the finish line at exactly the same time. How many possibilities are there for the make-up of that pair? _____ List the possible combinations of two skiers who finish at the same time: _____

_____

SCORE: Total Points _____ out of a possible 100 points

Name

GRAPHING, STATISTICS, & PROBABILITY
SKILLS TEST ANSWER KEY

Questions are worth 1 point each.

1. e
2. b
3. a
4. h
5. d
6. f
7. j
8. i
9. g
10. c
11. jet skiing
12. 4
13. wakeboarding
14. barefoot skiing
15. all 3 (bathtub races, backward unicycle races, lawnmower races)
16. bathtub races
17. backward unicycle races
18. yes
19. 1996
20. backward unicycle races
21. 8
22. 15
23. 15
24. T. J.
25. 8
26. 7.2
27. 10
28. 0–16
29. 8.8
30. pancake toss
31. grape toss
32. egg toss, and boot toss
33. grape toss
34. spear toss
35. Texas Torture and Tsunami
36. Texas Torture
37. Terminator

38. July
39. The Terminator
40. snowboarding
41. ice climbing and snowboarding
42. snowmobile racing
43. freestyle skiing
44. no
45. 68%
46. snowmobile and ice climb
47. 74%
48. g
49. a
50. d
51. c
52. b
53. e
54. h
55. f
56. i
57. 1
58. $\frac{1}{6}$
59. $\frac{1}{2}$
60. 0
61. $\frac{2}{12}$ or $\frac{1}{6}$
62. 2
63. 6
64. 7
65. 12
66. 4
67. 6
68. 3
69. 5
70. 8, 9
71. W10, W20, W50, W100, L10, L20, L50, L100
72. $\frac{1}{2}$

73. $\frac{1}{4}$
74. $\frac{2}{4}$ or $\frac{1}{2}$
75. $\frac{3}{6}$ or $\frac{1}{2}$
76. $\frac{4}{6}$ or $\frac{2}{3}$
77. $\frac{5}{12}$
78. $\frac{1}{12}$
79. $\frac{3}{12}$ or $\frac{1}{4}$
80. $\frac{3}{12}$ or $\frac{1}{4}$
81. $\frac{6}{36}$
82. $\frac{6}{36}$ or $\frac{1}{6}$
83. $\frac{5}{36}$
84. 25
85. $\frac{2}{25}$
86. $\frac{16}{25}$
87. $\frac{5}{25}$ or $\frac{1}{5}$
88. $\frac{3}{42}$ or $\frac{1}{14}$
89. $\frac{5}{18}$
90. 20
91. 500
92. 400
93. 1500
94. 600
95. a. $\frac{2}{1}$
    b. $\frac{1}{2}$
    c. $\frac{2}{3}$
96. a. $\frac{2}{7}$
    b. $\frac{5}{2}$
    c. $\frac{2}{5}$
97. 6
98. ABC, ACB, BCA, BAC, CAB, CBA
99. 120
100. 3; A & B, A & C, B & C

ANSWERS

page 218

Frequency Table Data:

JTSK-7	STLG-1
WSRF-4	HGGD-4
AILS-6	SKYS-4
BFJP-2	WKBD-5
BCYS-2	SPCL-4
SKBD-5	BNGY-7

page 219

Frequency Table Data:

AK-9	ID-6	NM-2
AL-2	LA-1	NY-1
AR-1	ME-4	OR-8
AZ-1	MI-2	SC-2
CA-17	MN-1	TX-3
CO-15	MO-1	WA-9
FL-5	MT-8	UT-4
GA-1	NC-1	VT-3
HI-20	NJ-1	

page 220

Some answers may be approximate. Give student credit if the answer is close for #8 and #9.

1. 40-45
2. 60-65
3. 35-40
4. 30-35
5. 20-25
6. 10-15
7. 50
8. about 12
9. about 75
10. 35-40 or 10-15
11. 60-65, 65-70, over 70
12. 45-50 and 55-60
13. 40-50
14. 35-40
15. 35-40
16. yes

page 221

Check graph to see that the heights of bars match these tallies from the tally sheet:

      0-500 mi . . . 58
     500-1000 mi . . . 73
  1000-1500 mi . . . 55
  1500-2000 mi . . . 61
  2000-2500 mi . . . 38
   over 2500 mi . . . 20

page 222

1. spear
2. grape
3. spear
4. 13 ft, 5 in
5. 638 ft, 9½ in
6. 19 ft
7. 846 mi, 1375 yd
8. spear
9. motorcycle jump
10. 34,872 ft

page 223

1. 47	13. 95
2. 74	14. 89
3. 11	15. 62
4. 64	16. Rapids Racers
5. 27	17. River Racers
6. 23	18. White Water Wizards
7. 48	19. Unsinkables
8. 65	20. Tuesday
9. 13	21. Friday
10. 15	22. White Water Wizards
11. 25	
12. 12	

page 224

1. 3–21
2. 11
3. 2-7; 4
4. 90 lb–140 lb; 109
5. 0–16; 8¼
6. 15–32; 19

page 225

Complete the chart with these totals.
Median, across . . . 15, 15, 15, 12, 14
Mode, across . . . 11, 27, 21, 20, 9

1. 15
2. 36
3. 12
4. circle 101 lb,
   squares around 77 lb and 77 lb

page 226

1. August	6. 450 m
2. 460 m	7. April
3. September	8. October and May
4. 220 m	9. 60 m
5. February	

page 227

Answers for 1, 2, 9 may not be exactly as given below. Give credit if the number is close.

1. 3600	5. Sue	9. 3500
2. 6200	6. Shirl	10. Shirl
3. Sly	7. 5000	11. Sara
4. 4	8. Sam	12. Sam or Sly

page 228

Check student graph to see that the data from the table has been accurately plotted and line has been drawn in order from dive 1–12.

page 229

Check student graph to see that the data from the table has been accurately transferred to the graph.

page 230

Check student graph to see that the data from the table has been accurately transferred to the graph.

page 231

1. 6	9. no
2. 10	10. yes
3. 6	11. 4
4. 11	12. 11 and 12 ft
5. 5 ft	13. 8
6. 1 ft	14. 14
7. 7 ft	15. a, d, f
8. no	

page 232

1. Nicole	7. yes
2. Jennifer	8. above
3. Brandy	9. 8 and 9
4. Nicole	10. 5 and 6
5. Amanda	11. Jennifer
6. Jennifer	12. Nicole

page 233

Check student graph to see that the data from the table has been accurately plotted and that each line has been drawn in proper color and in correct sequential order of the years.

page 234

1. 5½ or 6 min
2. Midnight Kings
3. Sleepwalkers
4. 11
5. 1 min
6. 3 min or 3½ min or 4 min
7. 1 min
8. 32
9. Snooze Crew and Sleepwalkers
10. Answers may vary. The teams with more experience have faster times.

page 235

Check student graph to see that the data from the table has been accurately transferred to the graph. Make sure alternate bars are green and yellow as instructed.

page 236

1. 230,200 mi
2. bicycle

3. 4900 mi
4. 847 mi
5. Answers will vary
6. Answers will vary
7. Answers will vary
8. Answers will vary
9. 2308 mi
10. Answers will vary

page 237

1. 6	7. yes
2. 13	8. 22
3. 4	9. half cab
4. 19	10. slob heli
5. 27	11. yes
6. 7	12. no

page 238

1. 45 years (answer is approximate)
2. 40
3. Bob, Boe, Brad
4. no
5. 25
6. 11 (answer is approximate)
7. x = Brett; y = Bev
8. x = Benjy; y = Brad
9. a = Brad; b = Bob
10. 30

page 239

1. 678 ft
2. 27 ft
3. Flo or Frank or Fred
4. Phoebe
5. Phillipe
6. Frank
7. Phyllis
8. 0
9. 195 ft
10. Phyllis
11. 6
12. 91 ft
13. 920 ft
14. 10

pages 240–241

1. 139 hours
2. MA
3. 39 hours
4. 113 hours
5. 103 hours
6. 1055 hours
7. CA
8. Black Widow
9. Swamp Fox
10. 16 hours
11. 67 hours
12. Maria; 2 hours
13. Big Bad Wolf

14. Brianna
15. Texas Twister, Tidal Wave, Twisted Sisters; 156 hours
16. Outlaw

page 242

1. 152	8. R. J.s
2. P. J.	9. P. J.
3. 17.25	10. B. J. and R. J.
4. yes	11. B. J.
5. R. J. and J. J.	12. R. J.
6. 13	13. J. J.s
7. J. J.	14. 17

page 243

1. $\frac{1}{4}$	13. $\frac{1}{50}$
2. $\frac{1}{4}$	14. 1
3. $\frac{2}{4}$ or $\frac{1}{2}$	15. 2
4. $\frac{2}{4}$ or $\frac{1}{2}$	16. 6
5. 1	17. $\frac{3}{12}$ or $\frac{1}{4}$
6. $\frac{1}{2}$	18. $\frac{2}{7}$
7. 1	19. 5
8. 0	20. E
9. 0	21. C
10. $\frac{1}{6}$	22. A and B
11. 1	
12. Answers will vary	

page 244

1. $\frac{1}{6}$	10. $\frac{2}{6}$ or $\frac{1}{3}$
2. $\frac{2}{6}$ or $\frac{1}{3}$	11. $\frac{2}{6}$ or $\frac{1}{3}$
3. $\frac{1}{6}$	12. $\frac{4}{6}$ or $\frac{2}{3}$
4. $\frac{3}{6}$ or $\frac{1}{2}$	13. $\frac{2}{6}$ or $\frac{1}{3}$
5. $\frac{4}{6}$ or $\frac{2}{3}$	14. $\frac{3}{6}$ or $\frac{1}{2}$
6. $\frac{2}{6}$ or $\frac{1}{3}$	15. $\frac{2}{6}$ or $\frac{1}{3}$
7. $\frac{1}{6}$	16. $\frac{5}{6}$
8. $\frac{3}{6}$ or $\frac{1}{2}$	17. $\frac{1}{6}$
9. $\frac{3}{6}$ or $\frac{1}{2}$	18. $\frac{2}{6}$ or $\frac{1}{3}$

page 245

Finish the graph:
Totals across bottom: AR = 50, AC = 80, M = 70, Total Tricks = 200
Totals down right: Japan = 50, Canada = 90, USA = 60, Total Skiers = 200

1. $\frac{90}{200}$ or $\frac{45}{100}$ or $\frac{9}{20}$
2. $\frac{140}{200}$ or $\frac{7}{10}$
3. $\frac{50}{200}$ or $\frac{1}{4}$
4. $\frac{30}{200}$ or $\frac{3}{20}$
5. $\frac{20}{200}$ or $\frac{1}{10}$
6. $\frac{120}{200}$ or $\frac{3}{5}$
7. $\frac{150}{200}$ or $\frac{3}{4}$
8. $\frac{130}{200}$ or $\frac{13}{20}$
9. $\frac{20}{200}$ or $\frac{1}{10}$
10. $\frac{50}{200}$ or $\frac{1}{4}$
11. $\frac{20}{60}$ or $\frac{1}{3}$
12. $\frac{40}{50}$ or $\frac{4}{5}$

13. $\frac{60}{90}$ or $\frac{2}{3}$
14. $\frac{10}{80}$ or $\frac{1}{8}$
15. $\frac{40}{50}$ or $\frac{4}{5}$
16. $\frac{40}{60}$ or $\frac{4}{6}$ or $\frac{2}{3}$
17. $\frac{30}{70}$ or $\frac{3}{7}$
18. $\frac{30}{50}$ or $\frac{3}{5}$
19. $\frac{50}{80}$ or $\frac{5}{8}$
20. $\frac{10}{50}$ or $\frac{1}{5}$

page 246

Outcomes for 2 spins . . . not necessarily in this order:
DD, DR, DN, RR, RD, RN, NN, ND, NR

Outcomes for 4 flips, not necessarily in this order:
HHHH, HHHT, HHTT, HTTT, HTHH, HTTH, HHTH, HTHT

TTTT, TTTH, TTHH, THHH, THHT, THTH, TTHT, THTT

1. $\frac{5}{9}$
2. $\frac{4}{9}$
3. $\frac{1}{9}$
4. $\frac{2}{9}$
5. $\frac{3}{9}$ or $\frac{1}{3}$
6. $\frac{6}{9}$ or $\frac{2}{3}$
7. $\frac{8}{16}$ or $\frac{1}{2}$
8. $\frac{6}{16}$ or $\frac{3}{8}$
9. $\frac{4}{16}$ or $\frac{1}{4}$
10. $\frac{2}{16}$ or $\frac{1}{8}$
11. $\frac{1}{16}$
12. $\frac{2}{16}$ or $\frac{1}{8}$

page 247

Outcomes for Rolling 2 dice, not necessarily in this orders;
1. 1.1, 1.2, 1.3, 1.4, 1.5, 1.6
2. 2.1, 2.2, 2.3, 2.4, 2.5, 2.6
3. 3.1, 3.2, 3.3, 3.4, 3.5, 3.6
4. 4.1, 4.2, 4.3, 4.4, 4.5, 4.6
5. 5.1, 5.2, 5.3, 5.4, 5.5, 5.6
6. 6.1, 6.2, 6.3, 6.4, 6.5, 6.6

1. $\frac{1}{36}$
2. $\frac{6}{36}$ or $\frac{1}{6}$
3. $\frac{9}{36}$ or $\frac{1}{4}$
4. $\frac{16}{36}$ or $\frac{4}{9}$
5. $\frac{9}{36}$ or $\frac{1}{4}$
6. $\frac{5}{36}$
7. $\frac{3}{36}$ or $\frac{1}{12}$
8. $\frac{5}{36}$
9. $\frac{18}{36}$ or $\frac{1}{2}$
10. $\frac{3}{36}$ or $\frac{1}{12}$
11. $\frac{6}{36}$ or $\frac{1}{6}$
12. $\frac{4}{36}$ or $\frac{1}{9}$
13. $\frac{4}{36}$ or $\frac{1}{9}$
14. $\frac{10}{36}$ or $\frac{5}{18}$
15. $\frac{2}{36}$ or $\frac{1}{18}$
16. $\frac{2}{36}$ or $\frac{1}{18}$

page 248

Outcomes:
GG, GO, GP, OG, OO, OP, PG, PO, PP
1. 9
2. $1/9$
3. $8/9$
4. $1/9$
5. $2/9$
6. $2/9$

page 249

Outcomes:

1, 1;	1, 2;	1, 3;	1, 4;	1, 5;
2, 1;	2, 2;	2, 3;	2, 4;	2, 5;
3, 1;	3, 2;	3, 3;	3, 4;	3, 5;
4, 1;	4, 2;	4, 3;	4, 4;	4, 5;
5, 1;	5, 2;	5, 3;	5, 4;	5, 5

1. $3/25$ (2, 5; 5, 2; or 4, 4)
2. $1/25$ (1, 1)
3. $1/25$ (5, 5)
4. $2/25$ (2, 3 or 3, 2)
5. $2/25$ (5, 4 or 4, 5)
6. $2/25$ (3, 4 or 4, 3)
7. $2/25$ (3, 5 or 5, 3)
8. 0
9. $20/25$ (every outcome except 3, 5 or 5, 3; or 4, 4 or 5, 5)
10. $1/25$ (5, 5)
11. $3/25$ (2, 2 or 1, 5 or 5, 1)
12. 0

page 250

1. 2
2. 3
3. 3
4. 2 x 3 x 3 = 18
5. $1/18$
6. 36
7. 72
8. 48

page 251

Chart: Balloon Permutations . . . not necessarily in this order on chart:
CH, C, M
CH, M, C
C, CH, M
C, M, CH
M, CH, C
M, C, CH
Example: 6; 6
1. 120
2. 24
3. 6
4. 40,320
5. 720
6. 5040
7. 3,628,800
8. 24

page 252

Example: 3
A. 5   Combinations do not have to be listed in this exact order: TPDM, TDMC, TPDC, TPMC, PDMC
B. 15   Combinations do not have to be listed in this exact order:
BC, BD, BE, BF, BG,
CD, CE, CF, CG,
DE, DF, DG,
EF, EG, FG

page 253

Outcomes not necessarily listed in this order: H1, H2, H3, H4, H5, H6, T1, T2, T3, T4, T5, T6

1. $3/12$ or $1/4$
2. $3/12$ or $1/4$
3. $1/12$
4. $4/12$ or $1/3$
5. $2/12$ or $1/6$
6. $4/12$ or $1/3$
7. $3/12$ or $1/4$
8. $5/12$
9. $2/12$ or $1/6$
10. $2/12$ or $1/6$
11. $2/12$ or $1/6$
12. $3/12$ or $1/4$

page 254

Outcomes not necessarily listed in this order: 2R, 2F,
3R, 3F,
4R, 4F,
5R, 5F,
6R, 6F,
7R, 7F

1. $3/6$ x $1/2$ = $3/12$ or $1/4$
2. $2/6$ x $1/2$ = $2/12$ or $1/6$

Table:
Answers across:
3. $1/2$; $1/2$; $1/4$
4. $1/6$; $1/2$; $1/12$
5. $1/2$; $3/6$ or $1/2$; $1/4$ or $3/12$
6. $1/6$; $1/6$; $1/36$

page 255

Table, across
1. $2/12$ or $1/6$; $3/11$; $1/22$
2. $10/40$ or $1/4$; $10/39$; $5/78$
3. $5/20$ or $1/4$; $5/19$; $5/76$
4. $2/12$ or $1/6$; $2/11$; $1/33$
5. $4/100$ or $1/25$; $32/33$; $32/825$

page 256

1. a. $3/4$
  b. $4/3$
  c. $3/7$
2. a. $1/3$
  b. $3/1$
  c. $3/4$
3. a. $5/3$
  b. $3/5$
  c. $5/8$
4. a. $2/4$ or $1/2$
  b. $4/2$
  c. $4/6$ or $2/3$
5. a. $7/3$
  b. $3/7$
  c. $3/10$
6. a. $8/9$
  b. $8/1$
  c. $1/8$
7. a. $1/10$
  b. $10/1$
  c. $1/11$
8. a. $3/12$ or $1/4$
  b. $9/3$ or $3/1$
  c. $3/9$ or $1/3$

page 257

1. $6/20$ or $3/10$
2. $16/20$ or $4/5$
3. $1/19$
4. $7/13$
5. $14/6$ or $7/3$
6. $6/19$
7. $2/19$
8. $3/50$
9. $7/200$
10. $7/400$
11. $49/400$
12. $4/400$ or $1/100$
13. a. $112/400$ or $7/25$
  b. $168/400$ or $21/50$
  c. 0
  d. $48/400$ or $12/100$ or $3/25$

page 258

Chart:
Totals across: 6, 4, 14
1. $6/24$ or $1/4$
2. $4/24$ or $1/6$
3. $14/24$ or $7/12$
4. $20/24$ or $5/6$
5. $18/24$ or $6/8$ or $3/4$
6. $20/24$ or $5/6$
7. 300
8. 200
9. 700
10. 180
11. a. 720
  b. 900
  c. 300
  d. 480

PRE-ALGEBRA

Skills Exercises

SKILLS CHECKLIST FOR PRE-ALGEBRA

✔	SKILL	PAGE(S)
	Identify opposites for positive and negative integers	270
	Give the absolute value of an integer	270
	Compare and order integers	271
	Add integers	272
	Subtract integers	273
	Multiply integers	274
	Divide integers	275
	Solve real-world problems with integers	276
	Describe relationships between numbers	277
	Evaluate mathematical expressions	278
	Write mathematical expressions	279
	Identify terms, variables, and coefficients in mathematical expressions	280
	Simplify mathematical expressions	281, 282
	Choose expressions to match statements	283
	Write equations to match statements	284
	Choose equations to solve problems	285
	Write equations to solve problems	286
	Rewrite equations using inverse operations	287
	Identify and use number properties	288, 289
	Solve one-step equations with one variable	290, 291
	Solve multi-step equations with one variable	292, 293
	Determine accuracy of solutions	293, 295
	Solve equations with rational numbers	294
	Use equations to solve real-world problems	296, 297
	Solve inequalities	298, 299
	Graph inequalities	299
	Solve equations with two variables	300, 301, 304, 305
	Locate ordered pairs of numbers on a coordinate plane	302, 303
	Graph equations with two variables	304, 305
	Identify transformations	306, 307
	Identify corresponding points in transformations	306, 307
	Identify and extend patterns and sequences	308, 309
	Solve proportions	310

SHOWING OFF INTEGERS

A bunch of friends are making plans for a camping trip. Each of them is wearing a T-shirt with a different integer. Figure out the opposites and values of their integers. Look at the T-shirt for each kid shown on these two pages (pages 270 and 271).

The absolute value of an integer is its distance from zero on a number line. **Opposites** have the same absolute value.

Give this information for the integer on the shirt:

1. **Chad**
   a. Is it positive (P) or negative (N)? _____
   b. What is the absolute value? _____
   c. What is its opposite? _____

2. **Zoey**
   a. P or N ? _____
   b. absolute value _____
   c. opposite _____

3. **Mike**
   a. P or N ? _____
   b. absolute value _____
   c. opposite _____

4. **Sam**
   a. P or N ? _____
   b. absolute value _____
   c. opposite _____

5. **Yolanda**
   a. P or N ? _____
   b. absolute value _____
   c. opposite _____

6. **Matt**
   a. P or N ? _____
   b. absolute value _____
   c. opposite _____

7. **Basha**
   a. P or N ? _____
   b. absolute value _____
   c. opposite _____

8. **Toni**
   a. P or N ? _____
   b. absolute value _____
   c. opposite _____

Name

A MATTER OF ORDER

Don't be fooled by integers! Some of them look bigger or smaller than they really are.

Look at the integers on pages 270 and 271. Answer these questions.

1. How many t-shirts have integers > Zoey's? _____

2. How many are > Chad's? _____

3. How any are < Basha's? _____

4. How many are > Toni's? _____

5. How many are < Yolanda's? _____

6. How many are < Toni's? _____

An integer is **greater than** all integers to the left of it on a number line.

An integer is **less than** all integers to the right of it on a number line.

Compare the two integers. Write > or < on each line.

7.	5	____	0	11.	0	____	–3
8.	–2	____	2	12.	–8	____	6
9.	3	____	–7	13.	0	____	–7
10.	–4	____	–8	14.	–6	____	–11

15. Put the T-shirt integers in order from smallest to largest. _____

Write the integers in order from smallest to largest.

16. **20, –20, 4, –7, 3, 0, 6, –1** _____

17. **–8, –16, 3, –4, –3, 5, 10** _____

18. **2, –2, 6, 8, –8, –4, 4** _____

19. **0, 2, 6, 8, 7, –7, –12** _____

20. **11, 0, 5, –6, 2, 9, –8** _____

Name _____

MOUNTAIN UPS & DOWNS

The easiest trail to the top of Mt. Blister is eight miles long. Toni and Chad are planning their trip up the mountain.

Last year, they covered 4 miles on Day #1 and 3 miles on Day #2. On Day #3, they went back down the trail 2 miles to recover from altitude sickness. On Day #4, they hiked up the mountain 1 ½ more miles. Where were they at the end of Day #4?

This problem will show their forward and backward movements.

4 + 3 + –2 + 1½ = (mile) 6½

these trails look great!

The sum of 2 positive integers is **positive.**
The sum of 2 negative integers is **negative.**
The sum of a positive integer and a negative integer may be **positive, negative, or zero.**

Solve these addition problems.

1. 7 + –3 = _____

2. –6 + –9 = _____

3. –63 + –36 = _____

4. –8 + 12 = _____

5. 5 + –9 = _____

6. 7 + –6= _____

7. –10 + 10 = _____

8. –41 + –34 = _____

9. –7 + –12 _____

10. –2 + –3 = _____

11. –12 + –11 + –6 = _____

12. 6 + –3 + –11 + 9 + 5 = _____

13. 10 + –2 + –30 = _____

14. 6 + 2 + 9 + –25 = _____

15. –4 + 3 + 4 + –3 + 3 = _____

16. –50 + –12 + 3 = _____

17. 27 + 18 + –3 = _____

18. –27 + –1 + 7 = _____

Name _____

The BASIC/Not Boring Middle

MOUNTAINOUS LOCATIONS

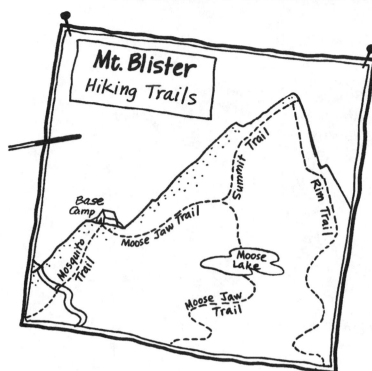

The hikers decide on the location for their Base Camp. They'll start their climb at 2 miles below Base Camp. By the end of the third day, they plan to be 4 miles above Base Camp. What is the difference between this goal and their starting location?

This problem will help to find the difference.

$$4 - -2 = \underline{\hspace{1.5cm}}$$

> **To subtract an integer, add its opposite.**

Finish these.

1. $8 - 10 = 8 + \underline{\hspace{1.5cm}}$

2. $8 - -10 = 8 + \underline{\hspace{1.5cm}}$

3. $-8 - 10 = -8 + \underline{\hspace{1.5cm}}$

4. $-8 - -10 = -8 + \underline{\hspace{1.5cm}}$

5. $5 - 7 = 5 + \underline{\hspace{1.5cm}}$

6. $5 - -7 = 5 + \underline{\hspace{1.5cm}}$

7. $-5 - 7 = -5 + \underline{\hspace{1.5cm}}$

8. $-5 - -7 = -5 + \underline{\hspace{1.5cm}}$

Subtract these.

9. $2 - 2 = \underline{\hspace{1.5cm}}$

10. $-8 - -4 = \underline{\hspace{1.5cm}}$

11. $20 - -3 = \underline{\hspace{1.5cm}}$

12. $-6 - 0 = \underline{\hspace{1.5cm}}$

13. $-5 - -8 = \underline{\hspace{1.5cm}}$

14. $12 - 22 = \underline{\hspace{1.5cm}}$

15. $44 - -20 = \underline{\hspace{1.5cm}}$

16. $-20 - -9 = \underline{\hspace{1.5cm}}$

17. $14 - -5 = \underline{\hspace{1.5cm}}$

18. $0 - -4 = \underline{\hspace{1.5cm}}$

19. $0 - 4 = \underline{\hspace{1.5cm}}$

20. $-33 - -4 = \underline{\hspace{1.5cm}}$

21. Hot Springs is 4.3 miles up the trail from Base Camp. Juniper Hollow is 1.5 miles below Base Camp. What is the difference between the locations?

Name _____

CHANGING BY DEGREES

Packing the right clothing for a camping trip is challenging, especially when mountains are a part of the trip plan. The temperatures on mountains are tricky, changing quickly with altitude or unexpected weather. The campers hear that there is a 5° temperature change for each thousand feet of altitude on Mt. Grizzly. The higher they go . . . the colder it gets!

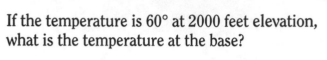

If the temperature is 60° at 2000 feet elevation, what is the temperature at the base?

This formula will help you find out.
(t = temperature; b = base temperature;
n = thousands of feet)
t = b + (n x 5 or –5)
t = 60 + (2 x 5)

If the temperature is 40° at the base, what is it at the 9000-foot peak?
 t = 40 + (9 x –5)

Finish the chart to compare temperatures on Mt. Grizzly.

The product of 2 positive integers is **positive**.
The product of 2 negative integers is **positive**.
The product of a positive integer and a negative integer is **negative**.

Expected Temperatures on Mt. Grizzly

	Temp at Base	1 thousand feet above base	2 thousand feet above base	4 thousand feet above base	6 thousand feet above base	9 thousand feet above base
1	30° F	25°	20°		0°	
2	42° F					
3	60° F					
4	16° F					
5	11° F					
6					- 20° F	

Multiply the integers.

7. 7 x –10 = _____

8. 14 x –3 = _____

9. –10 x –6 = _____

10. 7 x –9 = _____

11. –100 x –100 = _____

Estimate the products.

12. 5 x –498 = _____

13. –102 x –15 = _____

14. –202 x 1011 = _____

15. 78 x –4 = _____

16. –92 x –7 = _____

Name _____

COLD CALCULATIONS

Even in the summer, it gets awfully cold on Mt. Grizzly. Campers need to make plans for chilly nights. As they are planning their trip, the campers pay close attention to the past records of daytime and nighttime temperatures on the mountain.

**The quotient of 2 positive or 2 negative integers is positive.
The quotient of a positive and a negative integer is negative.**

Mount Grizzly Peak
Average Nighttime Temperatures

Month	Daytime *Farenheit Temp*	Nighttime *Farenheit Temp*
Jan	-18°	-45°
Feb	-16°	-32°
Mar	-6°	-14°
Apr	5°	-7°
May	18°	10°
Jun	24°	12°
Jul	50°	20°
Aug	48°	-1°
Sept	36°	-8°
Oct	-5°	-15°
Nov	-2°	-20°
Dec	-28°	-35°

Divide integers to find the month that fits the description.

1. Night temperature is half as cold as Dec. daytime. _____

2. Night temperature is one-fifth as cold as Dec. nighttime. _____

3. Day temperature is one-third as cold as Mar. daytime. _____

4. Day temperature is one-fourth as cold as Nov. nighttime. _____

5. Night temperature is one-seventh as cold as Apr. nighttime. _____

6. Its daytime temperature is one-tenth as cold as its nighttime. _____

7. Its daytime temperature is half as cold as its nighttime. _____

8. Night temperature is one-third as cold as Jan. nighttime. _____

Divide the integers.

9. $100 \div -10 =$ _____

10. $-78 \div -6 =$ _____

11. $-1000 \div 10 =$ _____

12. $-80 \div -4 =$ _____

13. $-44 \div 11 =$ _____

14. $4000 \div -40 =$ _____

Name

ELEVATOR PUZZLERS

A visit to the Super Camp Store is on the schedule for today. Sam and Basha will ride the elevator to the right floors for their supplies. Pay attention to the labels by the buttons, and use integers to solve these elevator problems.

Write and solve an integer problem for each question.

1. They leave the camera floor, ride up two floors, and down three. What floor are they on?

2. They leave the shoe & boot department and ride up ten floors. What floor are they on?

3. What is on the floor that is twice the distance from ground floor as the camera floor?

4. They leave the repair shop, ride up eight floors, and down one. What kind of merchandise will they find here?

5. To go from the tent department to the repair shop, how many floors must they travel?

6. What merchandise is on the floor that is 9 floors above the floor with kid's supplies?

1 2 3 4 5 6 7 8
4 3 2 1 ELEVATOR

↑ (8) CLIMBING GEAR
↑ (7) VIDEOS, SLIDES
↑ (6) BOOKS, MAPS
↑ (5) COOKING UTENSILS
↑ (4) CAMPING FOOD
↑ (3) CLOTHING
↑ (2) TENTS
↑ (1) BACKPACKS
GROUND LEVEL SLEEPING BAGS
↓ (1) KID'S SUPPLIES
↓ (2) CAMERAS
↓ (3) SHOES, BOOTS
↓ (4) REPAIR SHOP

7. What is on the floor that is one below the floor that is four floors above shoes & boots?

8. They leave the clothing floor, ride down 3 floors, up 8 floors, and down two. What kind of merchandise will they find here?

Name

276

WHO'S RELATED?

Some of the hikers are related to each other. Figure out these relationships while you explore the relationships between the numbers that describe their sizes and weights. The weights of the campers include the weight of the full pack.

MATT
Age: 8
Weight: 80 lb
Boot Size: 2

CHAD
Age: 15
Weight: 180 lb
Boot Size: 12

MIKE
Age: 18
Weight: 200 lb
Boot Size: 10

BASHA
Age: 16
Weight: 130 lb
Boot Size: 7

TONI
Age: 12
Weight: 120 lb
Boot Size: 6

1. Basha is 8 years less than twice the age of her cousin.
   Who is her cousin?_____

2. With pack, Matt weighs 20 pounds less than half as much as his brother.
   Who is his brother? _____

3. Chad's boot size is two less than twice his sister's.
   Who is his sister? _____

Which of these is true? Write T in front of the accurate relationships.

_____ 4. Basha's weight is greater than two other campers' weights.

_____ 5. Chad's age is 3 years less than twice Matt's.

_____ 6. Mike's boot size is half his age.

_____ 7. Mike's weight is equal to Matt's and Toni's combined.

Write a phrase that describes a way these two numbers are related.

8. Matt and Basha's ages: _____

9. Mike's and Toni's ages: _____

10. Chad's age and boot size: _____

11. Toni and Chad's weights: _____

12. Matt and Mike's boot sizes: _____

Name _____

TRUE EXPRESSIONS

4w < c + b !

This sentence makes sense to the shoppers.
Just look at the list of camping goods, and it will make
sense to you, too.

It's an expression that uses numbers instead of words
to tell you something.

In this case, it tells you that
the price of four water bottles is less than
the cost of a cook stove plus a pair of boots.

Is the above expression true? _____
You can tell by using the sale poster to find the money
value of each letter (variable) in the expression.

Circle the expression that is true.

$t < 2s$ $\qquad$ $s > 2t$ $\qquad$ $2s = t$

SALE ! ! !
CAMPING SUPPLIES

t   tents
s   sleeping bags $ 200
b   boots $ 180
p   packs $ 160
c   cook stoves $ 240
f   frying pans $ 32
w   water bottles $ 18
                           $ 6

Find the mathematical expression to match each group of words below.

1. cost of three water bottles and two packs

    $3w + 2p$ $\qquad$ $3(w + p)$ $\qquad$ $3w \times 2p$

2. cost of four frying pans and one sleeping bag

    $4(f + s)$ $\qquad$ $4f + 4s$ $\qquad$ $4f + s$

3. ten dollars more than two cook stoves

    $c + 2s + 10$ $\qquad$ $10 - 2c$ $\qquad$ $2c + 10$

4. cost of a pair of boots less three dollars

    $3b + 3$ $\qquad$ $3b$ $\qquad$ $b - 3$ $\qquad$ $b + 3$

5. cost of a frying pan is less than two tents

    $f > t$ $\qquad$ $2f < 2t$ $\qquad$ $2f < 2t$ $\qquad$ $f < 2t$

6. three times the cost of a pack and boots

    $3p + b$ $\qquad$ $3(p + b)$ $\qquad$ $3p \times 3b$

7. two dollars more than five water bottles

    $(5-2)w$ $\qquad$ $5w + b$ $\qquad$ $5w + 2$

8. the cost of a cook stove, two water bottles, and a frying pan is
    less than one hundred dollars

    $c + 2w + f < 100$ $\qquad$ $100 - 2(c + w + f)$

Name

EXPRESSIONS WITH TASTE

No hiker wants a back-breaking pack, so it's important to pay attention to weight while the supplies are gathered for the pack. These food items have weights (in ounces) that are represented by letter symbols.

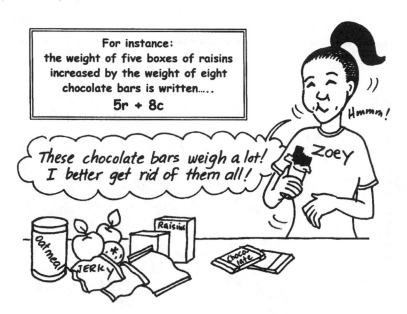

For instance:
the weight of five boxes of raisins increased by the weight of eight chocolate bars is written.....

5r + 8c

These chocolate bars weigh a lot! I better get rid of them all!

Hmmm!

Zoey

CAMPING FOOD	
weight in ounces	food
m	maple oatmeal
n	noodle packs
s	cans of stew
a	apples
h	hot chocolate packs
r	boxes of raisins
c	chocolate bars
g	bags of gorp
f	fruit leather sticks
b	bread rolls
j	jerky sticks
p	power bars

Use the letter symbols to write mathematical expressions about the food weights.

Write an expression to show the weight of . . .

1. 1 bag of oatmeal increased by 3 ounces: _____

2. 15 boxes of raisins decreased by 7 jerky sticks: _____

3. 4 power bars decreased by 2 packs of noodles: _____

4. 12 bags of gorp decreased by 4 bags of gorp: _____

5. 8 chocolate bars decreased by 5 ounces: _____

6. twice the sum of 2 bread rolls and 6 jerky sticks: _____

7. 3 times the difference between 2 stew cans and 5 fruit leather sticks: _____

8. 10 hot chocolate packets increased by 1 stew can and 2 power bars: _____

9. 2 apples weigh less than 3 power bars: _____

10. 5 times the weight of a bread roll and an apple: _____

11. the sum of ½ bag of raisins and ¼ bag of gorp: _____

12. ten times the product of bread and fruit leather: _____

Name

ALGEBRA ON THE TRAIL

Study the route the hikers plan to take to Mt. Grizzly. On the first day, they plan to hike from Bear Paw Pond to Lake Achoo. The second day, they'll go on to Horsefly Pond. On Day 3, their trip will be four times the length of their first day. The last day will take them to the summit. They'll hike half as far as the first day.

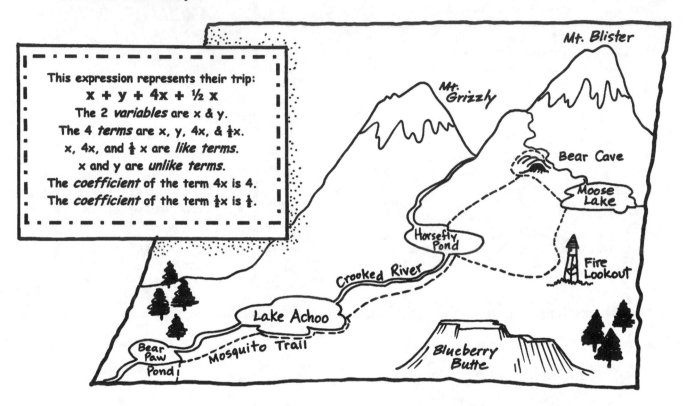

This expression represents their trip:
$$x + y + 4x + \tfrac{1}{2}x$$
The 2 *variables* are x & y.
The 4 *terms* are x, y, 4x, & $\tfrac{1}{4}$x.
x, 4x, and $\tfrac{1}{4}$x are *like terms*.
x and y are *unlike terms*.
The *coefficient* of the term 4x is 4.
The *coefficient* of the term $\tfrac{1}{4}$x is $\tfrac{1}{4}$.

How many variables in each expression?

1. $2z - 9x$ _____

2. $-4b + 2a + -7a$ _____

3. $-9k + 2m$ _____

4. $p + q + 2(r - s)$ _____

How many terms in each expression?

9. $y + \tfrac{1}{2}y$ _____

10. $-10p + 2\tfrac{1}{2}q + r - s$ _____

11. $2x + 3y + 9.9z > w$ _____

12. $3.5p$ _____

13. $a + 2b - 3c + 4d + f$ _____

Are the terms like(L) or unlike(U)?

5. $6x + 17x - 2x$ _____

6. $14y + 6x - x$ _____

7. $-3a + 2(c + b)$ _____

8. $-20p + 6q$ _____

14. $\mathbf{7z + 18m \div \tfrac{1}{2}b}$

What are the terms in this expression?

_____

What is the coefficient of z? _____

What is the coefficient of m? _____

What is the coefficient of b? _____

Name

SIMPLY FOLLOW THE TRAIL

Today's trip takes the energetic hikers a long way through the Mt. Blister Wilderness Area. They follow Mosquito Trail from Bear Paw Pond to Lake Achoo, then on to Horsefly Pond, the Fire Lookout, and Moose Lake. The day's final destination is Bear Cave.

This expression represents the distance of the day's hike:

$x + y + 2x + +x + z$

The expression can be simplified by combining like terms.

$3+x + y + z$

Simplify the following expressions.

DISTANCES	
Bear Paw Pond to Lake Achoo	x
Lake Achoo to Horsefly Pond	y
Lake Achoo to Fire Lookout	$y + 2x$
Fire Lookout to Moose Lake	$\frac{1}{2}x$
Fire Lookout to Horsefly Pond	$2x$
Bear Cave to Bear Paw Pond	$x+y+3z$
Moose Lake to Bear Cave	z

1. $3a + 5a$ _____

2. $x + x$ _____

3. $14k - 6k$ _____

4. $18c + c + \frac{1}{4}c$ _____

5. $y - 5 + 10y$ _____

6. $\frac{1}{2}x - \frac{1}{4}x + 2$ _____

7. $10t + 14 - 3t$ _____

8. $5.2k - 2k + 5$ _____

9. $4z + 5x - 3z + x$ _____

10. $2n + n + 4p$ _____

11. $y + x + y + x$ _____

12. $7g - 3s + 20g$ _____

13. $4m + 7m + 100$ _____

14. $4(w + 3) - 2w$ _____

15. $b + 2(b + 5)$ _____

16. $3(a + 2) + 4a$ _____

17. $n + 5(2 + 3n)$ _____

18. $6(x + y) - 3y$ _____

19. $12p \div 2 + 3p$ _____

20. $5s - 2(s + t)$ _____

Name _____

A SIMPLE TASK?

Setting up a tent ought to be simple for an experienced camper—right?
That's not quite the story for Chad. He's having some tent trouble today!
It took him a long, long time to get it right. It took Basha 25 minutes less. Toni set hers up in 38 minutes less than Chad, and Zoey took 30 minutes less. Matt beat them all by setting up his tent in 41 minutes less than Chad.

This expression shows how much time was spent setting up tents today, with Chad's time represented by **t**.

t + (t–25) + (t–38) + (t–30) + (t–41)

Here's the same expression simplified.

5t – 134

Simplify these equations by combining like terms.

1. $y + -3y + 10\,y + 7$

_____

2. $5(x + 7) + -x$

_____

3. $-p + 2p - -7p$

_____

4. $\dfrac{-x + 3x + x}{5}$

_____

5. $5z -2z + 12$

_____

6. $-t + 7t + 3t + 300$

_____

7. $2(100y + 3) + y$

_____

8. $12b + -8b + + b$

_____

9. $45 + 6(a + b) + a$

_____

10. $4(g + 6) - 6g$

_____

11. $b + -d - -c + 3d$

_____

12. $8x -14x + 12$

_____

13. $50 + 13p - 5 + 10p$

_____

14. $4.5z - x - 7.5z$

_____

15. $100j - -j + x -2j$

_____

16. $6(j + k) - 2j$

_____

Name _____

EQUATIONS TO BOOT

At the end of a long hiking day, the boots are quickly pulled off the hot, aching feet. Use the boot statistics to practice your skills with equations.

Sam's boots are 3 sizes less than twice the size of Toni's. One of these equations represents his boot size. (**s** = Sam's boot size; **t** = Toni's size)

$s = t + 3$

$s = t - 3$

$s = 2(3-t)$

$s = 2t - 3$

$s = 2(t-3)$

$t = 2s + 3$

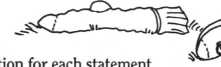

Circle the correct equation for each statement.

1. Basha's boots cost $80 more than Chad's.
    a. $b + 80 > c$
    b. $c = b + 80$
    c. $c + 80 = b$

2. Yolanda's boots cost $5 less than twice the cost of Sam's.
    a. $2s - 5 = y$
    b. $y + 5 = 2s$
    c. $5 + s = y$

3. Zoey's new boots cost $8 more than Toni's and Chad's combined.
    a. $z = t + c + 8$
    b. $2(t + c) = z - 8$
    c. $z + 8 = c + t$

4. Toni dried out her boots 4 hours more on Friday than on Thursday.
    a. $f + t = 4$
    b. $4f = t$
    c. $t + 4 = f$

5. On Monday, Mike's boots traveled 3 times longer than on Tuesday.
    a. $m \times t = 3$
    b. $t = 3m$
    c. $m = 3t$

6. On Sunday, Chad's boots traveled 6 miles less than on Wednesday.
    a. $w + 6 = s$
    b. $s + w = 6$
    c. $w - 6 = s$

7. Yolanda's boot size is one less than half the size of Chad's.
    a. $c = y - 1\frac{1}{2}$
    b. $y + \frac{1}{2} + 1 = c$
    c. $y = \frac{1}{2}c - 1$

8. Sam has 8 more than 4 times as many blisters on his left foot as on his right.
    a. $L = 8R + 4$
    b. $4R + 8 = L$
    c. $L + R = 4 \times 8$

9. Matt's right socks has 2 less than 6 times the holes as his left sock.
    a. $6L - 2 = R$
    b. $2(L + 6) = R$
    c. $R = (6 \times 2)$

10. Sam's socks have one more than twice the number of holes as Zoey's.
    a. $s = 2(z + 1)$
    b. $2z + 1 = s$
    c. $z = s + 1 \times 2$

Name

283

TO BUILD A FIRE

If there's going to be a good fire on a cold night, everyone needs to help collect the firewood. It looks as if Yolanda may have gathered the most. She has 12 times as many sticks as Sam and Toni combined.

You could write this equation for Yolanda's bundle:

$$y = 12(s + t)$$

Write an equation for each of these descriptions of the firewood situation.

1. Zoey *(z)* collected 3 more than twice Chad's (c) amount. _____

2. Toni gathered 5 less sticks than Matt and Basha did together. _____

3. Sam's bundle weighed 4 times Zoey's and Toni's together. _____

4. Yolanda searched for wood 5 less times than Sam did. _____

5. Toni carried 16 pounds less than Mike and Zoey together. _____

6. On Sunday, they burned 23 more pieces than on Thursday. _____

7. Basha collected 18 sticks more than Zoey collected. _____

8. On Saturday, they burned wood for 3 fewer hours than on Friday. _____

9. The fire burned for one-fourth as long on Monday as on Tuesday. _____

10. On Monday, they burned 3 logs less than
    twice the amount burned on Saturday. _____

11. The amount of wood burned on Monday and Wednesday
    totaled the same as the wood burned on Saturday and Tuesday. _____

12. The temperature by the fire *(t)* was 5° less than
    three times the temperature away from the fire *(a)*. _____

Name _____

MARSHMALLOW PROBLEMS

The best part of the day is sitting around the campfire toasting those creamy, gooey marshmallows. Tonight is no exception, but there are a few problems with the marshmallows. For each marshmallow problem, choose the equation that would find a solution.

1. Critters ate 73 marshmallows total from 4 bags. 23 were eaten from Sam's bag, 6 from Chad's bag, and 18 from Matt's bag. How many were eaten from Mike's bag?
   a. $73 - 4 - 23 - 6 - 18 = x$
   b. $x = 23 + 6 + 18$
   c. $23 + 6 + 18 + x = 73$

Answer: _____

2. Basha dropped 2 marshmallows into the fire. Mike dropped 4 and Toni dropped 3. Yolanda dropped 4 times as many marshmallows into the fire as the other three campers combined. Mike, Basha, and Toni combined. How many did she drop?
   a. $x = 2 + 4 + 3 + 4$
   b. $x = 4(2 + 4 + 3)$
   c. $2 \times 4 \times 3 = x$

Answer: _____

3. In the last three nights, 24 marshmallows have been burned. On Tues., 4 more burned than on Mon. On Wed., 3 times as many were burned as on Mon. How many burned on Mon.?
   a. $24 - 4 - 3 = m$
   b. $m + (m + 4) + 3m = 24$
   c. $24 = 4(3 + 4)$

Answer: _____

4. Someone (or something) ate ½ bag of marshmallows. 1¾ bags were left. How many bags of marshmallows were there to begin?
   a. $1¾ + ½ = x$
   b. $x = 1¾ - ½$
   c. $1¾ + x = ½$

Answer: _____

5. Zoey ate 6 marshmallows on Tues. and 3 less on Wed. and 4 times as many on Mon. as on Tues. How many did she eat?
   a. $m = 6 + 3 + 4$
   b. $m = 6 + (6–3) + (4 \times 6)$
   c. $4(6 – 3) + 6 = m$

Answer: _____

6. Three campers ate 50 marshmallows one night. Toni ate 6. Chad ate 4 times as many as Toni and Sam combined. How many did Sam eat?
   a. $50 - 6 - 4n$
   b. $50 = 6 + n + 4(n + 6)$
   c. $6 + 4(n + 6) = 50$

Answer: _____

7. The group cooked 18 marshmallows. Sam ate 2 less than ½ of these. How many did he eat?
   a. $n = 18 \div 2 - 2$
   b. $18 - 2 + ½ = n$
   c. $n = 18 \times 2 - 2$

Answer: _____

Name _____

CANOE CALCULATIONS

The whole time Toni is trudging across the path carrying her canoe, she's calculating how much further she has left to walk. Sometimes she even counts steps or seconds. It always seems endless!

Help her with some canoe calculations. Write an equation that will solve each of the problems. Then find the solutions.

1. Toni has carried the canoe for 14 minutes. The trip should take 21 minutes. How much more time (t) does she have to walk?

   Equation: _____

   Answer: _____

2. The canoe weighs thirty pounds less than Toni. She weighs 100 pounds. What is the canoe's weight (w)?

   Equation: _____

   Answer: _____

3. The trail is 280 feet long. She has walked 20 feet less than half of this distance. How far (d) has she walked?

   Equation: _____

   Answer: _____

4. Matt has rested 3 times. Zoey has rested 6 times. Toni has rested twice as many times as Matt and Zoey combined. How many times has she rested (r)?

   Equation: _____

   Answer: _____

5. Chad carried Mike's canoe for 25 minutes. The trip took 50 minutes. How many minutes did Mike (m) carry his own canoe?

   Equation: _____

   Answer: _____

6. Toni dropped her canoe 9 times. This was 3 times less than twice the number of times Basha did. How many times did Basha drop her canoe (d)?

   Equation: _____

   Answer: _____

7. The canoe weighs 70 pounds. Toni weighs 100 pounds. With her pack and canoe, she weighs 208 pounds. How much does the pack weigh (p)?

   Equation: _____

   Answer: _____

Name _____

REVERSE TRAVELS

The words reverse, inverse, opposite, or backwards could all be used to describe Sam's canoe trip through the rapids today. Whichever word you choose, he's still pointed in the wrong direction!

Inverse is a word that will help you solve equations. To find a solution, you will often need to get rid of the terms on the side of the equation with the variable. You do this by using inverse operations.

Add, subtract, multiply, or divide both sides of an equation by the same number to get an equivalent equation that will help you solve the problem. Use an inverse operation to rewrite and solve each equation caught in the rapids.

The examples will help you review this process.

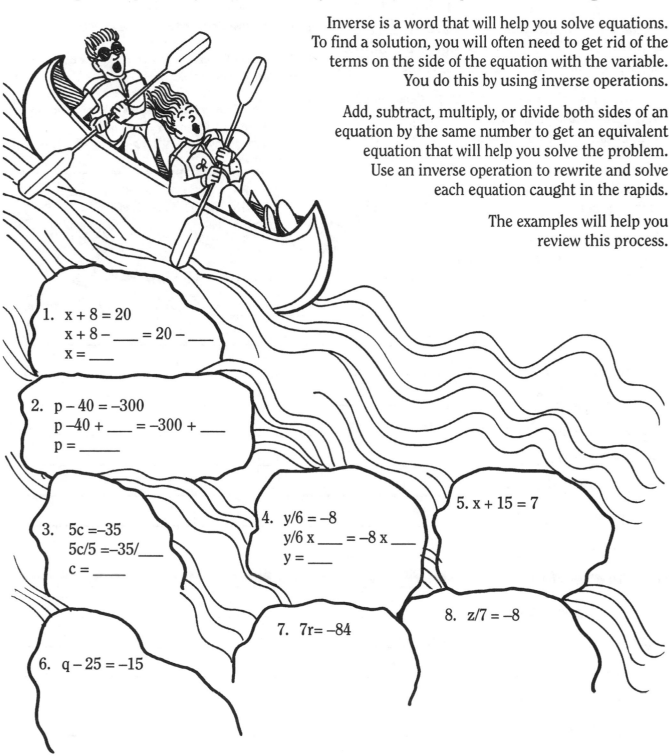

1. $x + 8 = 20$
   $x + 8 - \underline{\quad} = 20 - \underline{\quad}$
   $x = \underline{\quad}$

2. $p - 40 = -300$
   $p - 40 + \underline{\quad} = -300 + \underline{\quad}$
   $p = \underline{\quad}$

3. $5c = -35$
   $5c/5 = -35/\underline{\quad}$
   $c = \underline{\quad}$

4. $y/6 = -8$
   $y/6 \times \underline{\quad} = -8 \times \underline{\quad}$
   $y = \underline{\quad}$

5. $x + 15 = 7$

6. $q - 25 = -15$

7. $7r = -84$

8. $z/7 = -8$

Name

WHERE'S THE WATER?

On a hot, dusty trail, the climbers take out their water bottles. They have 7 water bottles. Each one has 0 ounces of water left in it. When they calculate how much water they have, they come up with ZERO. That's because 7 times 0 is ZERO. (It's also because they forgot to fill those bottles.)

The zero property for multiplication describes what happened to the thirsty climbers. The product of any number and zero is zero.

Here are examples of several number properties that are used when solving equations.

Which property is used?
Write the property for each equation.

Examples of Number Properties	
Identity Properties	$a + 0 = a$ and $a \times 1 = a$
Zero Property	$a \times 0 = 0$
Commutative Properties	$a + b = b + a$
and	$a \times b = b \times a$
Distributive Property	$a \times (b + c) = a \times b + a \times c$
Associative Properties	$(a + b) + c = a + (b + c)$
and	$(a \times b) \times c = a \times (b \times c)$
Opposites Properties	Dividing a number is the opposite of multiplying by that number. Subtracting a number is the opposite of adding that number.

I'm so dry!

Basha

1. $-40 \times 1 = -40$ _____

2. $-8 + (6 + -6) = -8$ _____

3. $-2 + (12 + 9) = (-2 + 12) + 9$ _____

4. $-9 \times 3 = 3 \times -9$ _____

5. $4 \times (-2 + 10) = (4 \times -2) + (4 \times 10)$ _____

6. $4 \times (-3 \times 2) = (4 \times -3) + (4 \times 2)$ _____

7. $7 \times -8 = -8 \times 7$ _____

8. $-200 + 0 = -200$ _____

9. $-200 \times 0 = 0$ _____

10. $-10 \times 1 = -10$ _____

11. $-9 + 4 = -5$ is the same as $-5 - 4 = -9$ _____

12. $(-20 + 5) + -3 = -20 + (5 + -3)$ _____

13. $3 \times -6 = -18$ is the same as $-18 \div -6$ _____

14. $14.5 + -99 = -99 + 14.5$ _____

15. $1 \times 16.5 = 16.5$ _____

16. $0 \times \frac{1}{2} = 0$ _____

Name _____

WHERE'S THE CHOCOLATE?

Basha is trying to figure out what has happened to all her chocolate bars. Her list tells how many she's borrowed, eaten, melted, or given away. However, she is not sure how many she has lost from friends. She uses the opposites property to help her solve the problem.

Use number properties to figure out which solution is correct for each equation.

Circle the correct solution.

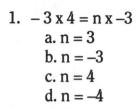

commutative   distributive

identity   associative

zero property   opposites

CHOCOLATE BARS

Started with	15
Gave away	4
Melted	2
Borrowed	5
Lost	?
Ate	9
Left over	2

How many lost ?

$15-4-2+5-x-9=2$
$5-x=2$
$5-x-5=2-5$
$-x=-3$
$x=3$

1. $-3 \times 4 = n \times -3$
   a. $n = 3$
   b. $n = -3$
   c. $n = 4$
   d. $n = -4$

2. $22 + -12 = y + 22$
   a. $y = 12$
   b. $y = -12$
   c. $y = -22$
   d. $y = 0$

3. $8 + (q + 3) = 0$
   a. $q = 11$
   b. $q = 5$
   c. $q = -5$
   d. $q = -11$

4. $15 \times d = 15$
   a. $d = 15$
   b. $d = 0$
   c. $d = 1$
   d. $d = -15$

5. $-6 + 3 = 3 + s$
   a. $s = 3$
   b. $s = -6$
   c. $s = 6$
   d. $s = 9$

6. $6 \times (3 + -9) =$
   $6 \times 3 + g \times -9$
   a. $g = 6$
   b. $g = -6$
   c. $g = 12$
   d. $g = 18$

7. $-20 + t = -20$
   a. $t = 20$
   b. $t = 1$
   c. $t = 0$
   d. $t = -20$

8. $1000 + (600 + 300) =$
   $(1000 + k) + 300$
   a. $k = 900$
   b. $k = 300$
   c. $k = 1900$
   d. $k = 600$

9. $25 \times 6 = j \times 25$
   a. $j = 25$
   b. $j = -6$
   c. $j = 6$
   d. $j = -25$

10. $-900 p = 0$
    a. $p = 900$
    b. $p = -1$
    c. $p = 100$
    d. $p = 0$

11. $4 \times (-4 \times 5) = -16 + b$
    a. $b = 4$
    b. $b = 5$
    c. $b = 20$
    d. $b = -4$

12. $-50 \times c = -50$
    a. $c = -1$
    b. $c = 1$
    c. $c = 0$
    d. $c - -50$

Name

WITH LIGHTNING ACCURACY

The storm has been raging for hours, and the campers have counted 150 lightning strikes in the last hour alone. To find out how many times lightning has struck per minute on the average, they've used the equation 60t = 150. Their solution is 2.5 times per minute.
Is this correct? _____

Examine their other solutions. If a solution is correct, circle the problem number. If it is not correct, cross out their solution and write the correct one.

1. $12x = 72$ $x = 6$ _____

2. $n \div 25 = 6$ $n = 150$ _____

3. $4 - -p = 27$ $p = 23$ _____

4. $1250 = \frac{1}{4}q$ $q = 250$ _____

5. $-10k = 360$ $k = 36$ _____

6. $d - 10.3 = 8.1$ $d = 18.4$ _____

7. $-100 = b + 6$ $b = 94$ _____

8. $-8x = -168$ $x = 21$ _____

9. $189 = 21r$ $r = 9$ _____

10. $\frac{m}{9} = 30$ $m = 270$ _____

11. $333 = \frac{1}{3}t$ $t = 999$ _____

12. $5\frac{1}{2}v = 99$ $v = 18$ _____

13. $\frac{n}{12} = -5$ $n = 60$ _____

14. $-7 - g = -49$ $g = 42$ _____

15. $x^2 = 64$ $x = 8$ _____

16. $\frac{s}{100} = -10$ $s = -1000$ _____

17. $-11g = 22$ $g = -22$ _____

18. $400 = 50y$ $y = 8$ _____

Name

PUDDLE PUZZLER

It has rained for 7 hours. The puddles are gathering in all the tents. If 1.75 inches of rain have fallen in that time, how many inches fell per hour?_____
The equation $1.75 = 7x$ will help you find the amount.

Solve the equations below to complete the puddle

Across

A. $x + 100 = 146$
E. $n/3 = 9$
G. $2200 - g = 89$
H. $p + 3000 = 10,000$
I. $2q = 128$
J. $z - -6 = 35$
L. $m/3 = 4$
M. $2r = 1850$
P. $k - 5 = 55,000$
R. $s/3 = 33$
S. $4p = 84$
T. $2t = 98$
U. $g + 92 = 400$
V. $120 = x - -9$
X. $r/7 = 9$
Y. $2004 = \frac{1}{2}p$
Z. $5f = 75$
BB. $400 - k = 25$
EE. $2q = 130$
FF. $176 \div 11 = w$
GG. $x + x = 128$

Down

B. $1000 - g = 400$
C. $n/9 = 9$
D. $500 - p = 184$
E. $14x = 280$
G. $\frac{1}{2}s = 101$
H. $107 = n/7$
K. $10,000 - 480 = d$
L. $5c = 75,050$
N. $140 - -159 = g$
O. $100 - w = 41$
Q. $2p = 1036$
T. $\frac{1}{4}t = 1029$
U. $999 = 3f$
V. $2000 - r = 994$
W. $63 = \frac{1}{3}n$
AA. $11z = 605$
CC. $-42 - -113 = b$
DD. $a + 14 = 70$

Name ____________________

LOST & FOUND

Matt got so wrapped up in his picture-taking that he wandered off the trail. Now he is totally lost in the woods. The solutions to these equations are lost in the woods, too.

Search the woods to find the correct solution for each equation. Show all the steps as you solve the equation.

1. $9 + 12x = 81$

   $x =$ _____

2. $31 = 8g - 9$

   _____ $= g$

3. $2r + 5 = 21$

   $r =$ _____

4. $(3 + p)22 = 88$

   $p =$ _____

5. $56 = 8(s - 6)$

   _____ $= s$

6. $40 = c + 2c - 101$

   _____ $= c$

7. $4x + x - 2x + 3 = 54$

   $x =$ _____

8. $2(n + 3)/2 = 23$

   $n =$ _____

9. $134 = 7k - 10 + 5k$

   _____ $= k$

10. $3z + 22 - z = 162$

    $z =$ _____

11. $20 = \dfrac{m + 4}{9}$

    _____ $= m$

12. $b + 3(b-4) = 48$

    $b =$ _____

Name

MAKING TRACKS

While wandering through a cave, Chad came face to face with the creature who called the cave "home." Find the path Chad followed as he escaped from the cave by finding the equations that are solved correctly. If the right solution is shown, color the box. Connect the colored boxes to show Chad's path.

A.
$3y + 13 = -20$
$y = -11$

B.
$5p - 4 = 31$
$p = -7$

C.
$200 = n + 310$
$n = -110$

D.
$-7r = 84$
$r = -12$

E.
$-2 + 8w = 30$
$w = 4$

F.
$3.6 + -7 = y$
$-3.4 = y$

G.
$5 + 3q = 50$
$q = 15$

H.
$s + 2s = -42$
$s = 14$

I.
$8(c-4) = -16$
$c = 2$

J.
$8(c + 2) = 16$
$c = 2$

K.
$g = 2(10 - 4)$
$g = 16$

L.
$x + -2 = 33$
$x = 35$

M.
$s + s = 100 - 10$
$s = 110$

N.
$3(x + 6) = 78$
$x = 20$

O.
$-8m + 2 = 482$
$m = -60$

Name

CLIMBING SOLUTIONS

Scale the rock wall along with Mike and Basha by solving the equations they encounter as they climb.

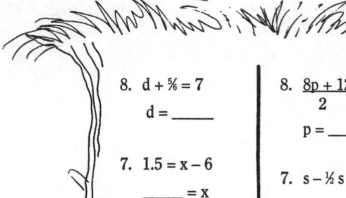

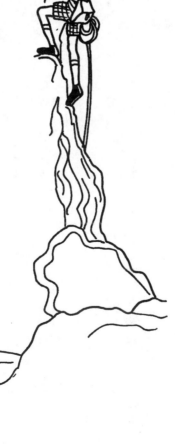

8. $d + \frac{5}{6} = 7$

  $d =$ _____

7. $1.5 = x - 6$

  _____ $= x$

6. $3p = 0.6$

  $p =$ _____

5. $\frac{b}{4} = 20$

  $b =$ _____

4. $3n = 4.5$

  $n =$ _____

3. $1\frac{1}{2} q = 9$

  $q =$ _____

2. $\frac{-z}{6} = -20$

  $z =$ _____

1. $6a = 180$

  $a =$ _____

ELEPHANT FOOT HILL

8. $\dfrac{8p + 12}{2} = 50$

  $p =$ _____

7. $s - \frac{1}{2}s + s = 18$

  $s =$ _____

6. $1.8 = 9m$

  $m =$ _____

5. $\frac{p}{5} = 6.5$

  $p =$ _____

4. $26 = \frac{1}{4}z - 14$

  $z =$ _____

3. $3w = -333$

  $w =$ _____

2. $\dfrac{m + 3}{5} = 7$

  $m =$ _____

1. $35 = y + .003$

  $y =$ _____

Name _____

CONFUSION AT THE CROSSROADS

"How much farther is Cripple Creek beyond Razor Rock?" Chad wonders. He's standing at the junction of many paths, trying to calculate some hiking distances. Examine these equations to see if Chad did his calculations right. Use the distances and letter symbols on the signs. Decide if each written equation is true. Write yes or no in front of each equation.

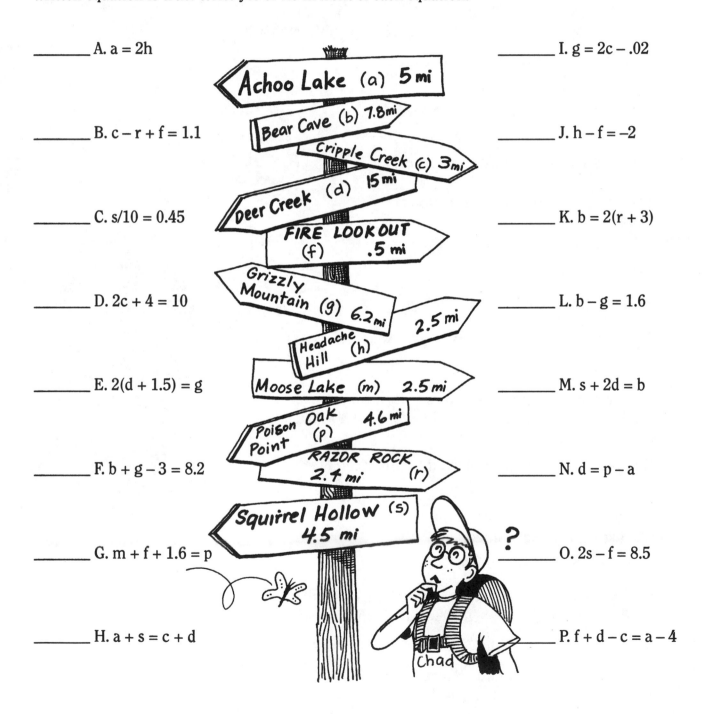

_____ A. $a = 2h$

_____ B. $c - r + f = 1.1$

_____ C. $s/10 = 0.45$

_____ D. $2c + 4 = 10$

_____ E. $2(d + 1.5) = g$

_____ F. $b + g - 3 = 8.2$

_____ G. $m + f + 1.6 = p$

_____ H. $a + s = c + d$

_____ I. $g = 2c - .02$

_____ J. $h - f = -2$

_____ K. $b = 2(r + 3)$

_____ L. $b - g = 1.6$

_____ M. $s + 2d = b$

_____ N. $d = p - a$

_____ O. $2s - f = 8.5$

_____ P. $f + d - c = a - 4$

Signpost labels:
- Achoo Lake (a) 5 mi
- Bear Cave (b) 7.8 mi
- Cripple Creek (c) 3 mi
- Deer Creek (d) 15 mi
- FIRE LOOKOUT (f) .5 mi
- Grizzly Mountain (g) 6.2 mi
- Headache Hill (h) 2.5 mi
- Moose Lake (m) 2.5 mi
- Poison Oak Point (p) 4.6 mi
- RAZOR ROCK 2.4 mi (r)
- Squirrel Hollow (s) 4.5 mi

Chad

Name _____

CULINARY MATTERS

Dig your fork (or your calculator) into these tasty problems about camping food. Write an equation to find the solution to each culinary problem.

1. Mike's stomach is a negative 6 when it comes to pancakes.
   It needs 6 pancakes to fill up.
   Mike eats 12 more than the amount needed to fill the stomach.

   How many pancakes does he eat? _____

2. Zoey ate 14½ pancakes.
   That's 6½ more than her stomach needed.
   How many did her stomach need? _____

3. Mike and Toni ate the same number of bags of gorp.
   This was 3 less than twice what Chad ate.
   Chad ate 5.

   How many bags of gorp did Mike and Toni each eat? _____

4. Matt's two water bottles were filled with 32 ounces each.
   At the end of the day, 7 ounces of water were left.

   How much did he drink? _____

5. Some critters got into the oatmeal. They ate 3 packages of Mike's, 2 of Chad's, and 6 of Matt's. Toni lost ½ as much as the others combined.

   How much of Toni's oatmeal did the critters eat? _____

6. Four campers left 18 chocolate bars in the sun.
   Yolanda lost 4. Sam lost 2 less than Yolanda.
   Chad lost twice what Sam lost.

   How many of Toni's chocolate bars melted? _____

7. Sam brought 3 more cans of stew than Basha, who brought 9.
   The two of them shared their stew with 2 other people.

   If each ate the same amount, how many cans of stew did each person get? _____

8. The group made 30 s'mores. Sam and Basha each ate 3.
   The rest were eaten (equally) by the other 6 campers.

   How many did each of the others eat? _____

Name _____

COOL COMPUTATIONS

There's nothing like the waters of a cool lake to soothe the hot, tired hiker at the end of a long day. Basha and the other campers are content to lie back and float, or dive and swim in Lake Achoo.

Use your problem-solving skills to find the answers to some of their water questions.

Write an equation to find the solution for each problem.

1. Basha's floating time is 15 minutes longer than Zoey's. Together, they float a total of 75 minutes. How long did Zoey float (f)?

    f = _____

2. Chad dives off a rock 4.6 ft above the surface. His dive takes him 8.3 ft below the water's surface. How much distance does he cover in the dive (d)?

    d = _____

3. Sam's dive covers 6.1 ft total. It began 4.3 ft above the surface. What distance did he travel below the surface (d)?

    d = _____

4. Mike can hold his breath for 72 sec. Yolanda can hold hers 26 seconds longer than ½ of Mike's time. How long does Yolanda hold her breath (t)?

    t = _____

5. Matt swam up the river. Toni followed him, swimming 31 ft less than ten times as far as Matt. Toni swam 469 ft. What distance did Matt swim (d)?

    d = _____

6. While snorkeling around the lake, Toni counted some fish. Mike counted 2 more than Toni. Basha counted 4 times the number seen by Mike and Toni combined. All together they counted 70 fish. Use (f) for the variable.

    How many did Toni see? _____

    How many did Mike see? _____

    How many did Basha see? _____

7. The temperature in the lake dropped 2° for each 10 ft below the surface. If the temperature was 70° at the surface, what is the temperature 40 ft below (t)?

    t = _____

Name _____

GHOSTLY INEQUALITIES

Basha told a ghost story. It went on for 45 minutes. Matt told a story, too.

His was not as long as Basha's.

This inequality describes Matt's story.
x < 45 and > 0

There are several possible solutions.
48 and –5 would not be solutions.

> < means less than
> \> means greater than
> ≤ means equal to or less than
> ≥ means equal to or greater than

For each inequality, circle the numbers that are solutions.

1. $x \geq 4$	6	–4	4	–2	0
2. $x \leq -1$	4	2	–1	14	6
3. $x > -8$	–8	–10	–6	–2	7
4. $x + 4 < 9$	8	5	–5	3	–2
5. $4x > -12$	–12	6	–3	–5	0
6. $x - 4 \geq 7$	11	–4	6	9	10
7. $\frac{1}{2}x < 2$	4	–4	3	9	–6
8. $3x > -9$	–4	–3	3	–2	0
9. $\frac{1}{4}x < 8$	7	16	20	–5	60
10. $4x + 2 \leq 7$	2	–1	3	–4	–6

Write an inequality for each of these.
Use x as the variable.

11. A number is increased by 10.
The result is greater than 18.

12. 6 is added to 3 times a number.
The result is less than or equal to 2.

_____   _____

Name _____

NOISES IN THE NIGHT

Yolanda and Zoey lost count of all the noises they heard in the night. Zoey heard at least 20. Yolanda knows she heard more.
This inequality represents the number she heard:

x > 20

The graph on the number line pictures the solutions for this inequality.

The open circle symbol at 20 shows that 20 is not included in the possible solutions.

This graph shows the solutions to the inequality x − 3 ≤ 2
The solid circle at 5 means that 5 is a possible solution.

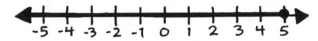

Write the inequality shown by each graph.

1. _____

2. _____

3. _____

4. _____

Draw a number line graph showing the solutions for each inequality.

5. **x ≤ -1**

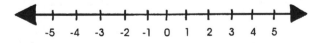

6. **x ≥ -3**

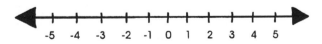

7. **x > -4**

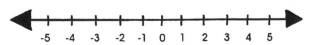

8. **x < 5**

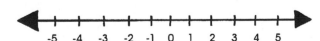

POISON IVY PROBLEMS

Chad and Zoey are covered with poison ivy. They're trying to cover all the spots on their bodies with soothing aloe lotion. Chad has 5 times as many spots as Zoey. How many does Chad have? You can't figure that out until you know the number of spots on Zoey.

The equation that represents this problem is **x = 5y**.
(x for Chad; y for Zoey)

This problem has two variables. The second one depends on the first.

Complete the table to show some possible solutions.

Complete Tables B-E to show possible solutions for the equations.

A $x = 5y$

x	y	(x, y)
40	8	(40, 8)
10		
5		
0		
-30		
-35		

B $x + 5 = y$

x	y	(x, y)
-3	8	(-3, 8)
-1		
0		
1		
2		
3		

C $x = 2y$

x	y	(x, y)
4	2	(4, 2)
-2		
0		
2		
4		
6		

D $x = 3y - 2$

x	y	(x, y)
-8	-2	(-8, -2)
	-1	
	0	
	1	
	2	
	3	

E $3x = y$

x	y	(x, y)
-5	-15	(-5, -15)
-3		
-1		
0		
2		
5		

Name _____

SCRAPES, BUMPS, & BRUISES

The numbers of cuts and scrapes, bruises and bumps, and blisters and bites are growing daily. Together, Basha and Matt have 14 bandaged cuts. How many does each of them have? You cannot find out unless you know the number for one of the campers.

This problem can be solved with an equation that has two variables.

The equation that represents this problem is x + y = 14. (x for Basha; y for Matt)
Complete the table to show some possible solutions.

1. If Basha has 7, what number does Matt have? _____

2. If Yolanda and Mike have 22 cuts between them, how many does Yolanda *(y)* have if Mike *(x)* has 7? _____

Complete Tables B-E to show possible solutions for the equations.

A

x + y = 14		
x	y	(x, y)
2	12	(2, 12)
4		
5		
8		
10		
12		

B

x = y + 3		
x	y	(x, y)
-5	-8	(-5, -8)
	0	
	-3	
2	-5	
5		
	-4	

C

y = -4x		
x	y	(x, y)
-3	12	(-3, 12)
	-8	
-1		
4		
	20	
7		

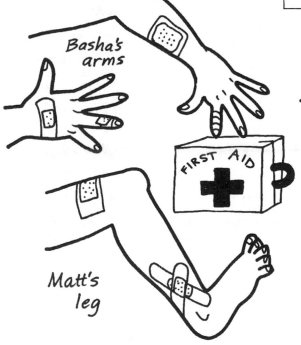

Basha's arms

FIRST AID

Matt's leg

D

2x + y = 3		
x	y	(x, y)
-5	13	(-5, 13)
-3		
-1		
0		
3		
6		

E

x - 2y = 6		
x	y	(x, y)
0	-3	(0, -3)
	-1	
	0	
	2	
	4	
	5	

Name _____

CREATURE COORDINATES

Bugs are a fact of life on a camping trip. Lightning bugs, beetles, spiders, mosquitoes, and other critters keep the campers company.

Find the location of the creatures on the coordinate grid. Write an ordered pair of numbers to show the location (coordinates) for each bug.

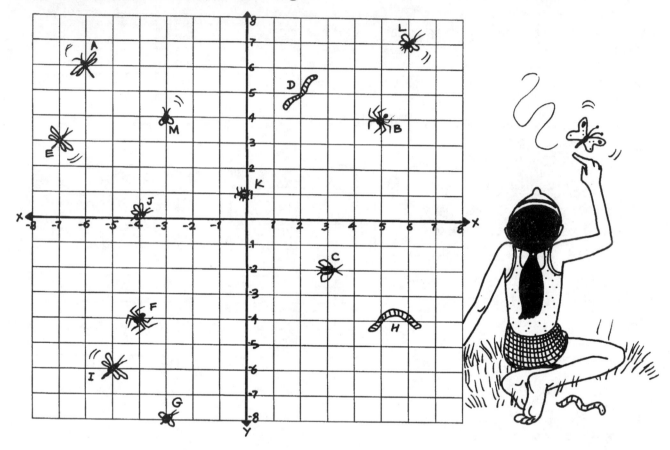

Write an ordered pair for each.

1. A _____
2. B _____
3. C _____
4. D _____
5. E _____
6. F _____
7. G _____

Write the letter.

8. What creature is at (6, 7)?

_____

9. What creature is at (–4, 0)?

_____

10. What creature is at (5, –4 and 6, –4)?

_____

11. What creature is at (–5, –6)?

_____

12. What creature is at (0, 1)?

_____

Draw a creature at each of these locations:

13. a spider at (5, 0)
14. a fly at (–8, –8)
15. a dragonfly at (0, –6)
16. a mosquito at (–7, –2)
17. a spider at (–2, 6)
18. a worm at (4, –7)
19. a fly at (–6, –2)
20. a bee at (–1, –2)

Name _____

A STARTLING MEETING

Mike has met an unexpected visitor! What creature has he stumbled upon?
To find out, follow the directions to plot points and draw lines on the coordinate grid.

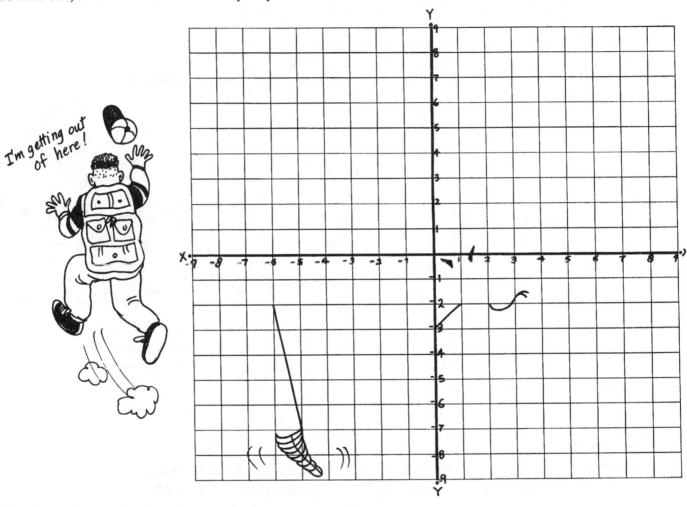

Plot the points in the first three columns.
When the points are plotted, connect them in the order given.

(0, –2)	(0, 4)	(8, 2)
(1, –4)	(–4, 3)	(6, 6)
(4, –2)	(–6, –2)	(2, 8)
(2, 2)	(–3, –7)	(0, 8)
(–2, 1)	(0, –9)	(–4, 6)
(–3, –2)	(2, –9)	(–6, 4)
(–2, –3)	(4, –8)	(–8, –1)
(1, –6)	(5, –7)	(–8, –4)
(6, –2)	(7, –5)	(–6, –7)
(4, 4)	(9, –3)	Stop.
Continue to the next column.	Continue to the next column.	Connect the points.

Plot these points.
Connect them in the order given.
(0, –1)
(2, –2)
(2.5, 0)
(1, 1)
(0, 1.5)
(–2, –2)
(–2, –3)
Stop.
Connect the points.

Name _____

LINEAR CONTEMPLATIONS

y = x + 2

x	y	(x, y)
-4	-2	(-4, -2)
-3	-1	(-3, -1)
-2	0	(-2, 0)
-1	1	(-1, 1)
0	2	(0, 2)
1	3	(1, 3)
2	4	(2, 4)

Mike has had no bites for hours, so he's fallen asleep contemplating the possibilities for his fishing line. Which hook in the graph is attached to Mike's line? You can find out by graphing the linear equation.

Graph the solutions shown on the table.
Connect the solutions with a line.
This will show which hook is attached to Mike's fishing line.

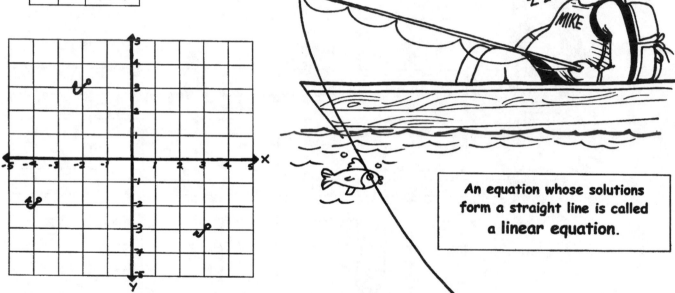

An equation whose solutions form a straight line is called a **linear equation**.

Complete the tables to find solutions for the linear equations on this page and the next page (pages 304 and 305). Then graph each equation to find the right hook for each line.

A. **y = 2x + 4**

x	y	(x, y)
-4	-4	(-4, -4)
-3		
-2		
-1		
0		

B. **x = y**

x	y	(x, y)
-3	3	(-3, 3)
-2		
1		
2		
3		
4		

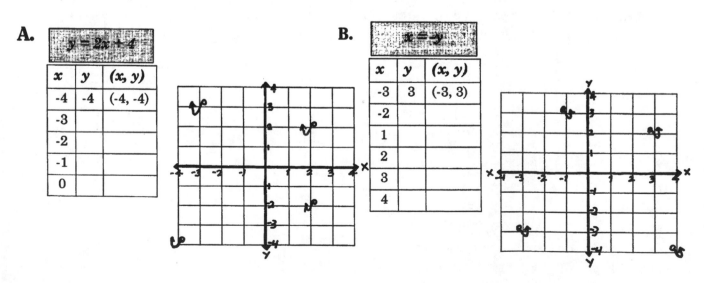

Name

LINEAR CONTEMPLATIONS, CONT.

Graph each "fishing line" equation. Draw a hook at the lower end.

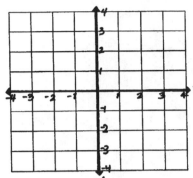

C. y = 2x

Finish these ordered pairs, then graph the solution.

(–2, –4); (–1, ___); (0, ___); (1, ___); (2, ___)

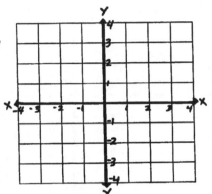

D. y = –2x + 1

Finish these ordered pairs, then graph the solution.

(–1, 3)

(0, ___)

(1, ___)

(2, ___)

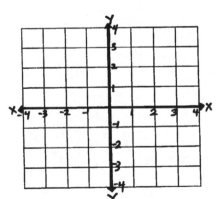

E. y = x + 5

Finish these ordered pairs, then graph the solution.

(–4, 1)

(–3, ___)

(–2, ___)

(–1, ___)

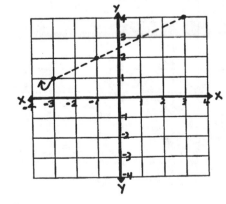

F. Which equation matches this graph? Circle the correct equation.

a. y = x –1   d. y = x + 1

b. y = 2x   e. y = 2x + 2

c. 2y = x + 5   f. y = 3x

Name

SLIDES, FLIPS, & TURNS

Reflections are exact opposites, or flips, of a figure. They are one kind of transformation to know and use. Slides and turns are the other two.

A figure can be moved on a coordinate plane.

For each point of a figure, there is a corresponding point in the moved (transformed) figure.

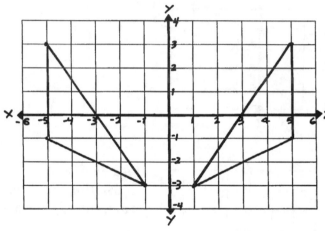

This shows a triangle and its reflection.

For each point on the first triangle, write its corresponding point on the flipped (reflected) figure.

1. (–5, 3) corresponds to _____ .

2. (–5, –1) corresponds to _____ .

3. (–1, –3) corresponds to _____ .

This is a translation (slide) of a rectangle.

For each point on the rectangle, write its corresponding point on the translated rectangle.

4. (–2, 7) corresponds to _____

5. _____ corresponds to _____

6. _____ corresponds to _____

7. _____ corresponds to _____

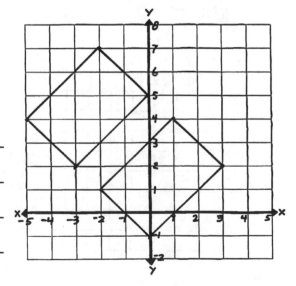

Name _____

SLIDES, FLIPS, & TURNS, CONT.

Identify the transformation for each pair of figures.
Write S for slide (translation), F for flip (reflection) or T for turn (rotation).

8. _____ 9. _____ 10. _____

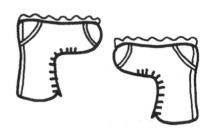  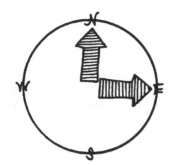

Draw a reflection of the figure on the grid.

Name the corresponding points.

11. (–1, 6) corresponds to _____

12. _____corresponds to _____

13. _____corresponds to _____

14. _____corresponds to _____

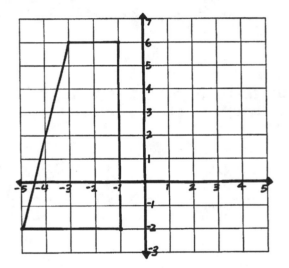

On this grid, draw a slide, flip, or turn of the hiker.

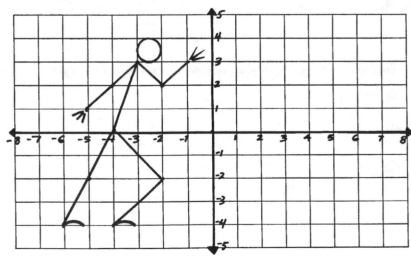

Name _____

CLOUD-WATCHING

Yolanda gazes up at a sky filled with unusual cloud patterns.
This is what she sees when she studies the clouds.

Find the pattern.

Draw the next two cloud formations to continue the pattern.

Study these sequence to predict the patterns.
Complete the next two figures in the sequence.

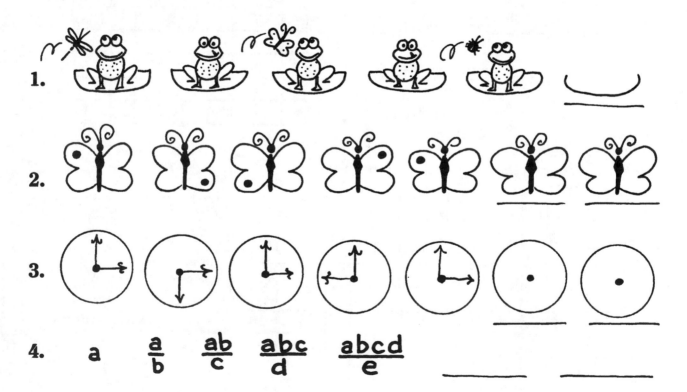

1.

2.

3.

4.   a $\dfrac{a}{b}$ $\dfrac{ab}{c}$ $\dfrac{abc}{d}$ $\dfrac{abcd}{e}$

Name _____

CLOUD-WATCHING, CONT.

Find the patterns.

Use them to predict the next one, two, or three figures in each sequence.

5.

6.

7.

8.

9. 107   108   106   109   105   110   104   _____   _____   _____

10.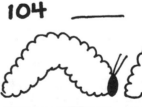

11.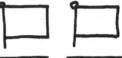

12.

13.

Name _____

THE END OF THE TRAIL

Write a proportion to show the relationship between the numbers in these problems from the last day on the trail. Use x as the unknown number in the proportion.

Then solve each proportion.

1. On the last day, the hikers covered 4.5 miles in 2 hours. If the total walking time was 6 hours, and they walked at the same rate all day, how long was the trail?

Answer: _____

2. Mike took 21 pictures with his camera in the first 3 hours on the trail. He continued his picture-taking at the same rate through the whole hike. How much time had passed when he'd taken 35 pictures?

Answer: _____

3. Toni drank 0.75 quarts of water in the first 3 miles of the trail. At this rate, how much will she drink in 13 miles?

Answer: _____

4. Matt rested 15 times in 5 hours. He rested at the same rate throughout his hike. How many times did he rest in 3 hours?

Answer: _____

5. The group ate 9 bags of gorp on their way out of the wilderness area. Their hike was 6 hours long. Assuming that they ate at the same rate throughout the hike, how much time did it take to eat 6 bags of gorp?

Answer: _____

Solve these proportions.

6. $\frac{n}{12} = \frac{5}{15}$

n = _____

7. $\frac{12}{n} = \frac{72}{108}$

n = _____

Name _____

PRE-ALGEBRA
ASSESSMENT AND ANSWER KEYS

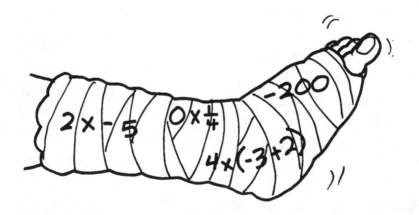

PRE-ALGEBRA
SKILLS TEST

Each answer is worth 1 point, except questions 36–40, which are worth 2 points. Total possible score: 100 pts.

Questions 1–10. For each definition, choose a matching term from the sign.
Write the term on the line.

_____ 1. A number that replaces the variable in an equation to make the equation true.

_____ 2. The point where the x-axis and the y-axis intersect on a grid.

_____ 3. A sentence that uses mathematical symbols instead of words.

_____ 4. The distance of a number from zero on a number line.

_____ 5. The variables and numbers in a mathematical expression.

_____ 6. The transformation of a figure through the motion of a slide.

_____ 7. The transformation of a figure through the motion of a flip.

_____ 8. A letter used to represent a number in a mathematical expression.

_____ 9. An equation whose solutions form a straight line.

_____ 10. Positive numbers (1, 2, 3 . . .), negative numbers (–1, –2, –3, . . .), and zero.

Write the absolute value:

11. $|-7| =$ _____

12. $|34| =$ _____

Write the integers in order from least to greatest:

13. 7, –9, 8, 0, 9, –3

_____

14. 20, –10, –5, 5, 10, –20

_____

Add, subtract, multiply, or divide the integers to find the answer.

15. $-22 + -1 =$ _____

16. $-17 - 4 - -4 =$ _____

17. $-6 \times -4 =$ _____

18. $-300 \div 60 =$ _____

19. $-11 + 14 - -6 =$ _____

20. $(-3 \times 2) \div -6 =$ _____

21. $(20 \times -5) - -100 =$ _____

The temperature was 18°F when the campers went to bed at 10:00 p.m. By 4:00 a.m., it had fallen 22°. By 6:00 a.m., the temperature was –12°F.

22. What was the temperature at 4:00 a.m.? _____

23. How far had the temperature fallen from 10:00 p.m. to 6:00 a.m. the next morning? _____

Choose the mathematical expression that matches each of these descriptions about packing camping supplies.

24. The difference between the weight of two packs (p) and 4 water bottles (w)

    a. 2p – 4w   b. p –4w
    c. 4(w + p) + 2   d. 2p + 4w

Name _____

The BASIC/Not Boring Middle Grades Math Book

25. The weight of three tents (t), increased by twice the sum of weights of a sleeping bag (s) and a frying pan (f).
    a. 3t + 2s + f
    b. 3 (t + s + f + 2)
    c. 3t + 2(s + f)
    d. 3 + 2 + t + s + f

26. The weight of one pair of boots (b) increased by four cook stoves (c), increased by six pairs of socks (p)
    a. b + 4 (c + 6p)
    b. b + 4c +6p
    c. b – 4c + 6s
    d. 4(b + c + 6s)

Write a mathematical expression to match each description.

27. Twice the sum of the weights of a tent (t), a sleeping bag (s), and four water bottles (w)

   _____

28. The weight of a pack (p) decreased by the weight of twelve tent stakes (s), two cook pots (c), and a pair of boots (b)

   _____

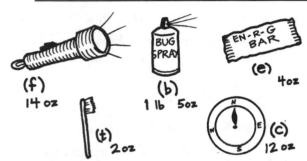

Use the information given in the above picture to answer questions 29–32.

Tell whether the expressions are true. Write T (true) or F (false) in front of each expression.

_____ 29. $2c < 2f$

_____ 30. $4e - 2 = f$

_____ 31. $10t > b$

_____ 32. $2c + b = 3f + t + \frac{1}{4}e$

33. How many variables?_____
$$12x + y - 3y = 42$$

34. How many terms? _____
$$4p + 9 + p - x + 35x = -7$$

35. What is the coefficient of y?_____
$$-7x + q - 13y$$

Simplify the expressions. (Worth 2 points each.)

36. $2(k + 9) + k$ _____

37. $4z + 6x - 7z$ _____

38. $(8g + 72) \div 4$ _____

39. $12y - 3y + q$ _____

40. $-25 + p - 10p$ _____

Circle the correct equation to match the statement or problem.

41. Toni had 14 fewer bug bites than Yolanda.
    a. $t - y = 14$
    b. $14t = y$
    c. $t = y - 14$

42. Mike swatted mosquitoes for 2 + hours. He killed 33. How many mosquitoes (m) did he kill (on the average) per hour?
    a. $33 \div 2\frac{1}{2} = m$
    b. $2\frac{1}{2} \div 33 = m$
    c. $33 - 2\frac{1}{2} = m$

43. Sam had 12 more than three times the number of bites as Chad.
    a. $s = c - 12 \times 3$
    b. $s = 3c + 12$
    c. $c = 2s$

44. The seven hikers used three cans of bug spray for the first week. At the end of two weeks, they had used six cans. How many cans (c) did they use the second week?
    a. $7 + c = 2 + 6$
    b. $3 + x = 6$
    c. $3 (6 + x) = 7$

Rewrite each equation using inverse operations.

45. $p + 200 = -100$

   _____

46. $-50 + p = 13$

   _____

47. $-5 = t + 9$

   _____

Name _____

Write an equation to match each statement or problem.

48. The campfire burned for an hour less than twice as long on Thursday night (t) as it burned on Wednesday night (w).

_____

49. Sam gathered 38 pieces of firewood. Together he and Matt gathered 50. How many did Matt find?

_____

50. The campers toasted 4 bags of marshmallows. One bag had 25. The other bags had a different number, equal to each other. They toasted a total of 119 marshmallows. How many were in each of the other bags?

_____

Tell if each equation is solved correctly. Write yes or no.

_____ 51. $0.9 + x = 0.18$
                $x = 0.27$

_____ 52. $\frac{1}{2} + y - 15\frac{1}{4} = 4\frac{1}{4}$
                $y = -20$

_____ 53. $6(p + 12) = 2$
                $p = 10$

Solve these equations.

54. $\frac{x - 37}{3} = 21$
      $x = $ _____

55. $g + -25 = 225$
      $g = $ _____

Write the property used to solve each equation. Use the first letter.

(A) Associative Propery
(I) Identity Property
(C) Commutative Property
(D) Distributive Property
(Z) Zero Property
(O) Opposites Property

_____ 56. $-35 \times 1 = -35$
_____ 57. $-3 + (12 + 6) = (-3 + 12) + 6$

_____ 58. $20 \times -7 = -7 \times 20$
_____ 59. $4 \times (5 + 9) = 4 \times 5 + 4 \times 9$
_____ 60. $0 \times -200 = 0$

Solve these equations:

61. $100 = -4n$
      $n = $ _____

62. $13p = -39$
      $p = $ _____

63. $\frac{s}{8} = 16$
      $s = $ _____

Solve these equations.

64. $67.5 = 7.5n$
      $n = $ _____

65. $7b + 8 - 2b = 48$
      $b = $ _____

66. $-8.2s + 3s = 20.8$
      $s = $ _____

67. Which inequality matches this graph? Circle one.

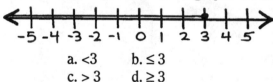

     a. <3 b. ≤ 3
     c. >3 d. ≥ 3

Write the inequality shown by each graph.

68.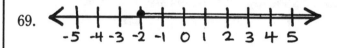

_____

69.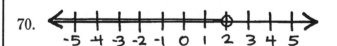

_____

70.

_____

71. Is $(-3, 8)$ a solution to the equation $x + y = 5$? _____

72. Is $(-3, 9)$ a solution to the equation $2x + y = 3$? _____

73. Is $(-13, -17)$ a solution to the equation $y = x + 4$? _____

Name _____

Is there a poison ivy leaf at each of these locations? Write yes or no.

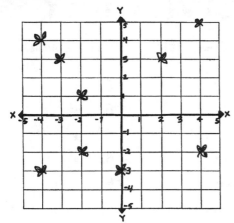

74. (2, –4) _____

75. (–2, –4) _____

76. (4, 5) _____

77. (–3, 0) _____

78. (–3, 3) _____

79. (–4, –3) _____

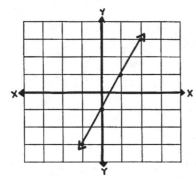

80. The above is a graph of which equation? _____

    a. y = x – 1   c. y = 2x –1

    b. y = x + 1   d. y = 2x

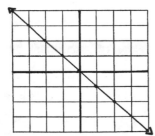

81. The above is a graph of which equation? _____

    a. x = y   c. 2x = y

    b. y = -x   d. y = –2x

Which transformation is shown? Write *slide*, *flip*, or *turn*.

82. _____

83. _____

84. _____

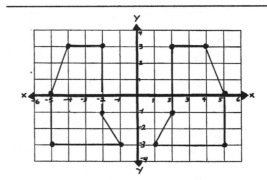

Which points in the reflection correspond to the above figure on the left?

85. (–2, –1) corresponds to _____

86. (–5, –3) corresponds to _____

87. (–4, 3) corresponds to _____

88. (–5, 0) corresponds to _____

89. **Finish the pattern. Draw the next item in the sequence.**

90. **Finish the pattern. Draw the next item in the sequence.**

   _____

SCORE: Total Points _____ out of a possible 100 points

Name _____

Pre-Algebra
SKILLS TEST ANSWER KEY

Each answer is worth 1 point, except questions 36–40, which are worth 2 points.

1. solution
2. origin
3. expression
4. absolute value
5. terms
6. translation
7. reflection
8. variable
9. linear equation
10. integers
11. 7
12. 34
13. –9, –7, –3, 0, 8, 9
14. –20, –10, –5, 5, 10, 20
15. –23
16. –17
17. 24
18. –50
19. 9
20. 1
21. 0
22. –4°
23. 30°
24. a
25. c
26. b
27. $2(t + s + 4w)$
28. $p - 12s - 2c - b$
29. T
30. T
31. F
32. T

33. 2
34. 4
35. 13
36. $3k + 18$
37. $-3z + 6x$
38. $2g + 18$
39. $9y + q$
40. $-25 - 9p$
41. c
42. a
43. b
44. b
45. $p + 200 - 200 = -100 - 200$
46. $-50 + 50 + p = 13 + 50$
47. $-5 - 9 = t + 9 - 9$
48. $t = 2w - 1$
49. $38 + x = 50$
50. $25 + 3x = 119$
51. no
52. no
53. no
54. 100
55. 250
56. I
57. A
58. C
59. D
60. Z
61. –25
62. –3
63. –128

64. 9
65. 8
66. 4
67. b
68. > -1
69. ≥ -2
70. < 2
71. yes
72. yes
73. no
74. no
75. no
76. yes
77. no
78. yes
79. yes
80. c
81. b
82. turn
83. flip
84. slide
85. (2, –1)
86. (5, –3)
87. (4, 3)
88. (5, 0)
89. Check student drawings to see that they follow the sequence.
90. Check student drawings to see that they follow the sequence.

ANSWERS

page 270

1. a. P
   b. 3
   c. –3
2. a. N
   b. 2
   c. 2
3. a. P
   b. 12
   c. –12
4. a. P
   b. 5
   c. –5

5. a. P
   b. 8
   c. –8
6. a. N
   b. 7
   c. 7
7. a. N
   b. 4
   c. 4
8. a. N
   b. 6
   c. 6

page 271

1. 4
2. 3
3. 2
4. 6
5. 6
6. 1
7. >
8. <
9. >
10. >
11. >
12. <
13. >
14. >

15. –7, –6, –4, –2, 3, 5, 8, 12
16. –20, –7, –1, 0, 3, 4, 6, 20
17. –16, –8, –4, –3, 3, 5, 10
18. –8, –4, –2, 2, 4, 6, 8
19. –12, –7, 0, 2, 6, 7, 8
20. –8, –6, 0, 2, 5, 9, 11

page 272

1. 4
2. –15
3. –99
4. 4
5. –4
6. 1
7. 0
8. –75
9. –19
10. –5
11. –29
12. 6
13. –22
14. –8
15. 3
16. –59
17. 42
18. –21

page 273

Answer to equation at top of page: 6 miles

1. –10
2. 10
3. –10
4. 10
5. –7
6. 7
7. –7
8. 7
9. 0
10. –4
11. 23
12. –6
13. 3
14. -10
15. 64
16. –11
17. 19
18. 4
19. –4
20. –29
21. 5.8 miles

page 274

Chart

1. 10° –15°
2. 37° 32° 22° 12° –3°
3. 55° 50° 40° 30° 15°
4. 11° 6° –4° –14° –29°

5. 6° 1° –9° –19° –34°
6. 10° 5° 0° –10° –35°°

Bottom

7. –70
8. –42
9. 60
10. –56
11. 10,000
12. –2500
13. 1500
14. –200,000
15. –320
16. 630 or 700

page 275

1. Mar
2. Apr
3. Nov
4. Oct
5. Aug
6. Nov
7. Feb and June
8. Oct
9. –10
10. 13
11. –100
12. 20
13. –4
14. –100

page 276

Equations may vary slightly, depending on what arrangement of terms the student chooses. Check to see that equations accurately reflect the problems, and to see that student has used integers in the equation.

1. $-2 + 2 + -3 = -3$
Answer: Shoes, Boots
2. $-3 + 10 = 7$
Answer: Videos, Slides
3. $2 x -2 = -4$
Answer: Repair Shop
4. $-4 + 8 + -1 = 3$
Answer: Clothing
5. $2 - -4 = 6$
Answer: 6
6. $-1 + 9 = 8$
Answer: Climbing Gear
7. $-3 + 4 + -1 = 0$ or $-3 + -1 + 4 = 0$
Answer: Sleeping Bags
8. $3 + -3 + 8 + -2 = 6$
Answer: Books & Maps

page 277

1. Toni
2. Mike
3. Basha
4. T
5. blank or F
6. blank or F
7. T
8. –12. answers will vary

Check phrases to make sure they give an accurate statement of a relationship between the two numbers.

page 278

Top questions:
  yes
  $t < 2s$
1. $3w + 2p$

2. $4f + s$
3. $2c + 10$
4. $b – 3$
5. $f < 2t$
6. $3(p + b)$
7. $5w + 2$
8. $c + 2w + f < 100$

page 279

Expressions may vary slightly, depending on what arrangement of terms the student chooses. Check to see that expressions accurately reflect the statements, and to see that student has used integers in each expression.

1. $m + 3$
2. $15 r – 7j$
3. $4p – 2n$
4. $12g – 4g$
5. $8c – 5$
6. $2 (2b + 6j)$
7. $3 (2s – 5f)$
8. $10 h + s + 2p$
9. $2a < 3p$
10. $5 (b + a)$
11. $\frac{1}{2} r + \frac{1}{4} g$
12. $10(bf)$

page 280

1. 2
2. 2
3. 2
4. 4
5. L
6. U
7. U
8. U
9. 2
10. 4
11. 4
12. 1
13. 5

14. $7z, 18m, \frac{1}{2} b$
    coefficient of z is 7
    coefficient of m is 18
    coefficient of b is $\frac{1}{2}$

page 281

Answers may vary somewhat, depending upon the order in which student chooses to place the terms of the expression.

1. $8a$
2. $2x$
3. $8k$
4. $19 \frac{1}{4} c$
5. $11y – 5$
6. $\frac{1}{4} x + 2$
7. $7t + 14$
8. $3.2k + 5$
9. $z + 6x$
10. $3n + 4p$
11. $2y + 2x$
12. $27g – 3s$
13. $11m + 100$
14. $2w + 12$
15. $3b + 10$
16. $7a + 6$
17. $16n + 10$
18. $6x + 3y$
19. $9p$
20. $3s – 2t$

page 282

Answers may vary somewhat, depending upon the order in which student chooses to place the terms of the expression.

1. $8y + 7$
2. $4x + 35$
3. $8p$
4. $3x/5$
5. $3z + 12$
6. $9t + 300$
7. $201y + 6$
8. $4\frac{1}{2}b$
9. $45 + 7a + 6b$
10. $-2g + 24$
11. $b + 2d + c$
12. $-6x + 12$
13. $23p+45$
14. $-3z - x$
15. $99j + x$
16. $4j + 6k$

page 283

Top correct equation to circle: $s = 2t - 3$

1. c
2. a
3. a
4. c
5. c
6. c
7. c
8. b
9. a
10. b

page 284

Answers may vary somewhat, depending upon the order in which student chooses to place the terms of the equation, and upon the letters chosen to represent the terms.

1. $z = 2c + 3$
2. $t = (m + b) - 5$
3. $s = 4 (z + t)$
4. $y = s - 5$
5. $t = (m + z) - 16$
6. $s=t + 23$
7. $b = 18 + z$
8. $s = f - 3$
9. $m = \frac{1}{4}t$
10. $m = 2s - 3$
11. $m + w = s + t$
12. $t = 3a - 5$

page 285

1. c; 26
2. b; 36
3. b; 4
4. a; 2 ¼
5. b; 33
6. b; 4
7. a; 7

page 286

Equations may vary somewhat, depending upon the order in which student chooses to place the terms of the equation, and upon the letters chosen to represent the terms. Answers (solutions to equations), however, should not vary.

1. $t = 21 - 14$
   Answer: 7 min
2. $w = 100 - 30$
   Answer: 70 lb
3. $d = 280/2 - 20$
   Answer: 120 ft
4. $2(3 + 6) = r$
   Answer: 18 times
5. $m = 50 - 25$
   Answer: 25 min
6. $9 = 2d - 3$
   Answer: 6 times
7. $p = 208 - 70 - 100$
   Answer: 38 lb

page 287

1. $x + 8 = 20$
   $x + 8 - 8 = 20 - 8$

$x = 12$

2. $p - 40 = -300$
   $p - 40 + 40 = -300 + 40$
   $p = -260$

3. $5c = -35$
   $5c/5 = -35/5$
   $c = -7$

4. $y/6 = -8$
   $y/6 \times 6 = -8 \times 6$
   $y = -48$

5. $x + 15 = 7$
   $x + 15 - 15 = 7 - 15$
   $x = -8$

6. $q - 25 = -15$
   $q - 25 + 25 = -15 + 25$
   $q = 10$

7. $7r = -84$
   $7r/7 = -84/7$
   $r = -12$

8. $z/7 = -8$
   $z/7 \times 7 = -8 \times 7$
   $z = -56$

page 288

1. Identity
2. Identity
3. Associative
4. Commutative
5. Distributive
6. Distributive
7. Commutative
8. Identity
9. Zero
10. Identity
11. Opposites
12. Associative
13. Opposites
14. Commutative
15. Identity
16. Zero

page 289

1. c
2. b
3. d
4. c
5. b
6. a
7. c
8. d
9. c
10. d
11. c
12. b

page 290

Top question: yes

Correct solutions are 1, 2, 3, 6, 8, 9, 10, 11, 12, 14, 15, 18
Correct answers to wrong solutions are:

4. 5000
5. –36
7. –106
13. –60
16. 1000
17. –2

page 291

Across

A. 46	M. 925	X. 63
E. 27	P. 55,005	Y. 4008
G. 2111	R. 99	Z. 15
H. 7000	S. 21	BB. 375
I. 64	T. 49	EE. 65
J. 29	U. 308	FF. 16
L. 12	V. 111	GG. 64

Down

B. 600	K. 9520	U. 333
C. 81	L. 15,010	V. 1006
D. 316	N. 299	W. 189
E. 20	O. 59	AA. 55
G. 202	Q. 518	CC. 71
H. 749	T. 4116	DD. 56

page 292

1. 6
2. 5
3. 8
4. 1
5. 13
6. 47
7. 17
8. 20
9. 12
10. 70
11. 176
12. 15

page 293

Path should follow these correctly-solved equations. NOTE: Student may connect these equations in a different order than this.

A.
C.
D.
E.
F.
G.
I.
L.
N.
O.

page 294

(left) Mike's path

8. 6 1/6
7. 7.5
6. 0.2
5. 80
4. 1.5
3. 6
2. 100
1. 30

(right) Basha's path

8. 11
7. 12
6. 0.2
5. 32.5
4. 160
3. –111
2. 32
1. 34.997

page 295

A. yes	E. no	I. no	M. no
B. yes	F. no	J. no	N. no
C. yes	G. yes	K. no	O. yes
D. yes	H. no	L. yes	P. no

page 296

The equations shown may not be exactly the equations written by student. Give credit for any equation that accurately reflects and solves the problem. The solutions, however, should not vary.

1. $-6 + x = 12$
   Answer: 18
2. $x = 14 \frac{1}{2} - 6 \frac{1}{2}$
   Answer: 8
3. $x = \dfrac{(2 \times 5) - 3}{2}$
   Answer: 3 + bags
4. $2 \times 32 - x = 7$
   Answer: 57 oz
5. $\dfrac{3 + 2 + 6}{2} = x$

Answer: 5 ½ packages
6. 4 + (4 − 2) +2(4 − 2) + x = 18
Answer: 8
7. $\frac{9 + (9 + 3)}{4}$ = x
Answer: 5 ¼ cans
8. $\frac{30 − (3 + 3)}{6}$ = x
Answer: 4

page 297

The equations shown may not be exactly the equations written by student. Give credit for any equation that accurately reflects and solves the problem. The solutions, however, should not vary.

1. (f + 15) + f = 75
   f = 30 min
2. d = 4.6 + 8.3
   d = 12.9 ft
3. d = 6.1 - 4.3
   d = 1.8 ft
4. t = 72/2 + 26
   t = 62 sec
5. 10 d − 31 = 469
   d = 50 ft
6. f + (f + 2) + 4(f + f + 2) = 70
   Toni saw 6
   Mike saw 8
   Basha saw 56
7. t = 70 − (2 x 4)
   t = 62°

page 298

1. 6, 4	7. −4, 3, -6
2. −1	8. 3, −2, 0
3. −6, −2, 7	9. 7, 16, 20, −5
4. −5, 3, −2	10. −1, −4, −6
5. 6, 0	11. x + 10 > 18
6. 11	12. 3x + 6 ≤ 2

page 299

1. x < 2	3. x > − 1
2. x > − 2	4. x < 3

5–8. Check student graphs to see that solutions are shown correctly. 5 and 6 should have solid circles at −1 and −3 respectively. 7 and 8 should have open circles at −8 and 6 respectively.

page 300

A.   x= 10, y = 2, (10, 2)
      x = 5, y= 1, (5, 1)
      x = 0, y = 0, (0, 0)
      x = −30, y = −6, (−30, −6)
      x = −35, y = −7, (−35, −7)

B.   x = −1, y = 4, (1, 4)
      x = 0, y = 5, (0, 5)
      x = 1, y = 6, (1, 6)
      x = 2, y = 7 (2, 7)
      x = 3, y = 8 (3, 8)

C.   x = 2, y = −1, (−2, −1)
      x = 0, y = 0, (0, 0)
      x = 2, y=1, (2, 1)
      x = 4, y = 2, (4, 2)
      x = 6, y = 3, (6, 3)

D.   x = −5, y = −1, (−5, −1)
      x = −2, y = 0, (−2, 0)
      x = 1, y= 1, (1, 1)
      x = 4, y = 2, (4, 2)
      x = 7, y = 3, (7, 3)

E.   x = −3, y = −9, (−3, −9)
      x = −1, y = −3, (−1, −3)
      x = 0, y = 0, (0, 0)
      x = 2, y = 6, (2, 6)
      x = 5, y = 15, (5, 15)

page 301

1.   7
2.   15
A.   x = 4, y = 10, (4, 10)
     x = 5, y = 9, (5, 9)
     x = 8, y = 6, (8, 6)
     x = 10, y = 4, (10, 4)
     x = 12, y = 2, (12, 2)
B.   x = 3, y = 0, (3, 0)
     x = 0, y = −3, (0, −3)
     x = −2, y = −5, (−2, −5)
     x = 5, y = 2, (5, 2)
     x = −1, y = −4, (−1, −4)
C.   x = 2, y = −8. (2, -8)
     x = −1, y = 4, (-1, 4)
     x = 4, y = −16, (4, −16)
     x = −5, y = 20, (−5, 20)
     x = 7, y = −28, (7, −28)
D.   x = −3, y = 9, (−3, 9)
     x = −1, y = 5, (−1, 5)
     x = 0, y = 3, (0, 3)
     x = 3, y = −3, (3, −3)
     x = 6, y = −9, (6, −9)
E.   x = 4, y = −1, (4, −1)
     x = 6, y = 0, (6, 0)
     x = 10, y = 2, (10, 2)
     x = 14, y = 4, (14, 4)
     x = 16, y = 5, (16, 5)

page 302

1. (−6, 6)	7. (−3, −8)
2. (5, 4)	8. L
3. (3, −2)	9. J
4. (2, 5)	10. H
5. (−7, 3)	11. I
6. (−4, −4)	12. K

13–20. Check to see that student has drawn creatures at correct locations.

page 303

If student plots points and draws lines correctly, the result will be the drawing of a coiled snake.

pages 304–305

a.   x = −3, y = −2, (−3, −2)
      x = −2, y = 0, (−2, 0)
      x = −1, y = 2, (−1, 2)
      x = 0, y = 4, (0, 4)
b.   x = −2, y = 2, (−2, 2)
      x = 1, y = −1, (1, −1)
      x = 2, y = −2, (2, −2)
      x = 3, y = −3, (3, −3)
      x = 4, y = −4, (4, −4)
c.   (−2, −4); (−1, −2); (0, 0);
      (1, 2); (2, 4)
d.   (−1, 3); (0, 1); (1, −1); (2, −3)
e.   (−4, 1); (−3, 2); (−2, 3); (−1, 4)
f.   c

pages 306–307

1. (5, 3)
2. (5, −1)
3. (1, −3)
4. (1, 4)
5–7. These three answers
     may be in any order:
     (0, 5) corresponds to (3, 2)
     (−3, 2) corresponds to (0, −1)
     (−5, 4) corresponds to (−2, 1)
8. F
9. S
10. T
11. (1, 6)
Check student grid to see that correct reflection of the figure has been drawn.
12–14. These three answers may be in any order.
     (−3, 6) corresponds to (3, 6)
     (−5, −2) corresponds to (5, −2)
     (−1, −2) corresponds to (1, −2)
Check student grid to see that transformation of the hiker has been drawn with correct corresponding points.

pages 308–309

Check student drawings to see that sequences are correct.

page 310

Proportions may differ, depending on the order student chooses to write the terms. These are likely proportions. The solutions should not differ.

1. 4.5/2 = x/6
   Answer: 13.5 miles
2. 21/3 = 35/x
   Answer: 5 hours
3. 0.75/3 = x/13
   Answer: 3.25 qt
4. 15/5 = x/3
   Answer: 9 times
5. 9/6 = 6/x
   Answer: 4 hours
6. n = 4
7. n = 18